SOCIAL IDENTITY

̶ial Identity provides a clearly-written accessible introduction to
̶iological and social anthropological approaches to identity.
̶oking at the work of Mead, Goffman and Barth, this book
̶kes clear their relevance to everyday life. Insisting that reflexive
̶f identity is not a modern phenomenon, the core argument is
̶at individual and collective identity can both be understood using
̶ame model, as 'internal' and 'external' processes.

Major concepts covered include:

̶odiment
̶al groups and social categories
̶ference and community
̶egorisation and resistance.

̶al *Identity* brings together sociological and social anthropo-
̶al theories of identity, and makes an original contribution to
̶heory. Focusing on identity as individual and collective, this
̶ings us a fresh perspective on the relationship between the
̶al and society. This book provides an essential guide to the
̶of social identity, offering students critical discussions of
̶Berger and Luckmann, Becker, Anthony Cohen, Giddens,
̶u and many others.

̶d Jenkins is Professor of Sociology at the University of
̶ld and the author of numerous books, including *Pierre
̶ieu* (Routledge 1992).

KEY IDEAS
Series Editor: Peter Hamilton
The Open University

KEY IDEAS

Series Editor: PETER HAMILTON
The Open University, Milton Keynes

Designed to complement the successful Key Sociologists, this series covers the main concepts, issues, debates and controversies in sociology and the social sciences. The series aims to provide authoritative essays on central topics of social science, such as community, power, work, sexuality, inequality, benefits and ideology, class, family, etc. Books adopt a strong individual 'line' constituting original essays rather than literary surveys and form lively and original treatments of their subject matter. The books will be useful to students and teachers of sociology, political science, economics, psychology, philosophy and geography.

THE SYMBOLIC CONSTRUCTION OF COMMUNITY
ANTHONY P. COHEN, Department of Social Anthropology, University of Manchester

SEXUALITY
JEFFREY WEEKS, Social Work Studies Department, University of Southampton

EQUALITY
BRYAN TURNER, School of Social Sciences, The Flinders University of South Australia

RACISM
ROBERT MILES, Department of Sociology, University of Glasgow

POSTMODERNITY
BARRY SMART, Associate Professor of Sociology, University of Auckland, New Zealand

CLASS
STEPHEN EDGELL, School of Social Sciences, University of Salford

CONSUMPTION
ROBERT BOCOCK, Faculty of Social Sciences, The Open University, Milton Keynes

CULTURE
CHRIS JENKS, Department of Sociology, Goldsmiths' College

MASS MEDIA
PIERRE SORLIN, University of Paris III

GLOBALIZATION
MALCOLM WATERS, University of Tasmania, Australia

CHILDHOOD
CHRIS JENKS, Department of Sociology, Goldsmiths' College

LIFESTYLES
DAVID CHANEY, Department of Sociology, University of Durham

SOCIAL IDENTITY

RICHARD JENKINS

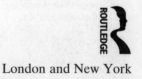

London and New York

LIVERPOOL
UNIVERSITY
LIBRARY

First published 1996
by Routledge
11 New Fetter Lane, London EC4P 4EE

Simultaneously published in the USA and Canada
by Routledge
29 West 35th Street, New York, NY 10001

© 1996 Richard Jenkins

Typeset in Times by Keystroke,
Jacaranda Lodge, Wolverhampton

Printed and bound in Great Britain by
Clays Ltd, Bungay, Suffolk

British Library Cataloguing in Publication Data
A catalogue record for this book is available from the
British Library

Library of Congress Cataloguing in Publication Data
Jenkins, Richard, 1952–
    Social Identity / Richard Jenkins.
        p.   cm.
    Includes bibliographical references and index.
    ISBN 0–415–12052–7. — ISBN 0–415–12053–5 (pbk.)
    1. Group identity.   I. Title.
HM131.J43   1996
302.5—dc20   96-7863
                                                   CIP

No man is an Island, entire of it self; every man is a piece of the Continent, a part of the main; . . . any man's death diminishes me, because I am involved in Mankind; And therefore never send to know for whom the bell tolls; It tolls for thee.

John Donne

It is not the consciousness of men that determines their existence, but their social existence that determines their consciousness.

Karl Marx

One is for the other what the other is for oneself; there is no exceptional place for the subject.

Emmanuel Levinas

Everybody needs somebody . . .

Solomon Burke

Contents

Get up to
32

public / private self

Acknowledgements

This book has been a long time in the making. Its intellectual thread began with my PhD, about the transition to adulthood in Belfast, continued through subsequent research into racism in the West Midlands labour market, moved on to work in South Wales about the transition to adulthood in different contexts, made a useful detour to sniff around informal economic activity, and has now turned into an interest in national identity in Denmark. Although the consistency of that thread was not necessarily obvious to others, it has kept me going in an institutional and higher educational climate which has not always been the most congenial.

As a result it is more difficult than usual – and it is never easy – adequately to acknowledge my debts. In one way or another all those with whom I have worked, whether as direct collaborators or interested colleagues, have influenced my thinking about the ideas which I present in this book. My students have been particularly important. Of my teachers and mentors, two in particular share most of the credit that is due. The late Milan Stuchlik started the ball rolling in the Department of Social Anthropology at Queen's, Belfast, and I have been trying to catch up with it ever since. John Rex, from the sidelines, has egged me on.

More directly, a particular text demands specific acknowledgements. Chris Rojek's initial encouragement was important. Since 1992 the intellectual support and inspiration supplied during my visits to the Institut for etnografi og social antropologi at the

University of Aarhus, Denmark, has been vital. The Department of Sociology and Anthropology at the University of Wales, Swansea, offered over the years a teaching context in which my disregard for the boundary between anthropology and sociology could survive, and the Department of Sociological Studies at the University of Sheffield allowed me sufficient space on taking up a new post to finish the writing. At Swansea John Parker deserves a broader acknowledgement than his specific mentions in the footnotes. Conversations with Jess Madge were helpful in orienting me to the post-Piagetian model of infant socialisation. Similarly, Pia Haudrup Christensen made a timely contribution to my thinking about embodiment. Finally, all or part of versions of the book have been read and commented on by Stephanie Adams, Steve Ford, Janne Bleeg Jensen, Melanie Jones, Sharon Macdonald, and two anonymous referees. I have done my best to pay them heed, and they all deserve my gratitude. However, the usual disclaimer applies. It is absolutely true that while I cannot take all the credit for the book's virtues, its failings are all my own.

Richard Jenkins
Sheffield

1

Knowing who we are

It is a cold Friday night, and windy. You are dressed for dancing, not the weather. Finally you reach the head of the queue outside the night club. The bouncer – although nowadays they prefer to be called doormen – raises his arm and lets your friend in. He takes one look at you and demands proof of your age. All you have in your pockets is money. That isn't enough.

You telephone the order line of a clothing catalogue to buy a new jacket. The young man who answers asks for your name, address, credit card number and expiry date, your customer reference number if you have one; all in order to establish your status as someone to whom, in the absence of a face-to-face encounter, goods can be dispatched in confidence. And also, of course, to make sure you're on the mailing list.

The immigration official asks you for your passport. She looks at your nationality, at where you were born. Your name. She checks your visa. These indicate your legitimacy as a traveller, your desirability as an entrant. She looks at the photograph, she looks at you. She asks you the purpose of your visit. She stamps the passport and wishes you a pleasant stay. Already she is looking over your shoulder at the person behind you.

On a train the stranger in the opposite seat excuses herself. She has noticed you reading last week's newspaper from a small town several hundred miles to the east. You explain that your mother posts it to you, so that you can keep up with the news from home. She recognised the newspaper because her husband is from your home town. You, it turns out, were at school with her brother-in-law. Before leaving the train she gives you her telephone number.

In everyday situations such as these, one's identity is called into question and established (or not). But the presentation or negotiation of identity is not always so ordinary or trivial: it can shake the foundations of our lives. Imagine, for example, the morning of your sixty-fifth birthday. With it, as well as birthday cards, will come retirement, a pension, a concessionary public transport pass, special rates every Tuesday at the hairdresser. Beyond that again, in the promise of free medical prescriptions and the beckoning Day Centre, hover the shades of infirmity, of dependence, of disability. Although it will be the same face you see in the bathroom mirror, you will no longer be quite the person that you were yesterday. Nor can you ever be again.

Sometimes a changed or strange situation makes the difference. An unfamiliar neighbourhood, an ethnically divided city: a casual encounter can transform one's taken-for-granted identity into a dangerous liability. Something as simple as the 'wrong' accent, or an 'ethnic' surname on your driving licence, can become a warrant for violence, even murder. Whether the ethnic identification is 'correct' or not – in your eyes – may make no difference. Identity is often in the eye of the beholder.

Or take a different time-scale, and another kind of transformation. What changes and negotiations are required by 'coming out', to assume a public identification as a gay man or a lesbian? What kind of response from others is the 'right' response? Which others matter? And what does such a process represent? The construction of a new identity, or the revelation of an authentic and primordial self?

Social identity is also important on a wider stage than the encounters or thresholds of individual lives. Imagine a contested border region. It might be anywhere in the world. There are different ways to settle the issue: warfare, a referendum, international arbitration. Whatever the means adopted, the outcome has implications for the identities of people on both sides. And it may not be accepted by those who find their new national identity uncongenial. Similarly, the referenda about the European Union in the early 1990s in Scandinavia were as much about the preservation and transformation of identity as anything else.

To return to gay and lesbian identity, mass public occasions such as Gay Pride in London, or the Sydney Mardi Gras, are affirmations that being gay or being lesbian are collective identifications. For individual participants these occasions may (or, indeed, may not) affirm their own particular sexual identities, but they are collective rituals of identification and political mobilisation before they are anything else.

These scenarios, different as they are, exemplify social identity in everyday life. It is the most mundane of things and it can be the most extraordinary. But what does it mean, to say that these situations all involve social identity? What do they have in common? How do we know who we are, and how do others identify us? How does our sense of ourselves as unique individuals square with the realisation that, always and everywhere, we share aspects of our identity with many others? To what extent is it possible to become someone, or something, other than what we now are? Is it possible to 'just be myself'?

This book sketches out a sociological framework for thinking about social identity which addresses questions such as these. Among the most seductive attractions of the study of identity is that it brings the sociological imagination to bear on the mundane dramas, dreams and perplexities of everyday life. It is also perhaps the best device that I know for bringing together 'public issues' and 'private troubles' and encouraging us to use one to make sense of the other.

The obvious place to start is with the most basic questions: what is identity, and what is social identity? Social identity is a characteristic or property of humans as social beings. The word 'identity', however, embraces a universe of creatures, things and substances which is wider than the limited category of humanity. As such, its general meanings are worthy of brief attention, to provide a base line from which to begin our consideration of specifically social identity.

Consulting the Oxford English Dictionary yields a Latin root (*identitas*, from *idem*, 'the same') and two basic meanings. The first is a concept of absolute sameness: this is identical to that. The second is a concept of distinctiveness which presumes consistency or continuity over time. Approaching the idea of sameness from two different angles, the notion of identity simultaneously establishes two possible relations of comparison between persons or things: *similarity*, on the one hand, and *difference*, on the other.

Exploring the matter further, the verb 'to identify' is a necessary accompaniment of identity: there is something active about the word which cannot be ignored. Identity is not 'just there', it must always be established. This adds two further meanings to our catalogue: to classify things or persons, and to associate one*self* *with* something or someone else (for example, a friend, a hero, a party, or a philosophy). Each locates identity within the ebb and flow of practice and process; they are both things that people do. The latter, in the context of social relations, also implies a degree of reflexivity.

We are now firmly in the realm of social identity. Throughout this text I will talk about 'social identity' and 'identity' interchangeably, meaning the former. Doing so follows much contemporary usage and allows for some stylistic flexibility. All human identities are in some sense – and usually a stronger rather than a weaker sense – *social* identities. It cannot be otherwise, if only because identity is about meaning, and meaning is not an essential property of words and things. Meanings are always the outcome of agreement or disagreement, always a matter of convention and innovation, always to some extent shared, always to some extent negotiable.

Some contemporary writers about identity treat it as a basic datum that simply 'is'. This pays insufficient attention to how identity 'works' or 'is worked', to process and reflexivity, to the social construction of identity in interaction and institutionally. Understanding these processes is central to understanding what social identity 'is'. Identity can in fact only be understood *as* process. As 'being' or 'becoming'. One's social identity – indeed, one's social identities, for who we are is always singular and plural – is never a final or settled matter. Not even death can freeze the picture: there is always the possibility of a *post mortem* revision of identity (and some identities, that of the martyr, for example, can only be achieved beyond the grave).

So, how to define 'social identity'? Minimally, the expression refers to the ways in which individuals and collectivities are distinguished in their social relations with other individuals and collectivities. It is the systematic establishment and signification, between individuals, between collectivities, and between individuals and collectivities, of relationships of similarity and difference. Taken – as they can only be – together, similarity and difference are the dynamic principles of identity, the heart of social life:

the practical significance of men for one another ... is determined by both similarities and differences among them. Similarity as fact or tendency is no less important than difference. In the most varied forms, both are the great principles of all internal and external development. In fact the cultural history of mankind can be conceived as the history of the struggles and conciliatory attempts between the two.

(Simmel 1950: 30)

Social identity is a game of 'playing the *vis-à-vis*' (Boon 1982: 26). Social identity is our understanding of who we are and of who other people are, and, reciprocally, other people's understanding of themselves and of others (which includes us). Social identity, is, therefore, no more essential than meaning; it too is the product of agreement and disagreement, it too is negotiable.

Human social life is unimaginable without some means of knowing who others are and some sense of who we are. Since we cannot rely on our sense of smell or our animal non-verbals (although these are not insignificant in the negotiation of identity during encounters), one of the first things that we do on meeting a stranger is attempt to locate them on our social maps, to identify them. And not always successfully: 'mistaken identity' is a common motif of interaction. Someone we thought was Ms A in fact turns out to be Mrs Q, or we take someone for French when they are Belgian.

All kinds of people other than social scientists have cause to reflect upon social identity during their everyday lives. A common theme in everyday discourse, for example, is lost or confused identity, about people not knowing 'who they are', about a 'crisis of identity'. Sometimes people talk about 'social identity'; sometimes they simply talk about 'identity'. More often than not, however, men and women going about the business of their daily lives are concerned with *specific* social identities. We talk, for example, about whether people are born gay or become gay as a result of the way in which they were brought up. About what it means to be 'grown up'. About what the difference is between Canadians and Americans. We observe the family who have just moved in round the corner and shake our heads: what can you expect, they come from the wrong part of town. We watch the television news and jump to all kinds of conclusions about current events on the basis of identifications such as 'Muslim', 'fundamentalist Christian', or whatever.

Social change is often accompanied by rhetoric about 'identity under threat'. Take, for example, the public debate in the United Kingdom about the European Union. While the regulations governing sausage manufacture are presented as a threat to the 'British way of life', the prospect of monetary union in Europe conjures up centuries of strife with our continental neighbours and is interpreted as another attempt to undermine British national identity. Recent debates within the Scandinavian countries about the European Union have thrown a similar barrage of concerns, albeit triggered by different issues.

Whether in the abstract or the concrete, with reference to ourselves or to others, in personal depth or during superficial casual chat, with reference to individuality, nationality, social class, gender or age (etcetera . . .), it seems that we cannot do without some concepts with which to think about social identity, with which to query and confirm who we are and who others are. This is probably true no matter the language or culture; it has probably always been true. Without frameworks for delineating social identity and identities, I would be the same as you and neither of us could relate to the other meaningfully or consistently. Without social identity, there is, in fact, no society.

identities without considering the broader theoretical issues which may be at stake. Another common-sensical strand in much intellectual debate is the use of identity to refer almost exclusively to the collective or individual *self*-determination of identity.

One perspective which is more intellectual than popular is the argument that discourses reflecting on identity are relatively novel and diagnostic of post- or late modernity. This isn't convincing. *How* we talk about self-identity is certainly historically and culturally specific. And it is true that, at the end of the twentieth century, the sheer *volume* of discourse about identity has reached new magnitudes, if only because global noise and chatter has expanded as a consequence of population growth and increasingly efficient and sophisticated communication technologies.

But discourses reflecting upon identity are not dramatically new. An established sociological and psychological literature about social identity goes back to the turn of the century and before. In the present (post)modern hubbub it has been somewhat neglected, but it remains centrally important to the sociological constitution and understanding of identity, and to social theory. Behind that is a more venerable philosophical discourse about identity – it is worth remembering, for example, that the second edition of Locke's *Essay Concerning Human Understanding*, published in 1694, included a chapter on 'Identity and Diversity' – not to mention a variety of religious and legal traditions which are recognisably reflexive about identity.

Popular concern about identity is, in large part perhaps, a reflection of the uncertainty produced by rapid change and cultural contact: our social maps no longer fit our social landscapes. We encounter others whose identity and nature are not clear to us. We are no longer even sure about ourselves; the future is no longer so predictable as it seems to have been for previous generations. But change – the confrontation of languages, traditions and ways of life; the transformation of divisions of labour; demographic flux; catastrophe and calamity – is not in any sense modern. We do not, for example, need too much knowledge of European history to recognise 'crises of identity' in early modern witch-hunting or in the mediaeval persecution of heretics, Jews, lepers and homosexuals, nor to contextualise these in change and upheaval (Moore 1987).

The privacies of the person are among the themes of discourses of identity. Reflexive self-identity is one of the social phenomena which are hailed as diagnostically modern by many sociological commentators (e.g. Giddens 1991). This is at least an overstatement, which tells us more about the conceits of Western modernity than about anything else. It is not, for example, straining interpretive licence to perceive in the religions of personal redemption responses to what Giddens calls 'ontological insecurity' (1991: 53). Salvation is no less a project of the self – although that word begs as many questions in this context as it answers – than 'personal growth' or psychological integration. Ideologies of spiritual salvation seek to understand and identify the essentials of personhood and the meaning of individual conscious existence no less than philosophies of personal growth. Both offer a raft to cling to in the storms of life; in both the relationship between self-deception and self-knowledge is arguably intimate. Saint Augustine's *Confessions*, written more than 1,500 years ago, is a testament to the possibilities for reforging the self, offered as an example for others. Going back nearly another thousand years, one can understand Buddhism as a project for the reformation of selfhood (Carrithers 1985).

The social identities which are prominent at the end of the twentieth century are, of course, to some extent historically and culturally specific, as are the situational contexts and media in and through which contemporary discourses of identity find expression. It would be foolish to suggest, for example, that the women's movement has not been a major historical development. But some claims are too enormous to support. There is, for example, the argument that the individual 'subject', having first appeared as a definitive and unique product of the European Enlightenment, has disappeared under conditions of postmodernity (Jameson 1991). At best this rests upon a notion of subjectivity and agency which is too narrow, too trivial indeed, for sociological use; at worst it takes the presumptions of modernity too much at their own, self-serving face value.

It is nothing new to be self-conscious about social identity – what it means to be human, what it means to be a particular kind of human, what it means to be a person, whether people are what they appear to be – to be uncertain about it, or to assert its importance. To suggest otherwise is to risk a conceit that consigns most of human experience to a historical anteroom, and to reinvent ethnocentrism and historicism under the reassuring sign of postmodernism's break with both.

3
Common sense

A distinction has been drawn between intellectual discourse and common sense. Although too much can be made of this, it is of considerable significance with respect to social identity. I have, for example, suggested that in everyday discourse identity tends to be taken for granted as the *self*-determination of identity, whether by an individual or a collectivity. There is, therefore, a need to clarify some things about this discussion before taking it further.

First, I am not concerned with the complete spectrum of debate about social identity. That would involve an acquaintance-ship with an enormous literature, and a diversity of traditions and ways of thinking and working, which is beyond me. For this reason, some important areas are absent. Recent literary criticism and theory, studies of sexuality, and lesbian and gay studies, are only the most obvious. Perhaps the relevances of my argument for these areas will be appreciated and taken up by others. Second, my word limit has prevented an adequate engagement with the substance of cultural variation, with the diversity of ways of thinking about selfhood, individuality, collectivity, and so on. Finally, I have side-stepped much of the debate about postmodernism. Most commentators on postmodernism are on a historicist mission by any other name, substituting a meta-narrative of fragmentation for the old story of progress. In the pursuit of such grand themes, the mundane is likely to be overlooked. My focus is firmly on the mundane: on how social identity *works*, on the interactional constitution of identity.

The intellectual scope of this discussion is, therefore, limited. My academic working life has been spent on the borders of social anthropology and sociology. These disciplines provide the framework, which for the sake of brevity I will generally describe as sociological,[1] of my argument. Other disciplines, particularly social psychology, philosophy and history, will be raided on occasions – for they have many affinities with sociology and anthropology, and much to say about identity – but this is essentially a sociological text.

So what is the relationship between sociology and common sense? To engage in sociology or social anthropology implies that their points of view are preferable to common sense. This is tricky. Many, perhaps all, of the topics in which sociology and social anthropology are interested – the whys and wherefores of social life – are no less interesting to the lay public. So this claim has to be justified. At least three justifications which don't depend upon dubious claims of epistemological privilege are available (R. Jenkins 1983: 10; see also Bauman 1990: 12–15).

First, sociology and social anthropology should draw upon more, and more detailed, information about the social world than is generally available in everyday discourse. This information is not only found, it is gathered and constructed for our specific purposes. Second, rather than adopting one positional or interested point of view, sociological knowledge should, ideally, encompass, as part of its data, different and even conflicting points of view within the social situation in question. Thus, finally, sociology is not 'part of the action', aimed at furthering particular ends and schemes within that action. Sociology's aims are communication, explanation and generalisation. Sociology is, in the first instance, its own end rather than a means to an end. In this strictly limited sense, sociology and social anthropology are not about *doing* things (other than themselves, that is).

This last point is not advocating a detached sociological enterprise, secure in its ivory tower, unsullied by the concerns of an 'outside world'. Not at all: there can never be an *outside* world. It is, rather, an argument for the primacy of sociology and social anthropology's particular intellectual concerns, which I take to be the production of a particular kind of understanding. Sociological knowledge, if it is to be something more than mere advocacy or administrative expertise, has in the first place to be a goal in itself, not a resource for the pursuit of other goals.

By contrast with common sense, then, sociology should be characterised by *systematic* inquiry, by a degree of *objectivity*, and by *theory*. This view may strike some readers as naive, particularly the bit about objectivity, but it is a defensible set of working assumptions. It is also the basis for expecting sociologists and social anthropologists to talk about social identity and social identities in ways which differ from the uses of these notions in everyday discourse. And they do. But, as in many areas of sociological inquiry, problems arise because sociologists and lay actors often, and unavoidably, use the same words. The distinction between common-sense understandings and sociological usages – or, to be more correct, the usages of some sociologists and social anthropologists – is not always clear.

Invidious though it may be to single them out, three books with 'identity' in their titles may serve to make the point. I selected these titles because they are recent, they are singly-authored, and they are all written by well-established scholars, and in order to include sociologists and anthropologists. The first is *Modernity and Self-Identity: Self and Society in the Late Modern Age* by Anthony Giddens (1991). This text expands upon his earlier critique of the notion of postmodernity (Giddens 1990) to take in the intimacies of selfhood and their transformations at the end of the twentieth century. Giddens argues that self-identity is a distinctively modern project within which individuals can reflexively construct a personal narrative which allows them to understand themselves as in control of their lives and futures. 'Life politics' have emerged in the capitalist democracies to fill the vacuum left by the decline of the politics of class. Giddens is concerned with the politicisation of the personal, the private, and the intimate. An expression with its origins in the women's movement of the 'sixties, 'the personal is the political' provides the sub-text to much of the contemporary concern with identity and, indeed, to Giddens' analysis.

My second example is *Appetites and Identities*, by Sara Delamont (1995), according to its subtitle, 'An Introduction to the Social Anthropology of Western Europe'. Western Europe in this context seems to mean primarily the rural and peripheral peoples of Europe, and, in terms of the ethnographies which are drawn upon for illustration, primarily southern Europe. Unlike Giddens,

Delamont is self-consciously offering a textbook for an uninitiated audience, focusing upon cultural variety among and between European peoples and the practices and beliefs – religion, tastes, values, food, gender roles, etc. – which provide indices of cultural difference and yardsticks of social change.

The scope claimed by my third example is the widest of all. Jonathan Friedman's *Cultural Identity and Global Process* (1994) is concerned with the implications for identity – particularly identity which is linked to local cultural membership – of the fact that we all, to some extent, inhabit a burgeoning world system of information, commerce and rapid transportation in which global similarities are becoming as marked as local differences. A new socio-cultural 'level' – the global – is emerging. This is another argument for the novelty and specificity of the late twentieth-century social scene. Along the way Friedman is also concerned with the implications of this new world order for anthropology, which has been shaped by its fieldwork encounters with the culturally local and exotic and prides itself upon its ability to inter-pret, if not translate, across cultural divides, to make sense out of difference.

These authors are discussed here only to exemplify a particular problem in the literature; they are not representative in any other sense. Friedman is an anthropologist, Giddens a sociologist, and Delamont a sociologist writing about anthropology. Although they cannot be dismissed as 'mere' common sense, these books illustrate, in their different ways, the influential and implicit place within sociology and social anthropology of two understandings of social identity which are widespread in Western societies (and perhaps further afield).

The first is the assumption that individual identity and collective identity are qualitatively, if not utterly, different. This is rooted in the foundational axiom that there are concrete things called individuals, over and against which stands something more abstract called 'society'. This distinction is neither stupid nor necessarily problematic. But taking it for granted *is* a problem, and theorisa-tions of the relationship between the two often treat the categories of individual and society as axiomatic. The distinction can be established in a number of ways. In Western common sense, for example, either the body or the soul/mind are commonly taken as referents of unique individuality. Society, by contrast, appears in everyday notions such as 'tradition', 'values', 'community' or 'the law'. Although it has been rigorously criticised, this ontology derives continuing sociological authority from the Durkheimian tradition and various strands of positivism.

Delamont presumes this division of the social world: there are individuals, on the one hand, and cultures and societies, on the other. Identity, despite being central to more than the book's title, goes untheorised as a matter of collective identities, particularly the cultural or the ethnic. Giddens is more sophisticated, but despite insisting that distinctions between the self and the social are problematic, he too assumes that personal identity and social identity are different:

> In many settings of pre-modern cultures . . . Appearance primarily designated social identity rather than personal identity. Dress and social identity have certainly not become entirely dissociated today, and dress remains a signalling device of gender, class position and occupational status.
>
> (Giddens 1991: 99)

Friedman explicitly relies upon an ideal-typical distinction between different systems of social (cultural) identity and individual (self) identity:

> The relation between the individual subject and social identity is generally poorly researched. . . . the way in which cultural identities are constituted is dependent upon the way in which individual selfhood is constructed.
>
> (Friedman 1994: 33)

This quotation is suggestive of the other common-sense view of identity which concerns me here. Having distinguished the individual–personal from the social–cultural, one is assumed to be more important – if not actually more 'real' – than the other. The greater is also often assumed, even if only in the last instance, to determine the lesser. This model exists in alternate versions, each of which can appear in different guises, rooted in different ontologies of society, reflecting different understandings of human experience.

In the least common-sensical version, social identity is taken to exist in a less problematic fashion than individual identity. This may – only apparently paradoxically – suggest that social identities, because of their greater robustness, are the more flexible. In this view individual personhood is often seen as vulnerable or fragile; as historically and culturally contingent; as socially determined; as in itself insecure. In this view social identities endure historically, persons are transient actors on the historical stage. Elsewhere in his book, and in apparent contradiction to the quotation above, Friedman, for example, suggests that, existentially at least, individual identity is so dependent upon the socio-cultural domain that it cannot be negotiable: 'Otherwise it has no existence' (p. 140).

In this model, social identity or – more exactly – social identities exist and persist in a relatively straightforward manner, although they may change or be changed, and particular identities may be more or less problematic or threatened, depending upon circumstances. They are spoken of as something which people 'have' or 'are' or 'belong to' (everyday idioms which can be difficult to abandon with any consistency). Social identities are thus liable to reification as solid or hard-edged, as phenomena which exert influence 'above our heads' or 'behind our backs'. Actions may be explained or predicted by reference to the identities of actors. Delamont and Friedman both at times talk in this way. This view finds a common-sense voice in opinions such as, 'Well, what can you expect from a so-and-so?' in justifications of individual behaviour by reference to group membership; in characterisations of conflict as 'tribal' or 'ethnic' (to say which is taken to be explanation enough).

Taking social identity for granted in this fashion leads to the confusion of common sense and sociology in other ways. Take, for example, the mild functionalism involved in characterising behaviour as productive or reproductive of identity. An innocent enough way of thinking, and seductive, it introduces the danger of confusing the sociologist's model of the situation for the local common-sense model. Delamont, for example, discussing Welsh wedding receptions, suggests that, 'What is being transmitted is a statement about proper food and the proper role of women' (1995: 35). Couched in different terms, this might be a legitimate, even revealing, *interpretation* of the organisation of wedding feasts, and of their consequences, but it is doubtful whether a *statement* about either food or women is being made, let alone *transmitted*.

The other version of the relationship between the individual–personal and the social–cultural is more characteristic of common sense. It expresses an ontology which privileges the person and the individual, as compared to society (which is either 'less real' or 'not real at all'). None of the authors mentioned can be arraigned for this kind of strong individualism, although Giddens sails close to that particular wind on occasion. For him, the self is distinctively modern: although it is vulnerable and contingent, it is available to individual actors for the purposes of personal narrative (re)construction and projects of 'personal growth'. Individualism is, unsurprisingly, most characteristic of disciplines such as psychology, philosophy and economics (although even liberal and neo-classical economists, for example, persist in their faith in the metaphysics and existence of 'the market'). Sociologists and social anthropologists may espouse methodological individualism – the view that the only acceptable *data* are statements about individuals and aggregates of individuals – but they are, with a few arguable exceptions such as ethnomethodology, unlikely to adopt a radical theoretical individualism. Most social scientists, although they may argue as to how best to apprehend or understand it, persist in the view there is such a thing as society.

The idea that individualistic views of identity characterise common sense more than sociology requires further comment. I could, for example, have argued that sociology is collectivist, while common sense is individualistic. I didn't because neither proposition is, in any straightforward sense, true. It depends, in the first place, on how one defines sociology. C. Wright Mills offers a view which still commands considerable support:

> The sociological imagination enables its possessor to understand the larger historical scene in terms of its meaning for the inner life and the external career of a variety of individuals ... to grasp history and biography and the relations between the two within society. ... Perhaps the most fruitful distinction with which the sociological imagination works is between 'the personal troubles of milieu' and 'the public issues of social structure'.
>
> (Mills 1959: 5, 6, 8)

There is nothing collectivist about this: the individual is, in fact, placed at the heart of the enterprise (although not more so than the collective). In Mills' understanding, the *social* is the field upon which the individual and the collective meet and meld. His view provides one basis for the understanding of social identity offered in this book.

A bald characterisation of common sense as individualistic raises different issues. For example, we must ask, *whose* common sense? Even if it is defensible to generalise for the sake of argument about 'Western common sense', or 'Western European common sense', in doing so we neglect considerable diversity within that category. How, for example, should we characterise the distinctively Scandinavian attachment to corporatist social democracy *and* individualist egalitarianism? Or what about Christianity, with its notions and practices of communion and congregation? And let's not forget that socialism is historically the product of Western Europe (as, indeed, is sociology). Further, a coarse-grained view ignores cross-cultural variation in models of the collective and the individual. What about the almost infinite plurality of 'non-Western' common senses?

In addition, there is more to individualism than the radical political ontology of liberalism. Recognising this offers the possibility of more flexible understandings of common-sense individualism. We move closer to the realities of everyday life, perhaps, by viewing the individualist viewpoint as a pragmatic interpretive framework which permits actors to construct a first line of sense and defence in a social world which, whatever else, is peopled by embodied individuals, of which we are each one, and with whom we each have to deal. We are all to some extent – and of necessity – pragmatic individualists in our dealings with others. As suggested by the quotation from Mills above, pragmatic individualism is a prerequisite for the exercise of the sociological imagination rather than a barrier to it.

4

Theorising social identity

I have argued that much sociological and everyday discourse
draws a distinction of type between *social* identity (or identities)
and *individual* identity. This underpins a further assumption that
one – it doesn't matter which for present purposes – is more real
or less problematic than the other. The relationship between
individual unique identity and collective shared identity is left
relatively unexplored, or treated as axiomatic. As a consequence,
even very sophisticated sociological arguments often offer a 'black
box' where there should be an understanding of how identity
works or is worked, of what it *is*. Something important is taken for
granted, something important is missed.

Among the central arguments of this book are that the
individually unique and the *collectively shared* can be understood as
similar (if not exactly the same) in important respects; that each is
routinely related to – or, better perhaps, entangled with – the other;
that the processes by which they are produced, reproduced and
changed are analogous; and that *both* are intrinsically social. The
theorisation of social identity must include each in equal measure.
Perhaps the most significant difference between individual and
collective identities is that the former emphasises difference, the

latter similarity. Even this, however, is never more than a matter of their respective emphases.

My intention in what follows is to begin the rehabilitation of the concept of social identity for sociological use; to put it (back?) in its proper place at the heart of our thinking about the relationship between our concrete models of individual behaviour, on the one hand, and our necessarily more abstract concepts of the collective, on the other. This perennial sociological issue, introduced to generations of students as the 'structure–action' problem or, more recently, following Giddens, as the 'structuration' debate, is the context within which my argument belongs. A theorised model of social identity is vital if that debate is to be moved forward.

The model that I propose is, however, in important respects not new. George Herbert Mead, Erving Goffman and Fredrik Barth have been particularly influential in shaping my argument. The line of theoretical kinship and development which connects them is the intellectual genealogy of this book. Many other authors have been influential – Gilbert Ryle, Howard Becker, Peter Berger and Thomas Luckman, Anthony Cohen, Pierre Bourdieu, and Anthony Giddens, most notably – but Mead, Goffman and Barth have been my inspiration.

The bare outlines of the argument can be summarised as follows. If identity is a necessary prerequisite for social life, the reverse is also true. Individual identity – embodied in selfhood – is not meaningful in isolation from the social world of other people. Individuals are unique and variable, but selfhood is thoroughly socially constructed: in the processes of primary and subsequent socialisation, and in the ongoing processes of social interaction within which individuals define and redefine themselves and others throughout their lives. This view derives from American pragmatism, via the seminal contributions of Cooley (1962; 1964) and Mead (1934). From their work, an understanding emerges of the 'self' as an ongoing and, in practice simultaneous, synthesis of (internal) self-definition and the (external) definitions of oneself offered by others. This offers a template for the basic model which informs my whole argument, of the *internal–external dialectic of identification* as the process whereby all identities – individual and collective – are constituted.

Mead distinguished the 'I' (the ongoing moment of unique individuality) from the 'me' (the internalised attitudes of significant others). Although this formulation requires considerable modification (see Chapter 7), the general idea does not: I argue for a unitary model of selfhood, but that unity is a dialectical synthesis of internal and external definitions. Mead further insisted that self-consciousness, indeed cognition itself, can only be achieved by taking on or assuming the position of the other, in his terms a social 'generalised other'. This is another idea which cannot be swallowed whole. But the view that 'mind' is an intrinsically social phenomenon, reciprocally implicated in identity, is central to the model which, drawing also upon Ryle's philosophy of mind, I propose here. In everyday terms, Mead suggests that we cannot see ourselves at all without also seeing ourselves as other people see us. For him society is, in a sense, no more than an extension of this basic theorem of identification.

Mead is equally clear that mind and selfhood are attributes of *embodied* individuals. The embodiment of social identity is another thread in my argument. That human beings have bodies is among the most obvious things about us, as are the extensive communicative and non-utilitarian uses to which we put them. The human body is simultaneously a referent of individual continuity, an index of collective similarity and differentiation, and a canvas upon which identification can play. Social identification in isolation from embodiment is unimaginable.

Individual identity formation has its roots in our earliest processes of socialisation. Recent post-Piagetian understandings of learning in infancy and childhood allow the development of cognition and the development of identity to be located side-by-side in primary socialisation. This further suggests that identities which are established this early in life – selfhood, human-ness, gender, and, under some circumstances, kinship and ethnicity – are *primary identities*, more robust and resilient to change in later life than other identities. Although change and mutability are endemic in all social identities, they are more likely for some identities than others. The primary identifications of selfhood, human-ness and gender, in addition to their deep-rooting in infancy and early childhood, are definitively embodied (as local understandings of kinship and ethnicity may also be). Where locally perceived embodiment is a criterion of any social identity, be it individual or collective, fluidity may be the exception rather than the rule.

To return to the internal–external dialectic, what people think about us is no less important than what we think about ourselves. It is not enough to assert an identity. That identity must also be validated (or not) by those with whom we have dealings. *Social identity is never unilateral*. Hence the importance of what Goffman

(1969) described as 'the presentation of self' during interaction. Although people have (some) control over the signals about themselves which they send to others, we are all at a disadvantage in that we cannot ensure either their 'correct' reception or interpretation, or know with certainty how they are received or interpreted. Hence the importance of what Goffman calls 'impression management strategies' in the construction of social identity. These dramatise the interface between *self-image* and *public image*. Impression management draws to our attention the performative aspect of social identity, and the fact that it is embedded within social practice.

An important assumption made by both Goffman (and indeed by Barth, about whom more below) is that individuals consciously pursue goals. They seek to 'be' – and to be 'seen to be' – 'something' or 'somebody', to assume successfully particular social identities. This raises two important questions. First: is a self-conscious decision-making model appropriate to the understanding of human behaviour? Second: is this kind of choice-making with respect to identity characteristic only of modern, industrialised societies? My answers to these questions, which underlie the whole discussion, are, to the first a qualified 'yes', and, to the second an emphatic 'no'. Bourdieu, another anthropologist much influenced by Goffman, offers a useful perspective on these issues when he emphasises (1977; 1990) the essentially improvisational quality of interaction. He talks about 'habitus', the domain of habit, which, in the presentation of self, operates neither consciously nor unconsciously, neither deliberately nor automatically. Although his notion of habitus is not without its problems (R. Jenkins 1992: 74–84), it is in a number of senses particularly resonant with the point of view offered here: habitus is both collective and individual, and definitively embodied.

Not only do we identify ourselves, of course, but we also identify others and are identified by them in turn, in the internal–external dialectic between self-image and public image. One – recently sadly neglected – understanding of this dialectic is offered by the labelling perspective in the sociology of deviance (e.g. Becker 1963; Matza 1969). It describes the interaction between (internal) self-definition and definition by others (externally) as a process of internalisation. Internalisation may occur if one is authoritatively labelled within an institutional social setting. A model of internalisation is not, however, sufficient. Significant in the processes whereby people acquire the identities with which they are labelled is the capacity of authoritatively applied identities effectively to constitute or impinge upon individual experience. This is a question of whose definition of the situation *counts* (put crudely, power). Identification by others has consequences; it is often the capacity to generate those consequences which matters. Labelling may also, of course, evoke resistance (which, no less than internalisation, is an 'identity effect' produced by labelling). Although the labelling perspective is typically concerned with deviance and social control, the model is relevant in other contexts – education and the labour market, for example – and with respect to positive as well as to negative labels.

Moving on to ever more collective identities, Karl Marx distinguished between a 'class in itself' and 'a class for itself'. The first is united only in the eye of the beholder, through the attribution to individuals of specific characteristics in common, in this case their relationship to the means of production. In the second, those individuals come to realise their shared situation and define themselves accordingly as members of the same collectivity. Appropriating the methodological distinction between groups and categories, a distinction can be made between a collectivity which identifies and defines itself (a group *for* itself) and a collectivity which is identified and defined by others (a category *in* itself).

More to the point, and in order to avoid reifying assumptions about the 'reality' of collectivities, it makes sense to distinguish processes of *group identification* and *social categorisation*. This is the internal–external dialectic once again. Both processes, group identification and categorisation, can feed back upon each other, and are likely to do so. Problematising the group–category distinction brings us back to the centrality of power (and therefore politics) in processes of identity maintenance and change. It is typically in political contexts that collective identities are asserted, defended, imposed or resisted. One of the core components of my argument is that the external or categorical dimensions of identity are not only centrally important but have been underplayed, if not ignored altogether, in most theorisations of identity.

Goffman's influence can be traced in the anthropological arguments of Barth (1969; 1981), who offers a model of ethnic and other social identities as somewhat fluid, situationally contingent, and the perpetual subject and object of negotiation. One of Barth's key propositions is that it is not enough to send a message about identity; that message has to be accepted by significant others before an identity can be said to be 'taken on'. As a consequence, identities are to be found and negotiated at their boundaries, where the internal and the external meet. Staying with Barth, and drawing also upon Anthony Cohen's discussion of the symbolic construction of communal identity (1985), group identity is characteristically constructed across the group boundary, in interaction with others. Boundaries are permeable, persisting despite the flow of personnel across them, and identity is constructed in transactions which occur at and across the boundary. It is in these transactions that a balance is struck between group identification and categorisation by others.

The distinction which Barth (1969) draws between 'boundary' and 'content' (the 'cultural stuff' which is supposed to characterise an ethnic group, for example) allows a wider distinction to be drawn between *nominal* identity and *virtual* identity. The former is the *name*, and the latter the *experience*, of an identity, what it means to bear it. It is possible for individuals to share the same nominal identity, and for that to mean very different things to them in practice, to have different consequences for their lives, for them to 'do' it differently. This distinction is related to the category–group distinction but not conterminous with it. It also brings us back to the consequences of identification by others, as in labelling. And the distinction is important. The name can stay the same – 'X' for example – while the experience of being an 'X' can change dramatically; similarly, the experience may stay relatively stable while the name changes. Or both can change. Processes of either group-identification or categorisation can contribute to this range of possibilities. Power and politics are central to questions of identity. To return to Marx, the mobilisation of a social category into a social group is a political process, which may be achieved from within or without the collectivity in question. That is a change of virtual identity, but it may also be associated, over time, with a nominal change. At the nominal level, the categorisation of people, for example by the state, may be subject to change and it may be resisted. It may also be part of a change in the virtual, in their conditions of life. Although the nominal and the virtual are analytically distinct they are in practice chronically implicated in each other.

Among the more important contexts within which identification becomes consequential are institutions. Institutions are established patterns of practice, recognised as such by actors, which have force as 'the way things are done'. Institutionalised identities are distinctive because of their particular combination of the individual and the collective. Particularly relevant are those institutions which the sociological literature recognises as *organisations*. Organisations are organised and task-oriented collectivities: they are groups. They are also constituted as networks of differentiated membership positions which bestow specifically individual identities upon their incumbents. In addition, identity is bound up with social classification practices. In order for persons to be classified, however, a classificatory lexicon must exist: positions and categories, for example. Since organisations – whether formal or informal – are made up, among other things, of positions, and procedures for recruiting individuals to them, they are important in social classification. The constitution and distribution of positions is the outcome of political relationships and struggles, within and without organisations. Institutional recruitment procedures, in allocating persons to those positions, authoritatively allocate particular kinds of identities to individuals (and draw upon wider typifications of identity to do so). This is one of the ways in which nominal and virtual identities are implicated in each other: the allocation of positions is also the allocation of resources and penalties. Consistency in individual recruitment practices – in the labour market, for example – contributes to the formation, maintenance and change of consistent collectivities, classes of persons characterised by similar life-chances and experiences.

Thus individual and collective identities are systematically produced, reproduced and implicated in each other. Following Foucault, Hacking (1990) argues that the classification of individuals is at the heart of modern, bureaucratically rational strategies of government and social control (which is not a back door admission of the distinctive modernity of discourses of identity, or reflexive identity itself). Social identities exist and are acquired, claimed and allocated within power relations. Identity is something *over* which struggles take place and *with* which stratagems are advanced: it is means and end in politics. Not only is the classification of individuals at issue but also the classification of populations.

So far two basic threads can be discerned in my argument. First, social identity is a practical accomplishment, a process. Second, individual and collective social identities can be understood using one model, of the dialectical interplay of processes of internal and external definition. The most persistent theme in social theory is the attempt to 'bridge the analytical gap' between the individual and society (action and structure, etc.). From Marx to Weber to Parsons to Berger and Luckmann to Giddens, the same questions are asked, albeit in different words and tones. How can we fruitfully bring into the same analytical space the active lives and consciousnesses of individuals, the abstract impersonality of the institutional order, and the ebb and flow of historical time? How to bring public issues and personal troubles into the same frame?

Social identity is a strategic concept in broaching these questions, for a number of reasons. First, identities are necessarily attributes of embodied individuals which are equally necessarily socially constituted, sometimes at a high level of abstraction. In social identity (or identities) the collective and the individual occupy the same space. Second, if social identity is conceptualised in terms of process, as here, a sharp distinction between structure and action may be avoided. Third, if those processes are conceptualised as a perpetual dialectic of two analytically (but only analytically) distinct moments – the internal and the external – then the opposition between the objective and the subjective may also be sidestepped. Fourth, since identity is bound up with cultural repertoires of intentionality such as morality, on the one hand, and with networks of constraint and possibility, on the other, it is an important concept in our understanding of action and its outcomes, both intended and unintended. Fifth, the institutional order is, at least in part, a network of identities (positions) and of routinised practices for allocating positions (and therefore identities) to individuals. Sixth, there is a direct relationship between the distribution of resources and penalties in society and social identity: identity is a criterion for distribution and is constituted in terms of patterns of distribution. Means and end again. Seventh, in identifying internal and external moments of identification a necessary connection is made between domination and resistance and processes of social identification. Lastly, the classification of populations as a practice of state and other agencies is powerfully constitutive both of the institutional order and of the experience of individuals in the interaction order.

There is more to be said about the distinction between the external and the internal. As with Mead's choice of 'I' and 'me' – one of the contexts in which the issue first appears and first appears as problematic – this may in some senses be an unfortunate usage. The danger exists of reifying or objectifying a distinction which is only pragmatic and analytical, which commits necessary violence to the complexities and subtleties of living in order to pin them down in the pursuit of better understanding. It is not meant to imply necessary sequence (first one, then the other): in principle they are simultaneous dimensions of ongoing social practice. This is what I hope to suggest by the expression 'moments of identification'. In this dialectical model the focus is firmly upon the synthesis. Nor is this usage meant to suggest difference of kind. Your external definition of me is an inexorable part of my internal definition of myself – even if only in the process of rejection or resistance – and vice versa. Both processes are among the routine everyday practices of actors. Nor is one more significant than the other. At best I am indicating different modes of mutual identification which proceed, not side by side, but in the same social space. It may be possible, and analytically necessary, to distinguish different kinds of collective identities – groups and categories – in terms of the relative significance to each of internal or external moments of identification, but this is only a matter of emphasis, and as far as one should take it.

That identity is, so to speak, both interior and exterior is one reason why it is so important for the integration within social theory of the individual and the collective. Something else which is significant in this respect is the centrality of time and space as resources for the social construction of identity. Philosophers – Aristotle in *Metaphysics* is a well-known example – have long remarked this with respect to identity in its widest sense, as a property of substantial 'things' in general. To identify something is to locate it in time and space. With respect to social identity the issue is different and more specific. The importance of the three dimensions of space, and their material coalescence into a 'sense of place', is implicit within the interior–exterior relationship. Identity is always constructed from a point of *view*. For individuals this is, in the first instance, located within the body. Individual identity is always embodied, albeit sometimes figuratively or imaginatively (in fiction or myth, for example). Collective social identities can be similarly located within territory or region, even if it is the imagined territory of a myth of return or a spatially modelled chart of organisational structure. Since bodies always occupy territories, the individual and the collective are to some extent superimposed.

Philosophers have also long understood that time is bound up with space in one's experience of self and others (Campbell 1994). Space makes no sense outside of time. Time is important in processes of identification because of the continuity which, even if only logically, is entailed in a claim to, or an attribution of, identity.

Social continuity necessitates the positing of a meaningful past. Social identities are in themselves one foundation upon which order and predictability in the social world are based. The past is an important resource upon which to draw in interpreting the here-and-now and in forecasting the future. Individually, 'the past' is memory; collectively, it is history. Neither, however, are 'real': both are fundamentally constructs and both are important facets of identity (Connerton 1989; Fentress and Wickham 1992;. Hobsbawm and Ranger 1983; Samuel and Thompson 1990). But that they are imagined does not mean they are imaginary.

This, then, is the basic framework for the arguments of the chapters which follow. I make no claim to be dramatically innovative. My aims are to restore to sociological usefulness points of view about identity which are presently somewhat neglected; to bring together discourses – particularly social anthropology and sociology – which occasionally frustrate me in their apparent mutual ignorance of each other; and to create a synthesis which is greater than the sum of its parts. That synthesis is a theoretical space within which 'self' and 'society' can be understood as different kinds of abstraction from the same phenomenon, human behaviour and experience. I shall begin with the 'self'.

5

Selfhood and mind

What do we mean when we talk about the self? According to the *Oxford English Dictionary*, the word has Germanic roots, and a known pedigree stretching back more than a thousand years. Four basic meanings emerge from pages of usages and examples. The first indicates uniformity, as in the 'self-same', for example. The second, and most common, denotes the individuality or essence of a person or thing: herself, yourself, myself, itself, etcetera. This simultaneously evokes consistency – internal sameness – over time, and difference from external others. The third meaning refers to introspection or reflexive action. Often expressed as a prefix, examples of this are self-doubt, self-confidence, or self-consciousness. Finally there is a sense of independence and autonomous agency, as in self-improvement, self-propulsion: 'she did it herself'.

   Thus the meanings of the word 'self' parallel the general meanings of 'identity' discussed earlier. There are the core features of *similarity*, *difference*, *reflexivity* and *process*. This is no coincidence. It leads me to propose a definition of the self as each individual's reflexive sense of her or his own particular identity, constituted *vis à vis* others in terms of similarity and difference, without which we would not know who we are and hence would not be able to act.

The literature about the self is vast, and so varied that I cannot pretend to survey it comprehensively.[1] A theme which runs through much of it is the distinction between the 'self' and the 'person'. The conventional understanding of these notions distinguishes the private, interior and psychological self from the public, external and social person (e.g. Harré 1983; Mauss 1985). The self is the individual's private experience of herself or himself; the person is what appears publicly in and to the outside world.

It is necessary to distinguish the internal from the external. Not everything that goes on in our heads and hearts is obvious to others. Nor is there always a fit between how we see ourselves and how others see us (or how we imagine they do). This is one aspect of the view of social identity I am offering here and we need some way of talking about it. However, too absolute a distinction between 'inside' and 'outside' obscures that view. So, against the widespread and well-established conventional distinction between 'self' and 'person', I want to insist that selfhood and personhood are completely, intimately and utterly implicated in each other.

Finding a metaphor for this simultaneity is not easy: 'different sides of the same coin' might catch it, describing them as eddies in the same stream is better. Each is an aspect of individual identity, and in each the internal and the external cohabit in one ongoing social process of identification. Talking about the internal–external dialectic of identification is an attempt to communicate this. The internal and external aspects of this process can be regarded as simultaneous moments. This implies temporality and process, but not necessarily sequence; one should not be seen as, by definition, following the other (although this doesn't mean that this can never happen). The word 'moment' is another metaphor, derived from applied mathematics: *moment* expresses the force around a central point as a combined function of mass and distance. The central point is, if you like, the identity at issue, the synthesis of the external and internal; mass and distance suggest the social factors which determine the strength of the identification process, whether internal or external.

Furthermore, it is important to recognise that we often don't differentiate self and person in everyday speech. If I speak 'personally' to you, my claim to authenticity relies upon the implication of an essence of self. In general terms, the difference between self and personality is not clear, a confusion which exists as much in psychology as in common sense. This might, as Mauss suggested (1985: 20), reflect a historical convergence of meanings in this respect in European culture: the public persona has increasingly been defined in terms of the psychological characteristics of the self. However, an equally plausible reason why selfhood and personhood are so difficult to distinguish might be that the 'internal' and the 'external' are, for each of us, inextricably entangled.

European intellectual traditions recognise two polar models of humanity, the 'autonomous' and the 'plastic' (Hollis 1977), each with its implicit model of the self. The autonomous self evokes reflexivity and independence. The emphasis is on the internal. Although this may be how we would prefer to see ourselves in the mirror, it is also an image of anxiety and uncertainty, of an existential world in which individual moral judgements derive internally from personal preference or feeling, rather than from external cultural canons of authoritative precept or the responsibilities of position. Resembling the fragmentation which Marx called alienation, and even more closely Durkheim's *anomie*, this has been characterised by Alasdair MacIntyre (1985: 31ff.) as the 'emotive self'. It is a self for which the most appropriate suffix might be '-indulgence'.

At the other end of the spectrum, the plastic self is an epiphenomenon of society, determined rather than determining. Here the emphasis is on the external. Structural functionalism and structuralism, each drawing upon Durkheim, are conventionally regarded as the exemplary sociological variations on this theme (although closer inspection of the work of, say, Parsons or Lévi-Strauss reveals more moderation in this respect than textbook caricatures suggest). This model of the self reaches its logical end in Althusser's argument – which finds resonance in Foucault – that the 'autonomous subject' is an ideological notion which fools individuals into misunderstanding their own domination as self-willed. Therefore they 'freely' accept it: 'There are no subjects except by and for their subjection' (Althusser 1971: 182).

Images of autonomy and plasticity each offer more than a grain of the truth. Each, just as obviously, is inadequate. There is as much and as good reason for rejecting a model of selfhood defined in terms of individual interiority, autonomy and reflexivity, as for refusing to accept a view of the self as externally determined by society. The first suggests an essential self which is, at least in part, untouched by upbringing, knowing its own mind but little else. The second denies the reality of a 'creative' or 'authorial' self (A.P. Cohen 1994: 21–54), able to make up its own mind and to act. To borrow Dennis Wrong's famous expression (1961), where one is undersocialised, the other is oversocialised. Both are unsatisfactory. Neither offers a convincing account of the exercise of rationality within culture by thinking actors. This suggests that in order to come to terms with the self, an account of the mind – of consciousness and thought – is required.

The mind is more and less than the brain. But what? A sociological approach to this question needs an initial definition which doesn't reduce 'it' to either physiology or metaphysics. Something along these lines: the mind consists of the organised processes of consciousness, communication and decision-making which we detect as much in individuals going about their everyday business as in the peaks of intellectual or artistic creativity. We need some model of this combination of perception, information handling, and intentionality if we are to understand human agency. For this reason, if no other, it is a prerequisite for understanding identity.

The mind is axiomatically synonymous with the self for many authors. This is reasonable. A self without a mind is unimaginable, and vice versa. But to say this raises difficulties. Does a damaged mind mean a damaged self? Does 'greater' or 'lesser' intellectual competence have implications for selfhood? These are awkward questions to ask, let alone answer. They are, for example, at the heart of debates about the treatment of impaired foetuses or neonates, or about the social and personal status of individuals with learning difficulties. The issues are ambiguous and delicate. For the moment, suffice it to say that although mind and selfhood are so closely related as to be in some respects inseparable, they are not the same phenomenon.

Another pertinent difficulty is familiar to philosophers as the 'other minds' problem (Wisdom 1952): how can we know what is going on in someone else's mind, since we cannot watch it or hear it? Hence, how can we understand someone else's selfhood? This is a mundane question, of a type which confronts us throughout everyday life, which is also fundamental to social science epistemology. According to one answer, the only mental processes to which we can ever have access are our own. Reflecting upon these, all we can do is to assume that those of other humans are similar in their workings if not in their content. This view often entails a second presumption that there *is* something special upon which to reflect, which differs from – and is causally prior to – overt behaviour. Anthony Cohen adopts both positions, arguing for 'the primacy of the self'. Whether it be soul, spirit or mind, in this view every individual has a cloistered essence of selfhood/ 'Selfhood rests on the essential privacy of meaning; in what else might it consist?/ (A. P. Cohen 1994: 142).

Before attempting to answer Cohen's question, his argument also raises epistemological issues. For example, his scepticism about the 'reasonable' assumption that uniformity of behaviour within a group indicates uniformity of thought, is 'purely intuitive' (p. 89). The issue is not whether he is wrong (I'm sure that he's not). Nor is it that he seems to have missed Wallace's convincing logical argument (1970: 24–38) in support of such scepticism: for Wallace, 'cognitive non-sharing' is, in fact, a 'functional prerequisite' of society. No, the problem is that in *presupposing* the existence of a private self which has 'primacy' – as a core of individual being – Cohen is lead into metaphysical assertion rather than defensible argument. His position is inscrutable; it can be neither wrong nor right.

Why should there be an epistemological problem about the self and, by extension, the mind? Well, first, the 'other minds' problem is real. We cannot 'read' other people's minds. But this doesn't mean that we must accept an interior–exterior model which identifies a domain of selfhood that is accessible only privately, and uniquely, to each individual, and about which others can only intuit at best. If that was true, everyday life would be very difficult indeed. How would we come to know other people at all, let alone get to know them well? Life is full of surprises, but it would be impossibly unpredictable if we couldn't know something – enough to be going on with – about the minds of others. And much sociological research would be in vain. So perhaps the wisest thing to do where possible is to sidestep, as incapable of resolution, issues concerning the ontology of the self. Instead, making a simplifying assumption that there is a self – as defined earlier[2] – I will ask, what is it possible to know about it?

Gilbert Ryle, in his robust critique of the Cartesian dualism of the mental and the physical, argues that an individual's understanding of herself or himself is no different in kind from her or his understanding of others:

> The sorts of things that I can find out about myself are the same as the sorts of things that I can find out about other people, and the methods of finding them out are much the

same. A residual difference in the supplies of the requisite
data makes some differences in degree between what I can
know about myself and what I can know about you, but
these differences are not all in favour of self knowledge.

(Ryle 1963: 149)

The data Ryle has in mind are visible behaviour, talk (whether
silent to oneself, vocal to oneself, or vocal to others), and other
communicative practices – such as writing – and their products.
'Unstudied talk', which is 'spontaneous, frank, and unprepared'
(p. 173), is particularly important. Our methods for deciding what
we are about and what others are about are observation and
retrospection.

For Ryle, introspection is implausible, requiring a capacity to
do something and to think about doing it – thus to do two things
– simultaneously. He uses this very particular definition of introspection to argue that actors possess no privileged way of knowing
themselves, compared to their ways of knowing others. But he
overstates the case about doing two things at once. The point is
literally true. Just as no two physical 'things' can occupy the
same space at the same time, no two words – whether uttered or
thought – can issue from the same speaker simultaneously. But
I can, for example, engage in a conversation while, during the
same performative flow of time, reflecting on the conversation and
the behaviour of all the parties to it (including myself). Although
this is, strictly, *retro*spection, it can be understood as a kind of introspection: my reflections will always be at least a micro-second
behind the action, but interactionally they are contemporaneous
with, and part of, their object. By this argument, retrospection isn't
possible until the business of interaction is finished. If this is
correct, introspection doesn't actually require privileged access: it
is observing oneself rather than observing others.

Reflexivity, therefore, involves observation and retrospection,
and is essentially similar whether I am considering myself or others.
Potentially I have different data available in each case. I may have
more information about myself, including recollections of my talk
with myself, and biographical data only I know. On the other hand,
I cannot observe myself in *quite* the way that I can observe others.
Ryle is correct: self-knowledge is not necessarily more accurate
than our knowledge of others, and self-awareness does not entail
'privileged access' to the mind. Accepting this, we can begin to
account for the common realisation that our understanding of

ourselves is at least as imperfect as our understanding of others (something which Cohen, for example, doesn't sufficiently acknowledge).

A possibility that Ryle doesn't consider is projection. And yet to know what we are doing and who we are, we must have some idea of what we are going to or might do. Intentionality is thus an important aspect of mind (and therefore selfhood). But more than intentions are involved: planning involves drawing on direct and indirect experience, on theoretical reasoning, and on the hunches of implicit practical logic, in the attempt to make the future more predictable. However, projection is about more than reducing uncertainty. It is a human characteristic to look beyond the here and now, to locate oneself as the link between a past and a future (Clark 1992). Thus it makes sense to include projection with retrospection and observation in the repertoire of reflexivity.

For Ryle, minds are neither occult nor secret: 'Overt intelligent performances are not clues to the workings of minds; they are those workings' (p. 57). If the mind is conceived of as mental processes, then these are to be found 'out there' as much as 'in here'. This doesn't uncouple individual minds from individual persons; that would reduce the argument to the absurd (and, anyway, individual persons are also 'out there'). But it does suggest that minds work as much *between* individuals as *within* them. Ryle's is a model of 'mind' – rather than, or as well as, 'the mind' – which offers the prospect of a theoretical framework for integrating individuals and the cultural domain without either being seen as determinate of the other.[3]

Although this view doesn't sit easily beside the presumptions of common sense, other models of the mind offer general encouragement. Among the most intriguing is Bateson's 'ecology of mind' (1972). This pictures the relationship between individual organism and environment as a cybernetic network within which information flows backwards and forwards: 'mind obviously does not stop with the skin' (Bateson 1991: 165). Bourdieu's notion of the 'habitus' (1977: 72–95; 1990: 52–65) is also suggestive, and in the same way. Habitus is a corpus of dispositions, embodied in the individual, generative of practices in ongoing and improvisatory encounters with social fields of one kind or another. The point is that habitus only 'works' in the context of a social field, which itself is constituted as a kind of collective habitus: the one seems to flow into and out of the other. Which is not too dissimilar to Wittgenstein's well-known argument (1974) that for humans the 'outside world', rather than existing in the eye of the beholder or in objective reality, is a contingent product of socially negotiated language-games.

Also drawing upon Wittgenstein, Harré and Gillett's notion of the 'discursive mind' is more straightforward. Coming out of what Harré (1979) calls the ethogenic revision of social psychology, with its emphasis on meaning and agency, and drawing upon recent critiques of behaviourism's model of mental process as a 'black box', unavailable for inspection, Harré and Gillett understand 'mental life as a dynamic activity, engaged in by people, who are located in a range of interacting discourses and at certain positions in those discourses' (1994: 180). Mental processes are thus always social processes. More thoroughgoing again, the mutualist perspective, rooted in the ideas of James, Dewey and Vygotsky, argues that even to talk about 'interrelations' is insufficient (Still and Good 1991).[4] Through the use of metaphors such as 'steeped in' and 'dyed in' – drawn from William James – and dialectical models of process, mutualism emphasises the utter perceptual and cognitive interdependence of human beings.

William James and John Dewey belonged to the diverse, largely American, philosophical tradition known as pragmatism. Pragmatism emphasises the purposive dimension of human behaviour, and derives meaning and criteria of judgement from behaviour's practical outcomes ('the proof of the pudding is in the eating'). Sociologically, the key pragmatists are Cooley and Mead, and the direct sociological descendant of their arguments about mind and self is symbolic interactionism. Charles Horton Cooley used the metaphor of an orchestra to emphasise that mind, the 'social mind', is an organic whole, though not necessarily one that is either 'made up' or in agreement. It is a system of which individuals are active parts: 'everything that I say or think is influenced by what others have said or thought, and, in one way or another, sends out an influence of its own in turn' (Cooley 1962: 4). Writing in 1909, Cooley did not mention Durkheim. It would have been perfectly appropriate had he done so. Each, in his different fashion, flirted with metaphysical notions of the 'group mind' (Parsons 1968: 64), and each tended towards a consensual view of society. However, the difference between Cooley's 'social mind', and Durkheim's *conscience collective*, systematically discussed in 1893 in *De la division du travail social*, is in their starting points. Durkheim begins with society, Cooley with the individual. For Cooley, 'society really has no existence except in the individual's mind' (Mead 1934: 224 n.).

Although critical of Cooley, George Herbert Mead was influenced by him.[5] Describing his own position as 'social behaviorism', Mead begins with two related assumptions: that 'no sharp line can be drawn between individual psychology and social psychology' (1934: 1), and that social interaction produces consciousness, not the other way around:

> the whole (society) is prior to the part (the individual), not the part to the whole; and the part is explained in terms of the whole, not the whole in terms of the part or parts ... from the outside to the inside instead of from the inside to the outside, so to speak.
>
> (ibid.: 7, 8)

Mead argued that our perception of a world of objects – the consciousness which creates meaning – depends upon being able to see *ourselves* as objects (something which bears more than a passing resemblance to Lacan's notion [1977: 1–7] of the 'mirror stage' in the development of human subjectivity). The perceptual basis of cognition is an internal–external dialectic between mind and environment. Socially, consciousness emerges within the pre-linguistic 'conversation of gestures' with others, and in the basic social behaviour of taking up attitudes (which doesn't here mean 'values' or 'views') towards others.

However, the development of language, the symbolisation of that conversation of gestures, is the crucial step. Speech, says Mead,

> can react upon the speaking individual as it reacts upon the other ... the individual can hear what he says and in hearing what he says is tending to respond as the other person responds.
>
> (1934: 69, 70)

Thus an individual can adopt the attitude *of* the other as well as adopting an attitude *toward* the other. The point made earlier, that I cannot observe myself as I can another, indicates the limitations of gesture and attitude without language. Mead argues that with language one can hear oneself in the same 'objective' way that one can *hear* another, and the situation is transformed: 'Out of language emerges the field of mind' (p. 133). In language, reflexivity, which is for Mead the principle uniting mind, self and society, comes into its own:

> It is by means of reflexiveness – the turning-back of the experience upon himself – that the whole social process is

thus brought into the experience of the individuals
involved in it; it is by such means, which enable the individual to take the attitude of the other toward himself,
that the individual is able consciously to adjust himself to
that process, and to modify the resultant of that process
in any given social act in terms of his adjustment to it.
Reflexiveness, then, is the essential condition, within the
social process, for the development of mind.

(ibid.: 134)

Reflexive interaction doesn't just 'bring society in' to the individual's
interior world. Without language there is no distinctively human
interior world; without the stimulus of interaction with others there
would be nothing to talk about or think. (The) mind is thus internal
and external.

Collins argues persuasively (1989: 15) that, although Mead's
great contribution is to demonstrate the *possibility* of a sociology
of mind, his theory is underdeveloped; that he overemphasises
the impact of the social on the individual, and like Durkheim (or,
indeed, Cooley) 'slides into the assumption that society is unified'.
It is, however, less easy to agree with Collins that Mead reduces
consciousness to mere behaviour or reflex. In fact, Mead's insistence that mind emerges out of cooperative social interaction is
reminiscent of Marx rather than of Durkheim: 'language, like
consciousness, only arises from the need, the necessity, of inter-
course with other men' (Marx and Engels 1974: 51).[6] Mead offers
the prospect of placing the thinking of individuals at the centre
of the social world without lapsing into either precious subjectivity
or mechanical objectivity. Mental processes become neither wholly
interior nor wholly exterior.

This may all seem some distance from social identity. However, a
social view of (the) mind is vital for an understanding of social
identity. The self is unimaginable without mental processes, and
vice versa. Social identity without the self is similarly implausible.
Both mind and selfhood must be understood as embodied
within a *social* framework, neither strictly individualist nor strictly
collective. To make safe the foundations of my account of identity,
mind and selfhood must be understandable within the internal–
external dialectic model. The arguments of Ryle and Mead offer a
perspective which allows us to do that.

6
Social selves

Ian Burkitt calls 'the idea that there is a basic division between society and the individual . . . a nonsense' (1991: 189). If he's right – and on balance I think he is – why is it such plausible and popular nonsense? Are the issues involved so difficult that they encourage simplification? Perhaps. Ryle calls the notion of the self – in his terms the concept of 'I' – 'systematically elusive' (1963: 178). In everyday life people find it perplexing. Yesterday's self seems to be substantial and easy enough to account for and explain, but the self of the ongoing moment is fugitive; like the shadow of my head I can never quite step on it.

According to Ryle, 'I' – in English – is an 'index word'. It locates what is being referred to with respect to the speaker. Like 'here' or 'now', it is always uttered from a point of view, and those points of view are always changing: spatially, over time, from individual to individual. There cannot be *an* 'I'; only my 'I', your 'I', her 'I', etc. Further, he argues (p. 186) that the one item of my behaviour about which any commentary of mine must necessarily be silent is itself. This is the argument about introspection again. Self-reflexivity, for Ryle, is always penultimate: the 'I' that does something has to wait until later before it can be considered.

'I' cannot look at itself: I can look at 'her' or 'you', but not at 'I'. Once again, this is logically correct, but interactionally wrong. Social action takes place within or over *periods* of time – even if very short periods – not in successive split seconds. I can, to some extent, approach myself in the here and now. I can, for example, tell someone over the 'phone that 'I'm sitting in the garden enjoying the sun'. Or I can say that 'I'm pissed off', and explain why. And so on.

Giddens also argues that 'I', compared to 'me', is specially problematic (1984: 43), and he is no more convincing. It is not clear why 'I' should be more elusive than other index words: here, there, you, now, then, etc. Despite all of the confusion which Giddens and Ryle accuse it of producing, 'I' is a much-spoken word which is relatively unproblematic in use: when I use it I know who I am referring to and so do you (as do I when you use it, and so on). Tellingly, individual difficulty with the word's use may be taken to indicate cognitive or emotional disorder (Erikson 1968: 217).

So why the problem? In rejecting the dualism of mind and body, Ryle argued that Mind and Matter are different, non-comparable, kinds of things. This allowed him to restructure the philosophy of mind, but prevented him from recognising the embodiment of mind and selfhood. He simply ruled the body out of court. Since the point of view of index words is *always* that of a speaker existing in time and space, and hence embodied, we may begin to appreciate why 'I' seemed so elusive to Ryle. This centrality to selfhood of an embodied point of view (Burkitt 1994) is probably the major reason for the plausibility of the categorical distinction between individual and society. Embodied individuals exist in common sense and experience in a way that 'society' does not; hence the 'pragmatic individualism' discussed in Chapter 3. Embodied individuals are the space–time coordinates of minds and selves and are thoroughly and reciprocally implicated in, and constitutive of, social relations and the social order.

Cooley (1964: 168) called this the 'empirical self': actual people who appropriate and acknowledge their presence and their actions in the world. But for Cooley, the self always implies the presence of others; it is always a social self, similar to and different from others. Part of this is summed up in his image of the 'looking-glass self':

> A self-idea of this sort seems to have three principal elements: the imagination of our appearance to the other person; the imagination of his judgment of that appearance,

and some sort of self-feeling, such as pride or mortification.
... The thing that moves us to pride or shame is ... the
imagined effect of this reflection upon another's mind.

(Cooley 1964: 184)

This dimension of selfhood is fundamental to social life: to the
adjustment of self to others, the internalisation of collective norms,
and – typical of Cooley – the production of an ordered and orderly
society. It is particularly important, he suggested, in the early
socialisation of children.

This understanding of the self draws upon William James.
Cooley in turn provided part of the foundation upon which Mead
built his more systematic model of selfhood. But while praising
Cooley, Mead criticised his ideas about selfhood in terms similar
to his critique of Cooley's model of mind (Joas 1985: 111–12). For
Mead, also interested in actual, embodied people, society was
'objectively' something more than an idea in the consciousness of
individuals. And he wanted to establish a cognitive basis for the
essence of selfhood in the 'internalized conversation of gestures';
that 'the origin and foundations of the self, like those of thinking,
are social' (Mead 1934: 173). For Mead the self was more than
'the bare organization of social attitudes'; he characterised it as a
relationship between 'I' and 'me' (a distinction also derived from
William James). Mead appears to be talking about 'selves' or a
'plural self' rather than 'the self':

> The 'I' reacts to the self which arises through the taking of
> the attitudes of others. Through taking those attitudes we
> have introduced the 'me' and we react to it as an 'I'. . . .
> The 'I' is the response of the organism to others: the
> 'me' is the organized set of attitudes of others which one
> himself assumes.

(1934: 174, 175)

The 'I' is the acting self: the 'ego' that moves 'into the future', the
individual's often unpredictable answer to others, the custodian of
initiative (p. 177). The 'me' is the other side of the argument: it is
what 'I' react against, the voice in part of others, the foil which
gives form and substance to the 'I' (p. 209). It might catch the spirit
of the 'me' to call it the 'what me?'. Although it represents social
control, Mead's 'me' is not a censor in the Freudian sense: the 'I' is
capable of winning the argument. The 'me' exercises a moral, not a
mechanical, imperative over the 'I'. Mead's self is not determined
by the internalised voice of *others* to the same extent as Cooley's

looking-glass self. Reflexivity, which is of the essence for Mead, involves a conversation with *oneself* (Blumer 1986: 62–4; Burkitt 1991: 38).

Mead and Ryle have something in common.[1] Mead's 'I' cannot be apprehended in the here and now, either: 'I cannot turn round quick enough to catch myself' (1934: 174). As soon as someone remembers her 'I' of a minute ago, it has become a 'me', something with which 'I' can only enter into dialogue. The 'I' is not directly available in experience. In this Mead was trying to evoke the co-existence of the cumulative, organised resources of learned culture, which we draw upon in the ongoing production of our lives, with the evanescent immediacy of being in the world, which is perpetually in the present tense: 'the "me" is the individual as an object of consciousness, while the "I" is the individual as having consciousness' (Joas 1985: 83). By this, however, Mead didn't actually mean a split or plural self:

> The 'I' both calls out the 'me' and responds to it. Taken together they constitute a personality as it appears in social experience. The self is essentially a social process going on with these two distinguishable phases. If it did not have these two phases there would not be conscious responsibility, and there would be nothing novel in experience.
>
> (1934: 178)

Even so, the two are not on an equal footing. Ideally, the 'me' is more in charge than the 'I'; it is the source of an integrated personality.

At this point, Mead hypothesised the existence of a 'generalized other', representing the organised community to which an individual belongs and against which she is poised and defined. Simply taking the attitude(s) of specific individual others – a looking-glass self – might produce a series of 'me's, rendering the self inherently unstable over time (the 'me' would thus be similar to the 'I'). A degree of personal consistency in the self could, therefore, only be assured by taking on consistent attitudes. Hence the 'me' also adopts the internalised voice of a generalized other. This differs from Durkheim's *conscience collective* or Cooley's 'social mind' in that it is the product of ongoing encounters between individuals within group social relations. Each person will, in principle, have his or her own generalized other; but every group member will, also in principle, have much in common with every other. Without the generalised other, the Meadian self is incomplete:

only in so far as he takes the attitudes of the organized
social group to which he belongs toward the organized,
co-operative social activity or set of such activities in which
that group as such is engaged, does he develop a complete
self . . . only by taking the attitude of the generalized other
toward himself, in one or another of these ways, can he
think at all; for only thus can thinking – or the internalized
conversation of gestures which constitutes thinking – occur.

(ibid.: 155, 156)

We are back to the social origins of cognition. The generalised
other is acquired early in childhood, it is the parent of mind and self
(and its 'voice' is often literally a parent's). Although Mead didn't
say that society is all in the mind, he insisted that without the
generalised other 'organized human society' (p. 155) is impossible.
Unless society is *also* in the minds of its members – *as well* as
'out there' in actual people and their behaviour – there can be
no universe of discourse, no meaningful social relationships, no
society. Since for Mead 'mind' is as much 'out there' as it is
anywhere, it adds up to the same thing however you look at it.

In Mead's social theory, individual humans and society are not
opposed as different kinds of thing. Society is social relationships
between individuals, and individual humans cannot exist outside
social relationships. Without social relations human agency and
culture would not exist. Mead saw selfhood as an intrinsically
social identity, emerging from the reciprocal relationship between
the individual dialogue in the mind between 'I' and 'me', on the
one hand, and the individual's dialogue with others in social
relations, on the other. Society is a conversation between people;
the mind is the internalisation of that conversation; the self lies
within and between the two.

Giddens' remark, that 'the "I" appears in Mead's writings as
the given core of agency, and its origins hence always remain
obscure' (1984: 43), is representative of one common criticism of
Mead. There are several answers to this. First, questions about
origins are of doubtful value: it is not clear what criteria one would
have to satisfy to answer fully a question of this kind. Second, root-
ing the self in cognition, Mead argued that the human organism's
evolved physiology entails the capacity for/of mind (1934: 226 n.).
Given this capacity, mind – and therefore selfhood – emerges from
the conversation of gestures, from social interaction. The 'I' is thus
the response of the species-specific capacity for intelligence – 'the

physiological mechanism of the human individual's central nervous system' (p. 255) – to the stimuli of others. It is also, by this token, the expressor of 'human nature'; Mead never suggested that mind and self are *only* social constructs (Honneth and Joas 1988: 59–70). Finally, and most important, the 'I' doesn't exist in isolation: the dynamo of agency in Mead's model is the relationship between 'I' and 'me'.

Giddens's comments do, however, indicate difficulties with the terms 'I' and 'me', implying as they do a plurality of selves (if not a 'split personality'). Despite these problems – to which I return below – Mead's account of selfhood offers the basis for a general theory of social identity. In particular, it allows us to understand intimate processes of mind and selfhood within the model of an internal–external dialectic. But Mead doesn't provide the basis for an adequate theory of society. This point can be made in two ways. First, in a manner which recalls Cooley, Mead sees society as essentially consensual (and essentially simple): power and domination are not recognised. In particular, the 'generalized other' makes little allowance for differences and conflicts within society (Burkitt 1991: 52). 'Being able to see the other person's view' held out to Mead a vision of a defensible social rationality. Conflict, in this view, is largely the product of poor communication.[2]

Rational communication leads on to the second point. The Meadian self, because of its entailment in cognition, is a cerebral character, a pragmatist at best. Mead thought, for example, that Freudian psychoanalysis was 'fantastic' in focusing on 'the sexual life and self-assertion in its violent form', which were outside 'the normal situation' (1934: 211). Compared to Durkheim, for example, 'Mead has a flat, unidimensional world. Utilitarian actions of individuals are primary; social interaction enters merely as means to these ends' (Collins 1989: 14). Collins suggests that Mead overlooked the human drive to sociability as an end in itself. We relate to each other because it is in our natures to do so; we cannot do otherwise. 'Sociality' is an adaptive feature of *homo sapiens sapiens* (Carrithers 1992). This criticism isn't wholly fair; Mead often discusses the intersubjectivity on which his theory depends as if it were part of the basic human repertoire. But it is true that we find little room for emotion or frivolity in Mead. We search more or less in vain in his work for passion, for doubt, for conflict.

Bringing the emotions in suggests a need to explore further the social genesis of intimate psychology and personality (Burkitt 1991; Giddens 1984: 41–109; Harré 1986). This is beyond the reach of this book. However, one related matter does require further attention. There appears to be an affinity between Mead's 'I' and 'me', and Freud's 'ego' and 'superego' (Freud 1984: 351–401).[3] The superego, as the internalised parent(s) and also the internalised voice of social control, resembles the 'me' and the 'generalized other'. And the similarity goes further than Freudian analysis: when Transactional Analysis, for example, redesigned the architecture of the self as a tripartite structure of ego states – parent, adult and child – the internalised parental voice remained (Berne 1968: 23–32). These models support the notion that the self is socially constructed within an internal–external dialectic of social identification. They also attempt to bring together internally regulated autonomy and externally determined plasticity within an integrated framework. However, they share one serious shortcoming, their characterisation of the self as a system of different 'bits': in Freud modelled as zones (which have frontiers or borders), in Mead and Berne as entities (who have identities and talk to each other).

This is a problem because most of the time most people don't seem to experience themselves as an assembly of different bits, and particularly not as a plurality of entities. Perhaps the most important source of this consistency – in the eyes of ourselves and others – is, as Burkitt argues (1994), the embodiment of selfhood. Although over time and across situations we recognise conflicts and different possibilities within ourselves, these don't constitute a committee or a cast of characters. Consider, for example, the notion of the internal conversation. Is it really a conversation? Probably not. I recognise the experience of 'talking to myself' and I don't confuse it with a conversation with some*body* else. To agree with Giddens (1984: 7–8), talking about the self as if it is inhabited by 'mini-actors' is unhelpful and unnecessary. 'Moral conscience' is, for example, a straightforward substitute for 'super-ego' (and for the 'me' and the 'generalized other' too). Giddens is also right (pp. 42–3, 60) to point to the definitional confusion created by the proliferation of usages of *das Ich*, the *ego*, and the 'I'.

Dividing the self up into bits thus risks losing sight of the fact that most humans most of the time live their lives as more or less unitary selves. But some people do not. When unity appears to be threatened or fragmented, a state of serious personal disorder may be diagnosed. The metaphors of diagnosis are revealing: 'possession', 'split personality', 'dissociation', 'multiple personality', and 'changeling' are examples from different cultural settings. They have in common images of invasion from outside and/or fragmentation or multiplication. If we are to acknowledge a continuum of differentiation between those who experience such states, and 'most people most of the time' who do not,[4] we need a model of the self as routinely more or less unitary. A similar point can be simply made by saying that although we can talk about someone 'being in two minds', there is no equivalent sensible remark about 'being in two selves'. To have two selves transgresses one of the root ideas of selfhood, a degree of individual consistency over time.

Principles of elegance and simplicity inform theoretical model-building. As a consequence, 'bits models' actually make the self too simple. To recognise the self in its many facets would require the proliferation of bits into potentially infinitely complex models. A unitary model, however, allows us to recognise the self as a rich repository of cultural resources: organised biographically as memory, experientially as knowledge; some conscious, some not; some of them in contradiction, some in agreement; some of them imperative, some filed under 'take it or leave it'; some of them pure in-flight entertainment; etc. The self is an umbrella under which this is organised. It may, in fact, be best understood as a way of talking about – of symbolising or imagining – the complexities of individuals in such a way as to bestow upon those complexities the minimal consistency that is an expected characteristic of people as individuals.

Retrospection offers access to some of the stuff under the umbrella: things that we have done or said, that others have done or said, etc. Some of what is going on we observe as it happens. Other material is not retrospective: it is knowledge about how things are or how they might be. Nor does this exhaust the possibilities. More complicated than a structure of a few bits, this model is also more plausible. It allows for disagreement and dissensus. It allows for variability: some people may, for example, have a rich vein of material deriving from their parents, others may not. For some who do, the parental stuff may be very controlling, for others not. Etcetera.

A related problem is that these 'bits models' tend to reduce process to structure. Mead, Freud and Berne each argue that selves are processual. But when they draw maps of the self or populate it with characters, even only metaphorically, the results are the problems described above *plus* misplaced concreteness. It also becomes more difficult to place the self in social context. Although Mead, for example, appears to imagine a unitary self, constructed within an intersubjective external social world, his manner of talking about it renders that image difficult to hold. The social world for the Meadian self often appears not to be actually happening 'out there': it is internalised, condensed into an over-simplified 'generalized other', part of the structure of the self.

Finally, what about the elusive 'I'? If Ryle and Mead can't turn round in time to catch their 'I', it is because they *are* it. The self is a unifying point of view, and the point of view is always *here*. Thus, so am 'I': always here. When I reflect upon myself I am not reflecting on someone – a 'me' – 'over there'. If I say, for example, 'That's just me, that is', I am either reflecting on myself *here*, which is also *now*, or I am reflecting on myself *then* (which could have been *here*, or in a range of *there*s). I am a complex character, capable of realising myself in different ways in different contexts, but I am me (and vice versa), and I am here, the centre of my own compass.

Where 'here' is, however, requires further consideration. It is embodied, certainly. Selves without bodies don't make much sense in human terms. Even ghosts or spirits, if we recognise them as human, once had bodies; even the disembodied world of cyber-space depends, in the not-so-final resort, on bodies in front of computer screens. We reach out with our selves, and others reach out to us. The self participates in an environment of others; to recall Bateson, like the mind the self does not stop at the skin. But it always *begins* – literally or figuratively – from the body. There is nowhere else to begin. But 'here' is not limited to the spot on which my body stands. When, for example, a large number of people gather by pre-arrangement in a big room, it is meaningful for someone to ask, 'Is everybody here?' Thus there can be different 'here's, depending on context. 'Here' from the point of view of an assembled group, and its individual members, is not the same as 'here' from the point of view of an individual performing solo. 'Here' can be a spot or a territory (as indeed can 'there'). This is a similar point to my earlier argument that it is possible to define the 'now' of introspection in social or interactional terms. As with all index words, the point of view is crucial. Each individual self is the embodied centre of a social universe of self-and-others, the locus of perpetual internal–external comings and goings, transactional inputs and outputs, some of which are incorporated by the self and some of which are not.

Selfhood is constitutive of our knowledge of who and where we are, which also implies knowing something about what we are doing. But the reciprocal entailment of minds and selves is more than logical. 'The mind' and 'the self' are different ways of referring to the same phenomenon, the embodied and developing point of view of the human individual, living in the society of other human individuals. Some of what we associate with the mind – perception, for example – is not what we think about when we think about the self. Similarly, *inter alia* the self is the terrain of emotion, which we commonly distinguish from cognition (although they coexist or overlap – it is not easy to communicate simultaneity – in the embodied point of view: we speak of our 'feelings' clouding our 'reason'). 'The mind' and 'the self' are not the same thing; but they are ways of *talking* about the same thing.

Culture – the domain of symbols – constitutes mind and selfhood. Exploring this point illuminates perhaps most clearly the difference between the two: mind is more universalistic or collective than selfhood. Selves are social and cultural, but they are by definition individual. Mind is something else. It makes as much sense to talk of individual minds, as of individual selves, but the ability to talk about 'mind', without the definite article, is telling. 'Mind' is not just cultural; in some senses it *is* culture. It is possible for us to be 'of one mind', whereas it makes no sense at all to say that 'we are of one self'.[5] Adopting this view confirms that the mind and the self should not be thought of as 'things', other than grammatically: they are processes. The mind and the self are perpetually in motion, even if it sometimes appears to be slow motion; they are perpetually in a state of 'becoming', even if what becomes is similar to what has been.

Minds and selves, whatever else they might be, are attributes of individuals. But this is not an argument for the 'primacy of the self': selves and minds are not definitively private essences of individuals which are causally prior to their behaviour. In what people do and say we witness minds and selves at work; minds and selves are thus knowable. Not perfectly knowable, perhaps, but nothing is. And how we 'know' ourselves is basically no different to how we 'know' others, depending upon observation, retrospection and projection.

However, the self can be thought of as a *primary* (that is, basic) social identity. This, it must be emphasised, is not a reference to psychoanalytic notions about the infant's primary identification with an other. It draws, rather, upon the useful basic distinction between primary and secondary socialisation (Berger and Luckmann 1967: 149–57). Selfhood is arguably the earliest identity into which an individual enters, and the most resistant to change (as

well as the most vulnerable in its earliest period of formation).
It can perhaps be understood as offering a template for all subsequent identities, offering a stem stock on to which they are
grafted. During the initial passage into self-recognition, the infant
becomes aware of her presence as against others: her difference
from and similarity to them. That she is one of them, but they
are not her. The sense of self may be coloured with secure self-
regard which is a reflection of the regard of others (or not).
The name enters into identity. The names of other peoples and
things. Subsequently, primary self-identity becomes elaborated or
embroidered in many ways: 'Mummy says I am a good girl', 'I hate
Aunty Meg', 'I love horses', 'I am bottom of the class', 'Nobody
loves me', etc. Selfhood is not the only identity which may be called
primary, in the sense of being found(ed) during primary socialisation and subsequently exhibiting great solidity. Gender is also,
for example, best understood as a primary social identity, organising experience from the earliest moment and integrated into selfhood (which is not to deny that gender may be manipulable);
depending on context, ethnicity may be too.

To characterise selfhood as a primary identity – or even as *the*
primary identity – doesn't imply that is simply or only individual.
Selfhood and mind are the products of interaction with others.
Paying attention to others is at the heart of the self from the
earliest age. It is a trait of the species:

> babies are born predisposed to learn about sounds and
> sights that are characteristic features of *people*. They are
> particularly attentive to shapes and patterns that are like
> faces and to sounds that fall in the frequency range of the
> female human voice. As babies they learn especially fast
> about stimuli that change in a way that is contingent upon
> their own behaviour.
>
> (Dunn 1988: 1)

The embodied point of view – mind and selfhood – arises within
the social world of intersubjectivity, the wider environment, and
the effects which the individual has upon both of them. Agency is
central to selfhood.

Mind and selfhood, then, are cultural and social, they operate
within and between individuals. To focus on selfhood and self-
identity, there are at least three senses in which this is so. First,
the human potential for individual selfhood is initially realised
vis-à-vis others: they are the necessary foils against which we come

to know ourselves. The human developmental process is a social process and cannot be anything other. This process continues, second, throughout our lives, as our individual identities (and our minds) adapt and change. Self-identification involves the ongoing to-and-fro of the internal–external dialectic. The individual presents herself to others in a particular way. That presentation is accepted (or not), becoming part of her identity in the eyes of others (or not). The responses of others to her presentation feed back to her. Reflexively, they become incorporated into her self-identity (or not). Which may modify the way she presents herself to others. And so on. As presented here, it appears simple, sequential and linear; it is multiplex, simultaneous and tortuous in practice.

Third, the presentation and elaboration of self-identity draws upon a wide palette of accessories in the environment. These are often other people: family, spouses or other partners, children, friends, employees, etc. Who I have relationships with, and the nature of those relationships, says something about me. Hence the importance of 'who one is seen with'. Other people, in their turn, can either validate what I think I am presenting, refute it, or attempt to float an alternative: power and authority are important in determining whose definition counts. Sometimes I know and they know what we are doing at the time; sometimes it only becomes apparent after the fact; sometimes I never know (although others might think that they do); and so on. Nor are people the only external resources which I can exploit to contribute to my self-identity: clothes, pets, religious practices, house, music, car, where I live, occupation. All sorts of things can be turned to use. The world, in this respect, seems to be our oyster.

The self is, therefore, altogether individual *and* intrinsically social. It arises within social interaction. It is constructed within the internal–external dialectic of social identification. It draws upon the external social environment of people and things for its content. Even though it is the most individualised of identities – we might call it customised – selfhood is absolutely social. It depends for its ongoing security upon the validation of others, in its initial emergence and in the dialect of continuing social identification.

I am proposing a unitary model of the self, rather than an image of the self as a collation of bits. A unitary self is not, however, a simple self. Quite the reverse. The self is complex and multifaceted, in reflection of the complexity of the lifelong social process of selfhood and self-identification. This involves a range of others in a range of situations, and draws upon a range of external resources. Nor is a unitary self in complete charge of itself. In the first instance, the foundational experiences of early life are largely outside the infant's control. And they are extraordinarily consequential for later life. During that later life, during the ongoing dialectic of identification, the responses of others are, at best, only predictable or manipulable to a limited degree. Their reception by the self, and their incorporation into self-identity, are unlikely to be within our full control. Everything that we know about individual psychology suggests that the early formation of selfhood – as insecure, secure, or whatever – is enormously influential in equipping us with the resources of selfhood required to respond to the categorisations of us offered or imposed by others.

Other constraints are grounded in embodiment. Where selfhood is entangled with identities that are *definitively* embodied, such as gender/sex, ethnicity/'race', or disability/impairment, the matter becomes infinitely more complicated than my attempts to deal with it via punctuation can communicate. Nor are the external accessories of identification equally available to each individual. The world is not really *everyone*'s oyster: a range of factors systematically influences access to the resources that are required to play this game. In any given context, some social identities systematically influence an individual's opportunities in this respect. The materiality of identity, and its stratification with respect to deprivation and affluence, cannot be underestimated.

I have called my point of view 'pragmatic individualism'. As a sociological perspective this permits an engagement with the 'empirical selves' of real people acting in the world, who know what they are doing and who they are (although it doesn't follow that they know everything about what they are doing or who they are). As actual people they are located in space and in time; as actual people they embody mind and selfhood as points of view within space and time. As actual people they talk about themselves and others as 'persons'. But 'selves' and 'persons' don't fit together with any consistency. As I argued in the previous chapter, the two are not systematically distinguished in common sense: a loose equivalency operates, with the presumption that each or either word has a taken-for-granted and understood referent. Even where they are defined and differentiated, as in much intellectual discourse, there is sufficient variety and lack of agreement, and so much conceptualisation by decree, that, when taken together with problems of translation between cultures and epochs, 'the risk of sheer incoherence is alarming' (Hollis 1985: 220).

So as far as possible I intend to avoid differentiating the *self* from the *person*. Instead I start from unitary selfhood, as defined earlier, as the embodied point of view of the individual. It is the individual's reflexive sense of her own particular identity, constituted *vis à vis* others in terms of similarity and difference, without which she would not know who she was and hence would not be able to act. That particular identity, in this model, is always a to-ing and fro-ing of how the individual sees herself and how others see her. These represent opposite ends of a continuum, one her *self-image*, the other her *public image*. Each is constructed in terms of the other and in terms of the individual's perceived similarity or difference to others. The difference is who is doing the perceiving, who is doing the constructing. This is the internal–external dialectic of individual identification.

And there are other issues concerning the choice of words. I have outlined two complementary understandings of the self: as the embodied point of view of the human individual in her or his social context, and as a way of talking about the complex consistency – or the consistent complexity – of those human individuals. Each of these suggests that it is better to talk about *selfhood* rather than about *the self*. This usage minimises the tendency towards reification implicit in '*the* self' and emphasises the processual character of selfhood. We are talking not about a 'thing', but about an aspect of the human social condition.

The definite article must be retained in some circumstances, however. It makes sense, for example, to talk about the self or selves of a specific individual or individuals: *their* embodied point(s) of view. Nothing else will do if we are to remember that selfhood is an attribute of actual individuals, 'empirical selves' in Cooley's words. And indeed all social identities must, at some point, refer to individuals if they are to have substance. Embodiment is not optional: just as all individual identities are social, so all social identities attach to individuals. But while some identities position individuals alongside other similarly identified individuals within collectivities, others primarily differentiate individuals, as individuals, from each other.

This distinction is crude and only analytical. Individuals differ from each other in their characteristic combinations of collective identities, and the similarities of members of a collectivity typically presuppose their difference from the members of other collectivities. The interplay of similarity and difference is the logic of *all* identification, whether 'individual' or 'collective'. Allowing for these reservations, however, it remains useful to distinguish *individual differentiation* from *collective assimilation*. The chapters immediately following focus upon social identities which are, to differing degrees, and in different ways, individual.

7

Entering society

A new-born baby is the product of social processes which begin
before birth. At least two people have to have had some interaction. There are family histories and a pre-existing social location.
There are ethical and metaphysical questions about the status and
identity of embryo and foetus. However, I am concerned here with
individual social identities, so birth is an obvious and convenient
point with which to begin. It is the point at which the embodied
individual enters the social world.

Questions of identity attend every birth: whether the baby is a
boy or a girl; who he or she resembles; naming; acknowledgement
of parenthood (particularly in its uncertain aspect, paternity);
perhaps ritual initiation into the community concerned (baptism,
circumcision, or a variety of other practices). These may be condensed
into one occasion. Modern civil society requires the bureaucratic
registration of name, place and time of birth, and antecedents,
which may establish the individual's claim to citizenship. In all
these cases, individual identification also locates the child within
collective identities.

There are, however, more pointedly individual questions of
identification. The risks and uncertainties of pregnancy and birth,

and the precariousness of life throughout most of human history, mean that these issues have been addressed by all cultures at all times. Perhaps the most pertinent questions arise out of perceived, typically bodily, impairments: is the neonate to be acknowledged as acceptably human? The question of individual human-ness is enormously consequential, but it is so largely by default. Although few, if any, mutual obligations are established simply on the grounds of fellow humanity, the attribution of 'non-human-ness' or 'sub-human-ness' is dramatic in its consequences.

Local understandings of human-ness are cross-culturally and historically varied. 'Being human', or being acceptably human, is socially attributed on the basis of explicit or implicit socially defined criteria (Hirst and Wooley 1982). As a categorical problem, philosophers perceive it better than they can resolve it (Cockburn 1991). 'Should the baby live?', is thus a question which rings no less loudly in our ears today than it has ever done. Medical progress in the twentieth century has, in fact, made the question more rather than less perplexing, and more common, as fragile lives can be maintained or prolonged (Kuhse and Singer 1985; Lee and Morgan 1989). On the other hand, modern times have also seen the most systematic attempt to routinise infanticide, in the 'euthanasia' of those falling short of eugenic standards of human-ness in National Socialist Germany (Burleigh 1994; Burleigh and Wippermann 1991: 136–67). Even here, however, where it might be thought that the identification of the 'ab-human' had been thoroughly collectivised, each decision required authoritative *individual* categorisation (in which it differed from the collective mass destruction of the Jews and other populations).

However, the question of whether a child should live need not always depend on the individual attribution of flawed human-ness. It may be a response to pertaining environmental conditions: abandonment, infanticide or abortion in times of famine or other stress are reported in the ethnographic and historical records (Williamson 1978). But even these practices are typically related to understandings of human-ness. Infanticide may be permitted at need by notions that full human status, whether in terms of spirit, naming, or whatever, is a developmental attribute of the child, not given at birth.

There are definitively collective identities – 'race', for example – which may compromise their bearers' human-ness in the eyes of others. At birth and in early infancy, however, the question of human-ness is posed in a distinctively individual way. If selfhood is the primary social identity of internal definition, human-ness is the primary identity of external definition. It is necessarily the work of others, with reference to criteria of perceived and interpreted bodily characteristics, to categorise individual neonates as acceptably human, or to decide the nature of their human-ness. More accurately, in the absence of evidence to the contrary, adequate individual human-ness is typically *assumed* at birth by significant adult others. Human-ness is largely taken for granted. And, once granted, human-ness is for most of us largely irrelevant thereafter. However, precisely because it is axiomatic and vague, the vagaries of life render this assumption vulnerable to repeal. Subsequently, factors such as perceived intellectual competence or acquired physical impairment may undermine it.

Human-ness and selfhood, as primary social identities, are typically entailed in each other. There is a close connection between perceptions of one and perceptions of the other. Anthropologist Robert F. Murphy, for example, in a moving account of his own progressive disablement by a spinal tumour describes profound disability as, in the eyes of others, 'a form of *liminality*' (a state of being betwixt-and-between), in which 'humanity is in doubt' (1990: 131):

> Alienation from others is thus a deprivation of social being, for it is within our bonds that the self is forged and maintained. This loss of self, however, is inherent in the social isolation of paralytics, who have furthermore become separated from their bodies by neural damage and from their former identities. Their plight is that they have become divided from others and riven within themselves.
>
> (p. 227)

This relocation – not merely on to the social margins but on to the margins of the human, a withdrawal of mutual recognition neither sought nor embraced by the individual concerned – is difficult to resist, even for adults equipped with resilient resources of selfhood. In this particular internal–external dialectic, others hold most of the cards. Human-ness is largely in the eye of the beholder. Murphy offers a first-hand account of his vulnerability when other people neglected, or refused to continue to recognise, his full human-ness and individual selfhood. Others' definitions of the situation became so dominant as to carry the day. Thus as alienation from others feeds back upon self-perception and reflexivity, individuals become alienated from themselves and their sense of selfhood. Public image may become self-image. Our own sense of humanity is a hostage to the categorising judgements of others.

Birth inaugurates the process whereby individual humans are initiated and initiate themselves into the social world and assume identities within it. This process takes place from an individually embodied point of view. But the social world is *always* a world of others, and, in the beginning, the balance is overwhelmingly in favour of the identificatory work that they do. If Shotter's account (1974) can be accepted, an infant is not a being independent of its mother (or, presumably, other consistent carers). Shotter draws on Spitz to characterise the relationship as 'psychological symbiosis'. While this image acknowledges the infant's activity and predisposition to learn, it emphasises the indispensable role of the other(s) in the infant's acquisition of mind, selfhood and identity. For Shotter, 'making' a social human infant is an intended project of the other(s).

Thus the symbiosis is neither symmetrical nor equal. Kaye, for example, reviewing the evidence in support of the notion of the 'mother–infant system', argues that, because the mother is in the first instance the locus of agency in the interaction, we should not consider it a system as such. Persons are not born, says Kaye, they are the creations of their parents:

> the temporal structure that eventually becomes a true social system will at first only have been created by the parent, making use of built in regularities in infant behavior rather than actual cooperation or communication. Another way of stating this is that evolution has produced infants who can fool their parents into treating them as more intelligent than they really are . . . it is precisely because parents play out this fiction that it eventually comes to be true: that the infant does become a person and an intelligent partner in intersubjective communication.
>
> (Kaye 1982: 53)

What does this process – by which the infant is 'routinely completed as a cognitive and social being' (Harré 1981: 98) – involve with respect to identity? First, it entails recognising self and significant others (in the beginning, perhaps, significant *other*). Interactional turn-taking is arguably the most basic – or even, recalling Mead's 'conversation of gestures', the *only* basic – interaction process (Goffman 1983: 7). It provides the framework for mutuality of recognition. It is also the context within which language is acquired:

recognising names, being able to ascribe them correctly, acquiring socially appropriate discursive forms. The capacity to make others respond bestows upon them significance, creating signifier and signified. Objects as well as persons fall into the identification process: their materiality, their uses, the practical possibilities which they afford (Gibson 1979). Learning who she is, and her place in the world of others and objects, is an integral part of the infant's acquisition of language, and vice versa.

Acquiring identity is a two-way process between infant and caretaker, but at its outset, and for a while thereafter, the exchange is dominated by incoming signals. Externalising the process further, some of the earliest identities may emerge, at least in part, out of transactions which do not involve the infant, taking place away from her, between significant others. Gendering, for example, often begins, unrecognised at that time by the infant, from day one (or before, now that the foetus can be sexed). In Britain, for example, naming aside, accessories such as clothing, toys, and nursery colour scheme may be brought in to play to create a gendered world which the infant gradually encounters and takes for granted as her social consciousness dawns, and which structures the responses to her of others.

Gender is only the most obvious aspect of individual identity which is constructed in interactions between others. Being 'a grand-child' is another, less momentous, example which comes to mind. Grandparents may open savings accounts for their grandchildren, or attempt to influence this or that aspect of their upbringing. They may vie with each other for position in the politics of the family. And in the process grandchildhood is constructed as much in transactions between others – largely in the circle of parents and grandparents – as between grandparents and infant grandchildren.

Infants, however, rapidly become children, as they move incrementally into a more autonomous social existence. They identify themselves as they identify others and as they are them-selves reciprocally identified. Dunn (1988) argues that self-efficacy develops in the child early in life, hand in glove with a concern about and with others. From as early as eighteen months, children exhibit an understanding of the world of self and others as a moral world in which actions have consequences; from about 3 years old they begin to show signs of interest in and understanding of their own mental states and those of others (that is, minds).

There is pattern in this process, although specialists may dispute its detailed chronology, and local variations modify it.

Poole, reviewing evidence from many cultures (1994: 847–52), suggests the following general sequence for the routine 'emergence of identity in childhood'.

- An individualised attachment to mothers and caretakers becomes apparent by seven to nine months.
- From twelve months onwards naming and categorisation emerges and is directed to an understanding of the social world.
- By the age of 2 basic conversational capacity is established.
- Thereafter the child's capacity to represent everyday individual others and act out their practices in the abstract – 'in pretend' – grows in complexity.
- By early childhood (2 to 4 years), the child's narratives and understandings of self and others indicate 'the appearance of a more elaborated map of persons in an experientially expanding sense of community', entailing 'Self-identification of and with other persons through observation, differentiation, imitation and affiliation' (Poole 1994: 850).
- During the same period, gender becomes an important dimension of selfhood.
- By middle childhood, from 5 or 6 years, the child begins to assume a degree of social and moral responsibility for her actions, begins to understand the statuses she occupies, with their related roles, begins to acquire a social 'face' to control how she is perceived by others, and (ideally!) begins to do as she would be done by.
- As the child moves through middle childhood, towards adolescence, the social world of the peer group, often segregated by gender, begins to replace the family as the primary context within which identification occurs and develops.

It is possible to question the universality of the classification of the early years of life into early childhood, middle childhood and adolescence. None the less, Poole's scheme offers a comparative perspective which draws upon a wider range of sources than most,[1] and is a useful ideal-typical model of what are likely to be very general processes (see also James 1993).

Poole identifies one of those processes as the assumption of 'social personhood' (1994: 851). He defines personhood, in contrast to selfhood, in terms of a public moral career, with connotations of responsible agency and jural entitlements (p. 842), and argues that it begins to develop in middle childhood. Unfortunately, Poole's version of the self/person distinction confuses institutional identity or status (jural entitlements) with understandings of individual cognitive and emotional development (responsible agency). He also conflates a general analytical category of 'the person' with necessarily local – common-sensical – categorisations of agency and status. One reading of his account, for example, might suggest an equivalence between adulthood – always socially defined – and personhood, while another might question whether, within many local definitions of gender differentiation, women can be persons at all.

A number of general themes can, however, be explored using Poole's model. In the first place, if selfhood and human-ness are the primary social identities *par excellence*, then, as touched upon previously, gender is something similar. Gender differentiations, socially constructed out of biological differentiation, are a ubiquitous feature of all human societies. Their specifics and content are locally variable, but that there *is* differentiation is not. Human infants are defined by others in terms of gender from their earliest appearance, and the environment of infancy is frequently structured by gender from the beginnings of interactive consciousness. Children come early to an embodied identification of themselves as gendered (Damon and Hart 1988: 30–1).

It may be objected here that gender is a collective, not an individual identity. Although it is certainly *also* a collective identity, the matter is complicated by the distinction between the general and the locally or culturally specific. The biology of sex differentiation has considerable generality, but it is not clear what implications this has for social behaviour. Gender, however, as the local sociocultural coding of sex differences, is enormously significant. But there is no *general* principle that obligation or mutual recognition, or even any actual relation, is collectively established between actors on the basis of gender. In any local context there may be, but that is a matter for investigation. To draw a distinction of which more will be made in the following chapter, gender is a *categorical* collective identity before it is a principle of *group* formation. In this it differs from kinship or ethnicity, which are in the first place typically – and by definition – principles of group identification. Furthermore, the gender of each embodied individual must be specifically identified at birth; it is not predictable from the local coordinates of birth. One is not born into a gender in the same way, for example, that one is born into a family, a lineage, or an ethnic community.

Despite these arguments for the individuality of gender, all human societies, and all cultural views of the world, are massively structured in gender terms. This is a collective matter. Gender is one of the most pervasive classificatory principles – arguably the most pervasive – with myriad implications for the life-chances and experiences of whole categories of people, and one of the most consistent identificatory themes in human history. Gender is thus simultaneously individual and collective, and in this it is distinctive. Although all human identities, individual or collective, are definitively social, where the individual emphasises difference, the collective is weighted towards similarity. Gender identities are fairly evenly balanced in this respect. Gender – as distinct from sexuality – is basically a binary classificatory scheme, and the demographic distribution of the root male–female differentiation is approximately equal. Thus each main gender is the classificatory intersection of one basic relation of difference and one basic relation of similarity.

The internal–external dialectic of identification is also relevant. Gender as a category, no matter what else it may be, is always massively externally defined. This is so with respect to initial individual identification, and subsequent practices of identification. In the institutional constitution of the social world and its rewards and penalties, an individual's gender is made socially real as membership of a collective category. On the other hand, gender – rooted as it is in sex differences – is at the centre of the embodied point of view of selfhood and the internal moment of the dialectic of individual identification (Sharpe 1976: 73–88). Collectively, the sharing of similar life-experiences, which may be powerfully embodied, also allows gender to be a principle of group formation; this is the internal moment of collective identification. The twentieth-century women's movement can, for example, be understood as an attempt to transform individual identification based on categorical differentiation into collective group identification asserting similarity.

How do the primary social identities of selfhood, human-ness and gender relate to each other? With respect to individual self-identification and self-image gender is typically powerfully incorporated into the embodied point of view of selfhood. On the other hand, local gender differentiation may relate to local conceptions of human-ness, via gendered notions about 'human nature' or embodied models of the 'natural' or the 'normal'. For example, behaviour which is locally gender-inappropriate may be identified by others as 'un-natural', and the individual may perceive herself to be 'un-natural' too, or must struggle not to do so.

Poole's account fits well with the model of an internal–external dialectic of identification. During the first years of life, however, the external moment of the dialectic is necessarily dominant: human infants and children are dependent, they must be taught about the world and their place in it. If they do not learn who they are from others, they will never know. This suggests that identities which are established during infancy and childhood may be less flexible than identities which are acquired subsequently. There are a number of reasons for suggesting this.

On the face of things, social identities are neither remorselessly permanent nor frivolously malleable. The most adamantine identity has some leeway in it, if only as a sense of possibility. Social identities are flexible because the dialectic of identification is, in principle, never wholly closed. Given the uncertainty and unpredictability of life this is useful, even vital. Arising within and out of bilateral processes of mutual recognition which are often rooted in specific social situations, social identities are generally contingent, 'for the time being', and somewhat tolerant of inconsistency or contradiction.

But the more unilateral the dialectic, the less negotiable the resultant identity is likely to be, and the smaller the room for manoeuvre. Identities entered into early in life are encountered as more authoritative than those acquired subsequently. At most, a child can only muster a weak response of internal definition to modify or customise them. Taken on during the most foundational learning period, they become part of the individual's axiomatic cognitive furniture, 'the way things are'. Very young children lack the competence to counter successfully their external identification by others. They have limited resources of experience and culture with which to question or resist, even were they disposed to. And they may not be: during and before the process of language acquisition the human learning predisposition leaves the individual open to forceful and consequential definition by others. Further, inasmuch as gendered identity (for example) is incorporated into individual selfhood, a powerful set of mutual reinforcements, with change posing a threat to the security of selfhood, is likely to be set in place.

The security of selfhood has, of course, sources other than authoritative inculcation during early childhood. As Giddens has argued (1984: 50ff.; 1990: 92–100), individual ontological security

– the common sense that all that is solid, including oneself, does *not* melt into air – relies upon routine and habit. This is arguably more so for children than for adults. Certainly children are famous for resenting the disruption of their routines; the insistence upon routine may be among their earliest interventions in the social world. Further, the early world of childhood is often largely, if not totally, sheltered within an immediate domestic group. Routine is easily established, carers well-known, and the social world relatively simple. Under such circumstances, primary identities are acquired in ordered social settings which the child experiences, and to some extent creates, as homogenous and consistent. Minimal situational and contextual change may encourage the experience of primary identification as universal, globally independent of context and situation, providing the individual with a subsequent taken-for-granted 'thread of life', to borrow a phrase from Wollheim (1984).

This is, of course an ideal-typical, even idealised, representation of early childhood.[2] None of it is inevitable: insecurity and inconsistency are to be expected. Not all parents and carers are or can be committed to their infants to the same degree. Interaction with baby, the all-important turn-taking, is perhaps as often neglected as not. The emotional climate of family life and kin relationships is variable. Local patterns of child-rearing practice vary enormously. For parents and carers, the demands of the adult world routinely conflict with the demands of child-rearing. More dramatically, children are rarely insulated from the tempests of the outside world: when life is turned upside down, they are turned upside down too.

Secure consistency and relative calm in the formative years may, therefore, be as much the exception as the rule. But this doesn't mean that the social world is peopled by individuals with utterly fragmentary or insecure senses of selfhood and identity. Rather, I am suggesting that although most people, most of the time, experience life from the embodied point of view of relatively unitary and consistent selfhood, they are no strangers to uncertainty and insecurity either. Usually we know who and where we are, but not always. And if on occasions our security is threatened (or worse), it need not mean our internal moments of identification are fragile or wavering. The social world of others can be unpredictable, challenging and unsupportive, and our bodies are vulnerable.

None the less, the primary identities of selfhood and gender are more robust than other social identities. Human-ness, as a taken-for-granted assumption, ascribed by default, is different, but it can still be described as primary: compromised or inferior human-ness is an unforgivingly robust identification. Certainly although both human-ness and gender are distinguishable from selfhood, they are are acquired so early, are so consequential across the broad spectrum of experience, and are so much a dimension of embodiment, that they should be regarded as reciprocally entailed in selfhood. But can any other identities be considered to be primary? One obvious candidate is kinship.

The kin group is an obvious source of enduring individual primary identity. No matter the time, place or culture, one of the most important elements in individual identification, by self and others, is kinship (Harris 1990; Keesing 1975). Kin-group member-ship epitomises the social-ness of identity. It is meaningful because it locates individuals within a social field independent of and beyond individually embodied points of view. Naming, the identification of individuals in terms of collective antecedents and contemporary affiliation, is central to kinship, but it is given consequential sub-stance by the rights and duties of kin-group membership. Kinship identity establishes relations of similarity with fellow kin in terms of descent; it differentiates the individual both from non-kin and, in classificatory terms, from other members of the descent group. Kinship can also establish equivalence – similarity – with non-kin: principles of exogamy and alliance relationships between kin groups identify potential marriage partners, ritual or exchange partners, etc.

Apropos the internal–external dialectic of identification, her individual name is among the earliest things a child learns; from it follows the ability to name her parents, other significant kin, where she lives, etc. Thus kin-group membership – name and place – is likely to be significantly entailed in selfhood. The experi-ence of kin-relations as emotionally charged is significant also. That kinship may be represented in terms of embodied family resemblance further encourages the incorporation of descent into self-identification. In the first instance, however, resemblance is in the eye of the beholder. Nor is our name usually an identity which we bestow on ourselves. In general, then, we should remember the old adage: unlike friends, one can't choose one's family.

There is no necessary universality about the salience of kinship as a primary identity: in some local socio-cultural settings kinship is all, in others it has limited significance. It may be less significant within the immediate kin group (where it may be taken for granted) than in relationships outside it. On the other hand, however, kin identities don't travel well. For example, outside the family itself my family membership only matters in the face-to-face local context from which it draws its relevance. Elsewhere, my family name ceases to be a multiplex identification *with* others, becoming instead a uni-dimensional means of differentiating me *from* others.

The other possibly primary social identity is ethnicity. There is debate about whether ethnicity is *primordial*, i.e. essential and unchanging, or *situational*, i.e. as manipulable as circumstances demand or allow (Bentley 1987; Eller and Coughlan 1993). If ethnicity can be considered a primary social identity, in my terms, it may offer a middle ground for this debate. So, how 'primary' is ethnicity? Ethnicity is a collective identity which may have a massive presence in the experience of individuals. Ethnic identity – including, for the moment, 'race' – is often an important and early dimension of self-identification. Individuals may learn frameworks for classifying themselves and others by ethnicity and 'race' during childhood, certainly by about ten years old (Goodman 1964; Heskin 1980: 132–4; Milner 1983; Troyna and Hatcher 1992). The ideologies of collective descent which frequently underpin ethnicity imagine it as distinctively embodied. And embodiment, even if stereotypical, is always individual and part of the point of view of selfhood. Although 'race' is likely to be more visible than ethnic differentiation based on cultural cues, either may be established relatively early, albeit perhaps not as early as gender. Ethnicity may involve emotion and affect (Epstein 1978; Memmi 1990), which suggests that it can be significantly entailed in selfhood. Ethnicity, when it matters to people, *really* matters. The circumstances under which it matters are relevant, however. Ethnicity depends on similarity rubbing up against difference collectively: 'us' and 'them'. Ethnic identification weaves together the fate of the individual with collective fate in a distinctive fashion, and it can be enormously consequential.

On the other hand, the work of Barth (1969) and others suggests that ethnicity can be negotiable. Individuals may, under the right circumstances, change their ethnicity, and sometimes they do. Even the firmly embodied categorisations of 'race' have their flexibilities: 'passing' is not unheard of and, more important, the definitions and significances of 'race' are historically and locally variable. Nor does ethnicity as a structuring principle of social relations, or a presence in early experience, have the same salience everywhere. All of which suggests that ethnicity is not primordial. It may however – depending on the situation – be a primary identity, and this need not deny it a certain situational flexibility.

Thus whether either kinship or ethnicity are primary social identities are local questions. Unlike human-ness, selfhood and gender, they are not *universal* primary identities. Kinship or ethnicity may become salient early in the individual dialectic of identification, they may be enormously consequential, they may be entailed in selfhood. The fact that both involve embodied criteria of identification – family resemblance, physical ethnic stereotypes, 'race' – can only reinforce this. But neither kinship nor ethnicity is necessarily a primary individual social identity. Depending on local circumstance and individual history, they can be more negotiable and flexible than human-ness or gender.

The final theme in Poole's model is a gradual shift in the dynamics of the dialectic of identification during childhood, towards increasingly bilateral relationships of mutuality and reciprocation. With time, selfhood develops and becomes more secure and consistent; the child becomes an increasingly knowledgeable and competent actor. These processes are systematically entangled, and on each count the child has greater resources with which to assert her internal moment of identification. She has a burgeoning, more confident, and fuller sense of who she is. Babies become infants, infants become children, children eventually become adults.

There is, however, more to it than individual development or the movement through age-based identities. As she gets older, and it begins quite early, the child moves in ever-widening social networks. Increasingly she has to relate to other children, with whom interaction is more equitable and more of a contest. Families may have their politics, but the peer group is definitively political. Social life becomes more negotiable and more negotiated (James 1993). And much less predictable. Other children need to know who she is; she needs to know who they are and what to expect of them. Skills of self-presentation are learned, as is the identification of others on the basis of a range of cues. Reputation, public image in the eyes of peers, becomes important. If indeed it ever was, the regard of others is no longer unconditional. Hierarchy must be negotiated and status begins to matter. Friendship begins to be an affective domain of its own, distinct from kinship. Projective play – 'let's pretend' – provides opportunities for role-playing and the rehearsal of identities. And increasingly children cultivate the capacity to mobilise 'face' and 'front'. A sense of private selfhood begins to be important.

Before long the peer group competes with the domestic group for the child's attention. Nor is it just the world of other children which looms increasingly large in her life. She has more adults to deal with, and proportionately fewer of them are familiar. Increasingly she is a member of formal institutional settings. Negotiating a path through and round these ever more complex environments, she is increasingly required to be self-resourcing and resourceful and is expected to function as an individual. This entails the gradual assumption of more and more responsibility for her actions. Something for which she may increasingly have to accept responsibility is her impact, *in the part of the other*, on the identification(s) of those with whom she interacts.

Most strikingly, the child has to learn to live with her public image. This may differ from her self-image, is not always within her control, and may vary from context to context. The internal–external dialectic of identification, the problematic relationship between how we see ourselves and how others see us, becomes a central concern and theme of her social life. Whether wholly consciously or not, identities are increasingly entered into as projects, or resisted when they are imposed and unwelcome.

The face-to-face social world of children quickly comes to resemble the adult world in its strategies, its games, its stratification, and its rules. It is a model for the world of adulthood. This is the everyday world which Erving Goffman called the 'interaction order'. Goffman's work is one of the places where the next pieces of the jigsaw of social identity are to be found.

8

Self-image and public image

Erving Goffman's work is approachable and subtle, combining sociology, social anthropology and social psychology in a manner which challenges pettifogging disciplinary propriety. He is also among the most mundanely useful of writers: how many other sociologists can illuminate the most routine face-to-face encounters, an evening in the pub, and the most formal of life-cycle rituals? He has no rivals in the sociological interpretation of everyday life.

There are four common criticisms of Goffman's work: first, that, if not merely descriptive, it doesn't amount to a systematic body of theory; second, that it doesn't integrate the 'micro' everyday world with the 'macro' world of social structure; third, that his analyses are so specific to modern (American) society as to be ungeneralisable; and fourth, that his actors are hollow shells, that he offers no account of the formation of selfhood and only a cynical account of motivation. Responses to the first three are not vital here. For those who are interested, Collins (1988) and Giddens (1984: 68–73) offer discussions of the issues which are sympathetic to Goffman's case.

The fourth criticism is relevant, however. Hollis, for example, argues that, 'Goffman owes us a theory of self as subject ... to sustain an active base for its social transactions. . . . Notoriously the debt goes unpaid' (1977: 88). He goes on to say, somewhat contradictorily perhaps (pp. 102–3), that Goffman's actors are pure individualists, bent only on the public pursuit of purely private ends. MacIntyre is one of the harshest voices of this strand of critique:

> Goffman ... has liquidated the self into its role-playing, arguing that the self is no more than 'a peg' on which the clothes of the role are hung. . . . For Goffman, for whom the social world is all, the self is therefore nothing at all, it occupies no social space.
>
> (MacIntyre 1985: 32)

This, too, seems contradictory: if MacIntyre is correct, if Goffman's self is merely its role-playing, then that self, such as it is, can *only* be social.

What does Goffman himself say? There are two interdependent major themes in his work. Perhaps the most widely recognised concerns the routines and rituals of social interaction. This can be summarised under four headings. First, there is the embodiment and spatiality of interaction. The individual has, and is, a presence in the world. The embodied actor is always, for Goffman, spatially situated: *vis-à-vis* others, and regionally, in terms of the local staging of interaction. The two main interaction regions are frontstage and backstage, the public and the private (Goffman 1969: 109–40). The body, particularly the upper body and most particularly the face, is the interactional presence of selfhood. Goffman's unit of analysis is the embodied individual, and the embodied self has its territories, preserves of space which can be respected or violated (1971: 51–87). So while Goffman's self is embodied, its boundaries extend into interactional social space.

Second, he uses two metaphors to understand the routines or rituals of everyday life: interaction as either a performance or drama (1969), hence frontstage–backstage, or as a game (1961; 1970). In each, interaction is cooperative, organised, ordered, rule-governed. However, it occurs in a world of negotiation and transaction which interactional routines enable and create: a universe in which implicit and explicit rules are resources rather than determinants of behaviour.

The variability and multiplexity of life and experience are

summed up, third, in Goffman's concept of framing (1975). From the individual point of view, and in the institutional constitution of the social world, specific social settings are 'frames' – each with characteristic meanings and rules – within which interaction is organised. Individuals experience life as a series of different sets or stages (which are formally or informally organised). While each individual may have different understandings of these settings, and of what's happening within them, the shared frame creates enough consistency and mutuality for interaction to proceed. Frames are bounded in space and time and are in this sense substantial. Frame analysis is thus a compromise between the relativism of social constructionism, in which the 'definition of the situation' is all (but all there is), and a common-sensical epistemology which recognises that there is a 'real' world out there.

All of these merge, fourth, in Goffman's notion of the 'interaction order' (1983): the 'face-to-face domain' of dealings between embodied individuals. Remote dealings, over the 'phone or by letter, are not excluded, but the emphasis is on the physicality of co-presence. It is an orderly domain of activity, in which the individual and the collective become realised in each other. Although, in Goffman's own words, this is the terrain of 'microanalysis', the notion of the interaction order may be regarded as his contribution to bridging the 'action–structure' gap. The interaction order and social structure are implicated in each other in a relationship of 'loose coupling' (1983: 11): each is entailed in the other, but neither determines the other.

One major problem with this framework is the picture which it presents of social life as rule-governed, scripted or ritualised. Goffman himself glossed these possibilities as 'enabling conventions' (1983: 5), which is helpful, but the image of explicit and directed organisation lingers. Another problem is the implication that individual means–ends calculative rationality is the wellspring of behaviour. Of course, much interaction is observant of rules or conventions, and means–end rationality is often important. But, *contra* rules or calculation, much behaviour is necessarily either habitual or improvised. There is no scriptwriter (although there are repertoires), and rules can never be sufficiently flexible to deal adequately with the variability and unpredictability of social life.

The importance of habit and habitualisation in social life is well-known (for example Berger and Luckmann 1967: 70–85). In fact habit provides the space within which rational decision-making operates: if we had to make a decision about everything, we'd

never be able to make a decision about anything.
emphasis upon ritual, routines and frames indicates
ness of this. Apropos rules, however, Goffman overstat
Bourdieu is on the right lines (1977; 1990), in theorisin᠎ ᵖᵣᵃᶜᵗⁱᶜᵃˡ
dispositions as embodied habit – habitus – and in emphasising
the improvisatory, non-rule-governed nature of much behaviour.
In many situations neither habit nor rules nor calculation offer a
way ahead; so, necessarily, we improvise. Improvisation can,
however, be reflexive, resembling rational calculation, or sponta-
neously unreflexive, in which case it looks more like habit.
Improvisation may also pay attention to rules and conventions in
the *ad hoc*ery of the moment. Habit, rule-observance, calculation,
and improvisation, as ways of doing things, are, at best, only
analytically distinct.

The other important theme in Goffman's work is identity.
Individuals negotiate their identities within the interaction order.
Mobilising interactional competences within situational ('framed')
routines, individuals present an image of themselves – of self – for
acceptance by others. In my terms, this is the internal moment of
the dialectic of identification with respect to public image. The
external moment is the reception by others of that presentation:
they can accept it or not. Individual identity is generated in the
relationship which is struck between self-image and public image.

Goffman's work suggests that, interactionally speaking, the
internal–external dialectic of individual identification involves a
number of elements. There are the arts of impression management:
the interactional competences which 'send' particular identities
to others and attempt to influence their reception. These include
dramatic style and ability, idealisation (by which Goffman means
individual identification with collectively defined roles), expressive
control, misrepresentation, and mystification. Many of these derive
from early socialisation, and are routinised in embodied non-verbal
communication in addition to language.

Interactional regions are resources for revealing and concealing
particular identities. Backstage one can to some extent be free of
the anxieties of presentation. It is the domain of self-image rather
than public image. Hence the idea that I can 'be myself' in private.
I can rehearse the presentation of an identity in a backstage area
before trying to carry it off in public. As a teenager, for example,
I learned to play the guitar in my bedroom, but I also practised
something more awkward, 'being a guitarist'. Frontstage, work is
required by performer and audience, to collude in the mutualities

of identification. Under some circumstances audience tact is required if the performance is to 'come off' and the public image established in the setting in question.

Burns (1992: 270ff.) discerns two understandings of self-presentation in Goffman. In *The Presentation of Self in Everyday Life* (1969) selfhood lies in expressive performance; hence the metaphor of all the social world as a stage (hence too the criticisms of Hollis and MacIntyre). In *Frame Analysis* (1975), however, the self – which is the thread of consistency from frame to frame – has become the source of the performance, sufficiently autonomous of context to be able at need to achieve distance from it. These visions of the self are complementary, not contradictory. Nor, arguably, is the second absent from *The Presentation of Self*: it is implicit in the discussion of discrepant roles (1969: 123–46), and clear in Goffman's distinction between the performed self-as-character, 'some kind of image, usually creditable, which the individual on stage and in character effectively induces others to hold in regard to him' (p. 223), and the performer, 'a harried fabricator of impressions involved in the all-too-human task of staging a performance' (p. 222). The individual as character is a social construct; the individual as performer is partly a psycho-biological creature and partly a product of the 'contingencies of staging performances' (p. 224).

In contradiction of Hollis and MacIntyre, Goffman's individual is a moral creature, inhabiting a moral universe. Giddens correctly stresses (1984: 70) the emphasis in Goffman on interpersonal trust: on tact, collusion, interactional damage-limitation and repair. Goffman's actors want to appear creditable to others; they want (or need?) to make a good impression. Thus most people most of the time extend to others the minimal interactional support which they require themselves if their own identity performances are to succeed (or, at least, not fail). Thus the dialectic – a word which Goffman himself uses (1969: 220) – of identification has a moral dimension, rooted in reciprocity:

> when an individual projects a definition of the situation and thereby makes an implicit or explicit claim to be a person of a particular kind, he automatically exerts a moral demand upon the others, obliging them to value and treat him in the manner that persons of his kind have a right to expect. He also implicitly forgoes all claims to be things he does not appear to be and hence forgoes the

treatment that would be appropriate for such individuals. The others find, then, that the individual has informed them as to what is and as to what they *ought* to see as the 'is'.

(1969: 11–12)

If this were all Goffman had to say, his would be a mildly utopian model of a social world in which actors do their best to get on with each other in a relatively equitable fashion. Fortunately he also understood that things do not always go smoothly. In particular, he recognised that identity can be 'spoiled'; that identification, particularly within institutions, can be heavily biased in favour of its external moment; and that in both cases identification is often a matter of imposition and resistance, claim and counter-claim, rather than a consensual process of mutuality and negotiation. Leaving institutional identity until later chapters, what does he mean by 'spoiled identity'?

The key text, *Stigma* (1968a) is the least satisfactory of Goffman's works. Under the rubric of spoiled or stigmatised identity he includes a range of things – from having a colostomy, to being a criminal, to being a member of an ethnic minority – which don't have much in common even at second or third glance. The book looks at how individuals manage discrepancies between their 'virtual social identity' – how they appear to others in interaction (often on the basis of superficial cues) – and the 'actual social identity' which closer inspection would reveal them to possess. Individuals with a discreditable actual identity want to be 'virtually normal': stigma is the gap between the virtual and the actual, and the shame which attaches – or which would attach – to its discovery by others. Stigmatisation is, moreover, a continuum of degree: we all have some disreputable aspects to our identities, and the information management skills required to control who knows about them, and in what degree, are normal items in our interactional repertoires.

Goffman also distinguishes social identity from personal identity. The latter combines relatively consistent embodied uniqueness and a specifically individual set of facts, organised as a history or a biography. This is not reflexive selfhood: 'Social and personal identity are part, first of all, of other persons' concerns and definitions regarding the individual whose identity is in question' (1968a: 129). These distinctions – social and personal, virtual and actual – are less rather than more helpful. Apropos the social and the personal, all human identities are social identities. Further, Goffman's notion of personal identity relies on the self–person distinction which I have been avoiding. The virtual–actual distinction is problematic in that the use of 'actual' implies that one is more 'real' than the other.

However, *Stigma* has much to say that is useful. It emphasises that others make demands on us, on the basis of our public image. We can have social careers, which are anything but those we would choose, thrust upon us as a consequence: others don't just perceive our identity, they actively constitute it. And they do so not only in terms of naming or categorising, but in terms of how they respond to or treat us. In the dialectic of individual identification the external moment can be enormously consequential.

In *Stigma*, Goffman drew upon the labelling perspective in the sociology of deviance.[1] Intellectually, this is an offspring of Mead, on the one hand, and Chicago sociologists such as W. I. Thomas and Everett Hughes, on the other. Beginning with the early work of Tannenbaum (1938), the labelling perspective was elaborated into a relatively coherent model by Becker (1963), Lemert (1972), Matza (1969) and others. Against the conventional view that social control was a reaction to deviance, the labelling school argued that social control necessarily produced deviance. There are three versions of the labelling theorem: first, that rule-breaking is routine and endemic and only becomes deviance when it is authoritatively labelled as such; second, that actors become deviants because they are so labelled; third, that rates of deviance are the product of the activities of social control agencies. From the perspective of classificatory logic, these arguments are unimpeachable. Compare, for example, Becker's view, that 'social groups create deviance by making the rules whose infraction constitutes deviance' (1963: 9), with Douglas's proposition, that 'Dirt is the by-product of the systematic ordering and classification of matter' (1966: 48). Disorder is the product of ordering; definition generates anomaly; and similarity begets difference.

The labelling perspective has its vigorous critics (Gove 1980; Taylor, Walton and Young 1973: 139–71). *Inter alia*, they argue that it isn't a systematic theory; that it is so relativist that nothing is *really* deviant; that it neglects power and social structure; that it is an over-simple model of process; and that it sees actors as unidimensional at best and socially determined at worst. Some of this resonates with the standard critique of Goffman. As with Goffman, the labelling perspective has its staunch defenders (Plummer 1979).

Most of the argument is not relevant here. But some aspects of the labelling model, as it applies to individual deviant identities, are important. Lemert distinguishes between primary and secondary deviance (1972: 62–92). Primary deviance is the basic act of deviance, with its origins in any number of physiological, psychological or social factors. Generally it is not dramatised as deviant, being normalised away or negotiated around. Excuses are made, mitigating circumstances discovered, the act re-defined as not 'really' deviant, or whatever. We all do deviant things sometimes (or could otherwise be considered deviant) but hardly any of us *is* 'a deviant'. This is an individual social identity which definitively requires the identificatory work of others. Depending on circumstance and the nature of the deviance, primary deviance may be recognised and defined as deviance, and the individual labelled deviant. Deviance is very much in the eye of the beholder. Secondary deviance is the identity of 'deviant' produced by the act of labelling and the subsequent deviance which that identity generates.

The labelling perspective emphasises secondary deviance, the process whereby people are identified as deviant and come to identify themselves as deviant. In terms of my model, the external moment of identification is turned round on and incorporated into the internal. The individual's subsequent behaviour and biography become organised – by herself and by others – with reference to an identification which is now internal as well as external. Becker (1963: 25–39) refers to this as the 'deviant career', the process over time which involves the initial external identification of 'deviant' becoming an internal identification. This occurs in the context of authoritative social control processes in which identification as deviant has social and experiential consequences, in which the identity of deviant is so powerful that it propels a rule-breaker in the direction of 'becoming a deviant'. It is a question of whose definition of the situation, *and of the individual*, counts. The affinities with Goffman, and with my argument that identity must be understood processually, are clear. Rather than fixed identities, we are always concerned with processes of identification, trajectories of being and becoming.

The labelling model is, of course, neither sufficient in itself to understand identity nor without its shortcomings. There needs to be more recognition of the capacity of individuals to resist external identification. More attention to the decision-making of individuals who are identified as deviant is required. Insufficient attention is paid to why primary deviance occurs, not least in terms of motivation. There is a failure to recognise that much deviance is not the secondary deviance of labelled individuals: unlabelled 'primary' deviants often know that they are being deviant, and precisely how deviant they are being. White-collar crime is illustrative of this. With respect to 'life-style' deviance – and the jazz musicians about whom Becker wrote are actually a good example – individuals may actively seek out an identification because it *is* deviant. Classifications of deviance are public knowledge, they are altogether cultural and collective, and they can be drawn on and manipulated in different ways with respect to identity.[2] An individual does not have to be labelled a deviant to know that some of the things she does count as deviance.

Allowing for these weaknesses, the labelling perspective offers a model with which to place the internal–external dialectic of individual identification in social context. Most significant is the insistence with which that model draws our attention to external identification in the constitution of individual identities. It offers a way of thinking about how external definition becomes internal definition. It reiterates the processual character of identity. It extends the dialectical model beyond primary socialisation and the interaction order. It offers a further view of the way in which collective identities – of deviance in this case – can become incorporated into self-conscious individual identities. Its emphasis upon the capacity of particular agents, occupying particular positions – in the case of deviance, the police, social workers, psychologists, judges and juries, etc. – to authoritatively identify others in consequential ways, moves us beyond Goffman's interaction order and into the institutional order.

Nor is it limited to the analysis of deviance. The educational progress of school children is just one area in which labelling models have proved insightful (Cicourel and Kitsuse 1963; Mehan *et al.* 1986; Mercer 1973). The perspective is particularly suited to examining institutionalised practices of identification, but labelling processes operate with as much force in the informal interpersonal settings of the interaction order. In fact, the labelling perspective arguably provides the basis for a general model of the external moment of individual identification. Nor is labelling something which only happens in the case of negative or stigmatising identities. There is no reason to suppose that positive, valorised identities aren't internalised in similar ways: they too are labels and they have their consequences. Perhaps the best known piece of research to make this point is Rosenthal's and Jacobsen's experiment (1968) in which the academic performance of individual children was found to be related to expectations of their progress which the researchers had foisted upon teachers via a spurious testing procedure. Those pupils who were identified as about to experience a learning 'spurt' subsequently achieved more academically than their peers, presumably as a consequence of the extra attention, stimulation and encouragement offered – whether consciously or unconsciously – by their teachers.

This 'expectancy' version of the labelling model brings me to the distinction between the *nominal* and the *virtual*. The nominal, in this context, is the label with which the individual is identified. The labelling perspective is so important because it insists that a label alone is not sufficient for an identity to 'take'. Just because I call you a deviant, or a gifted child, doesn't mean that you will think of yourself as a deviant or clever, or that other people will. Nor is it enough for *you* to think of yourself as a deviant or clever. What is required is a *process* of labelling: a cumulative process over time in which the label has consequences for the individual (even better if that labelling process is endowed with institutional legitimacy and authority). The consequences lie in the responses of others to the labelled individual as well as in her own responses to the identification. Which means that labelling individuals with the same identification doesn't mean that they will be similarly affected by it: in each of their lives, for myriad reasons, the consequences of being so identified – generated in the internal–external dialectic between the behaviour of others and their own actions – may differ widely. Being labelled is neither uni-directional nor determinate.

It is in the consequences of identification that the virtual can be discerned. A virtual identification is what the nominal identification means, in practice and over time, to its bearer. Distinguishing clearly the nominal and the virtual is important for several reasons. First, identification is never just a matter of the formal semantics of name or label: the meaning of an identity lies also in the difference that it makes in individual lives. Second, the label and the consequences may not always be in agreement (and only if they are is there likely to be substantial internalisation). Third, the consequences or meaning of any specific nominal identification can vary from context to context and over time. The nominal may be associated with a plurality of virtualities. Finally, individual identities and differences are to some considerable extent constructed out of collective identities. We need, therefore, a means of distinguishing the unique particularities of the individual from the generalities of the collective. Distinguishing the virtual from the nominal allows us to do that: some part of the virtual will always be individually idiosyncratic.

Two examples may illustrate these points. First, there is the situation where the virtual and the nominal are in disagreement. Nominally, people with learning difficulties over the age of about 19 or 20 in Wales (and elsewhere in the United Kingdom: Wales is simply where I have done research) are regarded by those who make policy about and for them, and provide them with services, as adults. This is a matter of public record on the part of Social Services and other agencies. However, the wider legal framework defining the adult status of people with learning difficulties is less clear: the matter is ambiguous (R. Jenkins 1990). On the other hand, the routine everyday responses to people with learning difficulties of most significant others – family, friends, care workers, or the anonymous public – rejects their adulthood (even though paying it due lip service). They are subject to almost constant supervision which is generally inappropriate to their competences (Davies and Jenkins 1995). Nominally adult, they remain virtually children. Although they may be called adults, they are treated otherwise. As a result it is difficult for them to become adults, in their own eyes or in the eyes of others.

Apropos the individual and the collective, being a gay male is an important identity which, in any individual case, becomes publicly nominal once it is 'out' and socially visible. But although there are relatively consistent collective templates or stereotypes of male homosexuality, what it means virtually depends on individual circumstances. It is one thing to be a gay television producer, another to be a gay doctor, and quite another to be a gay clergyman. Being gay in London, with a flourishing and supportive gay social scene, is likely to be quite different from being gay in, say, a village in rural Norfolk. The same nominal identity produces very different virtual identifications and very different experiences. Nor is it only the responses of others which constitute the virtual experience of an identity. Individuals construct the consequences of their own identification as and how they can, in engagement with a social world of others. There are many ways to be gay, in Norfolk as in London.

Neither the nominal nor the virtual is the more 'real' (hence the word 'virtual'). Nor are they separate in everyday life. They are aspects of the same *process*. We should speak not about nominal and virtual identities, but about nominal and virtual identification. On the one hand there is the labelling or naming of individuals, by themselves and by others. On the other, the individual's actions and the responses of others make up consequential experience. All identities combine the nominal and the virtual. It is in the inter-action between them that identity careers, drawing together the individual and the collective, emerge as meaningful elements in biography.

9

Groups and categories

Said 10 as diff + similarity

Individual identities, emphasising the differentiation of embodied uniqueness, are social products. In primary and subsequent socialisation, in the interaction order, and in institutionalised practices of labelling, individuals are identified, by themselves and by others, in terms which distinguish them from other individuals. Social identity is, however, also about similarity. Selfhood, for example, concerns the similarity or consistency over time of embodied individuals. Collective identities emphasise how people are similar to each other, what they are believed to have in common. People must have something socially significant in common – no matter how vague, apparently unimportant, or apparently illusory – before we can talk about their membership of a collectivity.

But it is a question of emphasis: similarity cannot be recognised without also delineating difference. Logically, *in*clusion entails *ex*clusion, if only by default. To define the criteria for membership of any set of objects is, at the same time, also to create a boundary, everything beyond which does not belong. Sociologically speaking it is no different: one of the things that *we* have in common is our difference from *others*. In the face of their difference our similarity often comes into focus. Defining 'us' involves defining a range of 'thems' also. When we say something about others we are often saying something about ourselves. In social terms, similarity and difference are always functions of a point of view: our similarity is their difference and vice versa. Similarity and difference reflect each other across a shared boundary. At the boundary, we discover what we are in what we are not. Even as superficially as this, it is possible to see an internal–external dialectic of identification at work collectively, to begin to understand how the same basic processual model of the social construction of identity may be applicable to individuals and to collectivities.

Collective social identities are vital building blocks in the conceptual frameworks of sociology and social anthropology. Without some means of talking about them it isn't possible to think sociologically about anything. Even selfhood incorporates identities such as gender, ethnicity and kinship which, whatever else they are, are definitively collective. However, although the 'individual' is an easy enough notion to grasp – in common sense at least – a 'collectivity' is more abstract and elusive. So what might 'collective' mean?

Similarity among and between a plurality of persons – according to whatever criteria – is the clearest image of the collective that I have offered so far. In sociology and social anthropology it is generally taken for granted that a collectivity is a plurality of individuals who either see themselves as similar, or who have in common similar behaviour and circumstances. The two facets of collectivity are often conceptualised together: collective self-identification derives from similar behaviour and circumstances, or vice versa. This understanding of collectivities dominated sociology during the late nineteenth and early twentieth centuries and still informs much contemporary social theory. It underpins most, if not all, attempts to apply models of causality to social phenomena, allowing regularities in behaviour to be translated into the principles which are believed to produce that behaviour.

It also exposes a major fault line within social theory: between an approach which prioritises people's own understandings of their social relationships and another which looks for and classifies behavioural patterns from a perspective which is outside the context in question. Somewhat crudely, this is the difference between the *verstehen* of Weber and Simmel, and the positivism of Durkheim, between 'the cultural' and 'the social' (Nadel 1951: 75–87), and between 'subjectivism' and 'objectivism' (Bourdieu 1977; 1990).

This might suggest that there are two different types of collectivity, and hence two different types of collective identity. In the first, the members of a collectivity can identify themselves as such: they know who (and what) they are. In the second, members may be ignorant of their membership or even of the collectivity's existence. The first exists inasmuch as it is recognised by its members, the second is constituted in its recognition by observers. Nadel is, however, correct to emphasise (1951: 80) that these are not two different kinds of collectivity. They are, rather, *different ways of looking at* social interaction, at 'individuals in co-activity'. He is equally right to insist that neither is more 'real' or concrete than the other: both are abstractions from data about 'co-activity'. These different kinds of abstraction provide the basis for the fundamental conceptual distinction between *groups* and *categories*:

> **category**. A class whose nature and composition is decided by the person who defines the category; for example, persons earning wages in a certain range may be counted as a category for income tax purposes. A category is therefore to be contrasted with a group, defined by the nature of the relations between the members.
>
> (Mann 1983: 34)[1]

This is a methodological distinction, concerned with how to constitute the social world as a manageable object for empirical inquiry and theoretical analysis. Whether a collectivity is seen as a group or a category is a consequence of how it is defined. However, since in each case the definition is that of the sociologist, the difference is less clear than it appears. By this token a group is simply defined sociologically according to a more specific criterion – perceived mutual recognition on the part of its members – than a category, which may, in principle at least, be defined arbitrarily, according to any criteria.

At this point Bourdieu's strictures against substituting 'the reality of the model' for 'the model of reality' (1977: 29) are worth considering. He is warning – as indeed is Nadel – against the reification of social interaction, against the linked fallacies of misplaced concreteness and misplaced precision. We should beware, for example, of investing collectivities with the kind of substance or agency with which embodiment allows us to endow individuals. It is not that collectivities lack substance or the capacity to do things – if that were so they would be of little sociological interest

– but they differ in these respects from individuals. Similarly, the boundedness of a collectivity is different in kind from the bodily integrity of an individual. Where a collectivity begins and ends is not mappable using the sociometric equivalent of a dressmaker's tape. Nadel and Bourdieu are also reminding us that our necessarily systematised and draughted view of social reality is, after all, just that, a *view*. A necessarily abstract (and simplified) view which we should not mistake for social reality. And, what is more, it is always *from* a point of view.

However, groups and categories are not just sociological abstractions. Although the distinction between them is a product of processes of definition and abstraction – of identification – on the part of social scientists, social scientists have no monopoly over these processes. Sociologists engage in the identification of collectivities, but so does everyone else, in a range of common-sense discourses and practices of identification. The sociological definition of 'group', above, recognises this. Group identity is the product of collective internal definition. In our relationships with significant others we mobilise identifications of similarity and difference, and, in the process, generate group identities. At the same time, our self-conscious group memberships signify others and create relationships with them. Thus categorisation is also a general social process, this time of collective external definition. I have, for example, already suggested that the identification of others, *their* definition according to criteria of *our* adoption (which they may neither accept nor recognise), is often a feature of identifying ourselves. More generally, categorisation is a routine and necessary contribution to how we make sense of, and impute predictability to, a complex social world about which our knowledge is always partial. The ability to identify unfamiliar individuals with reference to known social categories allows us at least the illusion that we know what to expect of them.

Thus, although in the strictest of senses groups and categories exist in the eye of the sociological beholder, the conceptual distinction between them mirrors routine social processes, external and internal moments of collective identification: *group identification* on the one hand, *social categorisation* on the other. This means that groups and categories are something more than products of the sociological imagination. But what?

It is an article of sociological faith for all but the most obdurate positivists that if people think that something is real, it is real in its consequences (if nothing else). Therefore it is socially real.

Deriving from W.I. Thomas at Chicago in the early decades of this century, this injunction recommends that sociologists not bother themselves too much with ontology and get on instead with the pragmatic business of trying to understand the social realities in terms of which people act. How people define their social situation(s) is thus among the most important of sociological data. From this point of view, a group is socially 'real'. Group members, in recognising themselves as such, effectively constitute that to which they believe they belong. It is in processes of internal collective definition that, in the first place, a group exists: in being identified by its members, and in the relationships between them. However, a group that was recognised *only* by its members – a secret group – would have only a very limited social presence, and its discovery (and categorisation) by others would be perpetually immanent. Furthermore, even if secrecy were maintained, such a group would necessarily be shaped to some extent by the categorising gaze of others: one of its identifying features in the eyes of its members would be precisely its freedom from external recognition. Thus categorisation by others is part of the social reality of any and every group.

A category, however, is less straightforward, since its members need not be aware of their collective identification. Here the emphasis falls on consequences. One useful place to begin is by asking whether the extreme case – a category which is unrecognised by those who are identified by others as belonging to it, and which has no impact upon their lives – can be said to have any social reality. Such cases are not common; a social category is not generally a secret to its members. But there is no reason why it could not be. Among the obvious possible examples are the classificatory schema of the social sciences.[2] These are often distant from the people to whom they refer, and their uses apparently arcane and remote. For instance, it seems unlikely that anthropological debates concerning the Nilotic peoples of the southern Sudan – about whether 'the Nuer' and 'the Dinka' are separate social entities, whether one is the other, or which one is which (for example Burton 1981; Newcomer 1972; Southall 1976) – were either audible to Dinka or Nuer themselves or had any consequences for their lives. A similar point could be made about sociological debates concerning the categorisation of populations in terms of social class (for example, Goldthorpe and Hope 1974; Marshall *et al.* 1988; Stewart *et al.* 1980; Wright 1985). It doesn't seem likely that technicians, for example, spend much time pondering whether they are members of the 'service class', the 'non-manual working class' or some other social stratum.

However, these examples oblige us to ask whether social categorisation can ever be aloof or disinterested. In the first place, neither example is wholly divorced from the people who are the objects of the classificatory exercise: 'Nuer' and 'Dinka' are locally recognised identities in southern Sudan, are part of the present political landscape, and earlier had resonance for colonial government. Similarly, people in industrialised societies routinely identify themselves according to class. The ways in which these categories are defined may not be part of the local knowledge of the people to whom they are applied, but the categories themselves are locally grounded. They are not secrets to their members.

The role of categorisation in the production of disciplinary power is also worth considering. Authors such as Foucault (1970; 1980), Hacking (1990), and Rose (1989) argue that the categorising procedures of the social sciences have a role in the bureaucratic practices of government of the modern state, and cannot be described as wholly disinterested. Scientific notions of 'objectivity' and 'truth' derive their epistemological power in part from their grounding in procedures of categorisation. In turn, objectivity and truth legitimise the bureaucratic rationality which is the framework of the modern state. The categorisation of individuals and populations that is the stock in trade of the social sciences is also one of the ways in which humans are constituted as objects of government and subjects of the state, via censuses, etc. The reference to taxation in the definition of 'category' quoted earlier was perfectly apposite. More pointedly, 'objective' knowledge about the social behaviour of humans provides one basis – whether that is its rationale or not – for the policing of families and the private sphere which characterises the modern state.

So, even the most apparently uninvolved categorisation is only apparently so. Whether directly, via the commissioning, direction and use of social science research by the state or other agencies, or indirectly, via the contribution of theory and research to the fecundity and potency of the categorical point of view of government (Foucault's 'governmentality'), categorising people is always *potentially* an intervention in their lives. And often more.[3] Although they may not be aware of having been categorised, the fact that they have been must always be considered as at least immanently consequential for a category's members.

More commonly, people know that they have been lumped

together in the eyes of others, but are not aware, or not fully aware, of the content and implications of that categorisation. A category may be recognised by its membership without its implications for their lives being clear or obvious to them. We have probably all had the experience of realising that we are being categorised in a particular fashion – in a new work place, perhaps, or on moving into a new neighbourhood – without knowing what to expect in terms of the responses of others, or their expectations of us. Imbalances of this kind may be institutionalised. People with learning difficulties, for example, are often aware of their categorisation by others as 'retarded', 'stupid', or whatever (Davies and Jenkins 1997). However, the extent to which that shapes their lives, or the relationship between that categorical identity and the cruelties of the world, is just as often systematically concealed from them. Here are situations in which the nominal may be clear but not the virtual.

Talking about individuals and categorisation highlights another characteristic of social categories. A group is distinguished by the nature of the relations between its members. In fact, group membership is a relationship between members: even if they do not know each other personally, they can recognise each other as members. Membership of a category is not a relationship between members; it doesn't even necessitate a relationship between categoriser and categorised. Any social relationships which may exist are strictly dyadic, involving the categorised as individuals. Once relationships between members of a category involve mutual recognition of that categorisation, the first steps towards group identification have been taken.

Categorisers are the other side of the coin. Categorisation may be more significant for categoriser(s) than for categorised. Our categories don't have to be consequentially 'real' to the people to whom they refer, in order to have consequences for us. Although categorising others is one aspect of identifying ourselves, this need not involve explicit notions of difference *vis-à-vis* ourselves and those others. Nor need we have any expectations of them. The examples of the Nuer–Dinka, or social class, which I discussed earlier, can help to make the point. The most important themes of these categorisations are not 'Nuer–Dinka are different from us anthropologists', or 'the working class are different from us sociologists' (although these sub-themes may be present). As aspects of their disciplinary world views, categorisations such as these do other kinds of identificatory work for anthropologists and sociologists. Disagreements over categories produce boundaries internally, between different 'sides' of the argument. Certainly in the case of class, different classificatory schema are associated with intra-disciplinary groupings and minor sociological feuds of some longevity.

Another example may further illustrate what I mean. Style is an arbiter of youth identities in western industrialised societies. One of the ways in which styles are delineated is through the categorisation of music and musicians. In my youth, for example, questions such as whether white musicians could play the blues, or whether Tamla-Motown counted as soul, had an urgency which seems disproportionate only in retrospect: how they were answered was a significant part of our style and who we were. Thus the categorisation of others is a resource upon which to draw in the construction of our own identities.

That categorisation has consequences, even if only trivial or immanent, returns the discussion to the distinction between the nominal and the virtual. Collective identification also has nominal and virtual dimensions. The nominal encompasses how the group or category is defined in discourse, the virtual how its members behave or are treated. As with individual identification these are conceptually distinct. In practice they are chronically implicated in each other, but there is no necessary accord between them.

The argument so far is that the internal–external dialectic of identification can be seen at work in the construction of collective as well as individual social identities. Collective internal definition is group identification; collective external definition is social categorisation. Each is an inter-related moment in the collective dialectic of identification. This suggests that neither comes first and neither exists on its own. But is this actually the case?

Group identification probably cannot exist in a social vacuum. Short of imagining an utterly isolated – and implausible – band, small enough to lack significant internal sub-groupings, then historically speaking it seems sensible to suggest that groups necessarily exist in relation to other groups: to categorise and to be categorised in turn. Group identification therefore proceeds hand-in-glove with categorisation. Although it makes figurative sense to talk about groups being constituted in the first instance by internal definition – after all, without their members relating to each other and defining themselves as such there would be nothing to belong to – this should not be misconstrued literally and chronologically, to mean *first* group identification, *then* categorisation.

There may, in fact, be situations in which group identification is generated by prior categorisation. But although categorisation necessarily conjures up an immanent group identity, it doesn't inevitably create an actual one. Marx understood this when he formulated his famous distinction between a 'class in itself' and a 'class for itself'.[4] He argued that the working class is constituted *in itself* by virtue of the similar situation of workers, their common alienation from the means of production within capitalism. By virtue of their shared situation, workers have similar interests (that is, things that are in their interest). Marx argued that these interests cannot be realised until workers unite into a class *for itself*, and realise for themselves what their interests are. This, for Marx, signifies the emergence of the working class as a collective historical agent. The process of group identification encourages and is encouraged by class struggle. Subsequent refinements of this model, particularly by Lenin in *What is to be Done?*, emphasised that class struggle would not 'just happen' as a consequence of the conflict of interests between classes; it has to be inspired or produced. Hence Lenin's notion of the 'vanguard party', and hence the need for politics.

Whether or not we agree with this argument historically, it illustrates my argument. Given appropriate circumstances, groups may come to identify themselves as such because of their initial categorisation by others. The point is that there was no class 'in itself' until its common interests were perceived and *identified*. The categorical constitution of the working class as a class in itself with a situation and interests in common – by socialists and other activists, on the one hand, and, as a 'dangerous class', by capitalists and the state, on the other – was a necessary although not a sufficient condition for the birth of the class for itself and, hence, for working-class politics (if not necessarily revolution). Before the working class could act *as* a class, working people had to recognise that it *was* – or they were – a class. In this recognition the working class was constituted as a politically effective group.

Distinguishing the necessary from the sufficient suggests that for a social category to be defined it must be definable. There has to be something which its members share. In principle this can be completely arbitrary. One could, for example, decide that all married persons with ingrowing toenails were a social category. But would this ever amount to more than an abstract, logical category? To become a social category, it would at the very least have to be recognised by appreciable numbers of others. In order for that to happen the combination of being married and suffering with ingrowing toenails would have to possess some social significance to those others. They would have to have an interest in the matter, there would have to be a point to it. In the case of the working class, capitalist wage-labour produced the common interest and the point, without which there would have been nothing 'in itself' to recognise. Although social categorisation may in principle be arbitrary, it is unlikely ever to actually be so.

People collectively identify themselves and others, and they conduct their everyday lives in terms of those identities, which therefore have practical consequences. They are 'socially real'. This is as true for social categories as for social groups. Or, to come closer to the spirit of this discussion, it is as true for social categorisation as for group identification, since neither groups nor categories are anything other than emphases in processes of identification.

Two further points flow from adopting this position. First, collective identities must always be understood as generated simultaneously by group identification *and* social categorisation. How we understand any particular collective identity is an empirical matter. In one case group identification may be the dominant theme, in another categorisation. But, as argued above, both will always be present as moments in the dialectic of collective identification, even if only as potentialities. Second, social processes are pre-eminently social practices, done by actually existing individuals. There is thus nothing idealist about this argument. Collectivities and collective identities do not just exist 'in the mind' or 'on paper'.

The conceptual distinction between groups and categories is an analogue of general social processes of group identification and social categorisation. Collective social identities are no less processual than individual social identities, and group identification and social categorisation have practical consequences. Rather than reify groups and categories as 'things', we should think instead about social identities as constituted in the dialectic of collective identification, in the interplay of group identification and social categorisation. In any particular case it is empirically a question of the balance between these processes. Group identification always implies social categorisation. The reverse is not always the case. Social categorisation, however, at least creates group identification as an immanent possibility.

10

The social organisation of difference

Social identity is the constitution in social practice of the intermingling, and inseparable, themes of human similarity and difference. Collective social identities emphasise – construct, even – similarity. This is the focus of the next chapter. With respect to difference, the practicalities of collective identification, as process and with respect to consequences, can be illuminated by the work of the Norwegian anthropologist Fredrik Barth.

Barth has not, perhaps, had the recognition he deserves. Compared to stars such as Bourdieu or Geertz, his work remains little known outside anthropology. This may be a consequence of being based in Oslo, rather than in Princeton or Paris; it may be a consequence of intellectual fad and fashion. Whatever the reasons, however, Barth's body of work is one of the richest and most imaginative in anthropology. He is a social theorist of greater significance than his lack of wider reputation might suggest. His project has consistently been,

> to explore the extent to which patterns of social form can
> be explained if we assume that they are the cumulative

result of a number of separate choices and decisions made
by people acting *vis-à-vis* one another ... patterns are
generated through processes of interaction and in their
form reflect the constraints and incentives under which
people act.

(Barth 1966: 2)

Barth wants to understand how collective social forms exist,
given that the social world is – before it is anything else – a world
of individuals. He understands collectivities as generated in and
out of interaction between individuals. This does not, however,
mean that 'society' is simply the sum of individuals and their
relationships:

Indeed, 'society' cannot defensibly be represented by *any*
schema which depicts it as a whole made up of parts. ...
The complexities of social organization can neither be
bounded in delimited wholes nor ordered in the unitary
part–whole hierarchies which the schematism of our
terminology invites us to construct.

(Barth 1992: 19)

In the paper cited immediately above, he cautions against identifying any 'particular area of the world' in which we are interested as
a 'society'. Along with its patterns and forms, we should recognise
the disorder and lack of closure of social life. This is another
consistent theme in his work.

In 1969 he edited *Ethnic Groups and Boundaries*, a symposium
on ethnic identity that was sub-titled 'the social organisation of
culture difference'. This indicated that ethnicity and cultural
difference are connected, and acknowledged that the social and
the cultural are not separate domains. Although his framework is
concerned with ethnic identity, it is, as I hope to show, applicable
to other collective identities.

Although Barth's model of ethnic identity broke new ground
for social anthropology, it was not an immaculate conception. Its
important elements all had their antecedents. Individual behaviour
and decision-making – social organisation rather than social
structure – had long been themes in the work of anthropologists
such as Malinowski, Firth and Nadel. Barth's key insight that ethnic
identities are flexible – if not totally fluid – over time can be found,
albeit less systematically theorised, in Leach's earlier study of
Burma (1954), and the situational variability of ethnic identity had

already been explored by, for example, Moerman (1965). Barth's theorising also has many affinities with Goffman and, through him, Chicago sociologists such as Everett Hughes.[1]

However, Barth went beyond existing conceptualisations in both depth and detail, theorising ethnic identity within a wider set of arguments about social process and social forms. This line of theoretical development began with his study of politics in Swat, north-western Pakistan (1959), in which he focused on how political groupings develop and change as the result of inter-personal strategising and transactions. His understanding that collective forms are not fixed, but are generated by, or emerge out of, interaction, was taken further in *Models of Social Organisation* (1966). The insight that the foundation of social pattern lay in the social processes of individual lives was the primary theme in Barth's thinking; it continued in his exploration of ethnic identity.

Barth began his 'Introduction' to *Ethnic Groups and Boundaries* (1969) by observing that the persistence of differences between ethnic groups, indeed the groups themselves, had been taken for granted. The existence of ethnic groups (or tribes) was just 'the way things were' and anthropology had not problematised how such groups maintained their distinctiveness or reproduced themselves. Although Barth made the pragmatic assumption that it was sensible to continue to talk about groups, he was moving away from a structural-functionalism which over-solidified them as Durkheimian social facts. 'Societies' are not to be seen as *things*. That groups are produced by people in social interaction is his basic theorem, and anthropologists need to look at how the membership of ethnic groups is recruited, rather than simply assuming an obvious process of birth-and-death reproduction.

He went on to insist that groups 'exist' even though the barriers separating them are osmotic rather than watertight: 'boundaries persist despite a flow of personnel across them' (1969: 9). Barth declared his interest in 'social processes of exclusion and incorporation whereby discrete social categories are maintained *despite* changing participation and membership in the course of individual life histories' (ibid.: 10). Bearing in mind that in his usage the word 'category' is not tightly defined as it is in mine, Barth is arguing that ethnic collectivities are independent of the individuals whose membership constitutes them. Members come and go, if only (but not only) as a consequence of human mortality. The ethnic group can also survive the fact that individuals in the course of their lives may change their ethnic identities. In Haaland's analysis (1969), for example, individual members of sedentary Fur communities in the western Sudan may adopt a nomadic lifestyle, eventually becoming members of Baggara communities. But a difference between Fur and Baggara collective identities remains clear even though it is blurred in individual biographies.

Barth's model of ethnic identity has three basic elements. First, ethnic identities are folk classifications: ascriptions and self-ascriptions, held by the participants in any given social situation. They thus contribute to the organisation of interaction. In Thomas's sense they are socially 'real'. Second, Barth is interested in the processes which generate social forms, rather than in their abstract structure. He is primarily concerned with what people do; his is a materialist (and pragmatist) concern with the behaviour of embodied individuals. As a consequence, third, rather than looking at the 'content' of ethnicity – cataloguing the history or cultural characteristics of ethnic groups – the focus of investigation shifts outwards to processes of ethnic boundary maintenance and group recruitment. This involves looking at inter-ethnic relations. By these tokens, cultural commonality is better understood as a product of processes of boundary maintenance, rather than as a defining characteristic of group organisation. In other words, the social construction of (external) difference generates (internal) similarity, rather than vice versa. It follows, only at first sight paradoxically, that:

> we can assume no simple one-to-one relationship between ethnic units and cultural similarities and differences. The features that are taken into account are not the sum of 'objective' differences, but only those which the actors themselves regard as significant. . . . some cultural features are used by the actors as signals and emblems of differences, others are ignored, and in some relationships radical differences are played down and denied.
>
> (Barth 1969: 14)

This characteristic of ethnic identities allows individuals to move in and out of them. It also means that ethnic identities are not immutable. They are capable of change over time. To be German in 1995, for example, involves emphasising or de-emphasising different things than being German would have done before reunification; and both would be very different to nominally equivalent identifications in 1938, or 1916, or 1871. There is also likely to be considerable variability between contexts. What it means to be

English – what is required to maintain the identification, and the kinds of responses from others which it generates – is one thing when an English person interacts with, say, a Nigerian person in England; it is likely to be another thing altogether in Nigeria.

Thus difference is socially organised, in the first instance by individuals in interaction. But not all interaction is equally significant in this respect: the continuity of ethnic units – which is a better expression for the moment than groups or categories – is particularly dependent upon boundary maintenance. This is managed during interaction *across* the boundary, with Others (for whom we are, in turn, their Other). Making at this point (p. 16) a specific reference to Goffman's 'presentation of self', Barth argues that all inter-ethnic relations require recognised rules to organise them. Although 'rules' may be too strong a word, implying a degree of conscious formulation which is implausible, these interactional conventions or habits do not just delineate difference. They define the limits of the interaction, and permit either side to participate with only the barest agreement about acceptable behaviour in common.

Relationships within the boundary, between co-members, are not neglected, however. Barth emphasises the importance to ethnic identity of shared value orientations, the 'standards of morality and excellence' with which behaviour is evaluated. His emphasis upon being recognised, as well as recognising oneself, is congruent with Mead and the symbolic interactionist tradition, not to mention Goffman. Internal and external meet, inasmuch as claiming an ethnic identity 'implies being a certain kind of person, having that basic identity, it also implies a claim to be judged, and to judge one-self, by those standards that are relevant to that identity' (Barth 1969: 14). In belonging to a collectivity, an individual accepts the right of co-members to judge, and seeks to be to be accepted and judged by Others only in particular ways.

For Barth, ethnic identities are processual or practical: 'for acting . . . rather than contemplation' (p. 29). All social identities are part of a larger universe of experience, a significant aspect of which is 'the material world of causes and effects' (Barth 1981: 3). Collectivities exist within the realities of ecological constraint and possibility,[2] which frame both their relations with Others, and relations among their members. Inter-group competition for resources within specific ecologies is important in the generation of boundaries. Further, in the embodied face-to-face world of everyday life, and making a distinction which is homologous to that between the nominal and the virtual, he argues (1969: 28) that although ethnic ascription does not require access to assets (conceived in the widest possible way), the satisfactory performance of an ethnic identity does. It is not enough to claim an ethnic identity, one must be able satisfactorily to perform it, to actualise it. That may require resources.

What counts as a successful performance varies from situation to situation, place to place, and time to time. Nor is success guaranteed. Nominal 'ethnic labels' and the virtualities of experience feed back on each other:

> under varying circumstances, certain constellations of categorization and value orientation have a self-fulfilling character, . . . others will tend to be falsified by experience, while others are incapable of consummation in interaction.
>
> (Barth 1969: 30)

By 'self-fulfilling', and drawing once again upon Goffman,[3] Barth means that participants will typically do their best, using 'selective perception, tact, and sanctions', to maintain identifications conventionally appropriate to the situation. If for no other reason, they do this because it is generally easier than coming up with alternative identifications or definitions of the situation. Thus although change and flux in ethnicity are possible – and common – the persistence of ethnic identity is likely to be routine. This is a tribute to the 'organizing and canalizing effects of ethnic distinctions' (ibid.: 24). Identity revision only takes place when it is either manifestly incorrect ('untrue in any objective sense') or proves to be consistently unrewarding. What counts as unrewarding is, of course, moot in terms of the pragmatics of the situation. What counts as 'objective' is more problematic; I will return to this below.

It is implicit that identity change occurs only when interaction must be maintained, when disengagement isn't a practical option. It is also implicit, given Barth's insistence that interaction across the boundary is the *sine qua non* of ethnic identity, that its persistence or revision are dialectical processes of collective identification, with internal and external moments. Ethnicity is always a two-way street, involving 'them' as well as 'us'. The fact that not all identificatory performances 'work' draws our attention to the role of significant others in validating identity. Internal identification and external identification are mutually entangled. It is, however, true to say that in Barth's own work, and in its appropriation within anthropology, the emphasis has tended to fall upon group identification ('us') rather than social categorisation ('them'). But this emphasis is not inevitable (R. Jenkins 1994).

Most of the comment on Barth's 1969 paper stressed the transactional and situational flexibility of ethnic identity. This understanding of ethnicity has become central to conventional anthropological wisdom in the field (e.g. Eriksen 1993). However, Barth's general theoretical stance has been sharply attacked with respect to exactly these themes by a number of critics (Asad 1972; Evens 1977; Kapferer 1976; Paine 1974) and these criticisms can be applied to his arguments about ethnicity. In particular, he was taken to task for individualist, means–ends voluntarism and a neglect of power. Barth has responded at length to these criticisms (1981: 76–104), so I shall be brief here.

Barth emphasised individuals and their decision-making to a degree which was at that time unusual – although not novel – within anthropology. That it is more routine today reflects a gradual recognition within the discipline of the need to acknowledge social action, practice and subjectivity. But Barth focuses on more than individuals anyway. His interest in the processual generation of collective social forms (such as identities) as the unintended consequence of interaction has been largely overlooked by his critics. He has described this aspect of his work as the most significant (1981: 76), and it is the theoretical path he has continued to tread (e.g. 1987; 1992). If a body of work of great substantive range and theoretical variety can be characterised in one keyword, 'generative' would undoubtedly do.

Since 1969 Barth has addressed issues which further mitigate the charge of individualism. Discussing pluralism in complex societies (1984; 1989), he talks about 'universes of discourse' or 'streams of tradition'. These are less clear-cut than 'cultures'; individuals participate in them differentially, typically in several at the same time, and with varying intensity or depth. Writing about Bali, Barth describes it thus:

> People participate in multiple, more or less discrepant, universes of discourse; they construct different partial and simultaneous worlds in which they move; their cultural construction of reality springs not from one source and is not of one piece.
>
> (1989: 130)

While the imagery suggests movement and activity, these universes or streams are to a considerable extent historically stable.

In part these ideas are a response to the persistence with which anthropologists and sociologists – despite his arguments of 1969 – still reify ethnic identity as possessing coherence and definite boundaries: 'We must abandon the physicalist comforts of seeking to anchor plural cultural components universally in some construct of population segments' (1984: 80). Ethnic groups are, let us remember, generated in and expressions of process, of interaction. For Barth, this implies that 'dichotomized cultural differences . . . are vastly overstated in ethnic discourse'; 'the more pernicious myths of deep cultural cleavages . . . sustain a social organization of difference' but are not 'descriptions of the actual distribution of cultural stuff' (1994: 30).

Criticisms about Barth's neglect of power are, of course, related to the accusation of individualism. And they have some force. Much of the relevance of Barth's argument with respect to power is not explicit in his work. That does not, however, mean it is absent. A consistent theme uniting Barth's work since the 1950s has been the fundamentally political nature of social interaction. Competition and manoeuvre are ubiquitous, as are constraints of ecology and resources. Emphasising choice and decision-making does not mean that they only take place in a situation of equality between persons. Quite the reverse (and the echo of Marx is surely no accident):

> choice is not synonymous with freedom, and men and women rarely make choices under circumstances chosen by themselves. What is more, the unfortunate circumstance of a gross disadvantage of power does not mean that strategy is unavailing – indeed it may be all the more essential to the actor and all the more pervasive in shaping his behaviour.
>
> (Barth 1981: 89)

In emphasising the importance of assets for successful performance, and exploring the circumstances under which ethnic identities are *not* validated, Barth is implicitly indicating the importance of power, in this case the power to define the situation successfully. Stressing that the dialectics of group identification and social categorisation (to use my terms) are rooted in interpersonal transactions does not mean that each is equally important in specific situations. One is likely to dominate; *which* is a question likely to be decided by power differentials.

Barth's argument is, however, vulnerable to other criticisms. In suggesting that cultural commonality (similarity) results from the construction of identity (difference) at the boundary, rather than vice versa, he misses the dialectical simultaneity of identification. Neither similarity nor difference 'come first'. Subsequently, and somewhat contradictorily, however, in emphasising the role of values in orienting decision-making, he takes a substantial degree of shared culture somewhat for granted. This is part of his concentration upon feedback (particularly in *Models*, 1966), upon how values change as a result of interactional experience. As Barth himself admits, he may have 'overestimated the potential power and adequacy' of the concept of 'value' (1981: 91). If nothing else, an emphasis upon values falls foul of the difficulty of attempting to know what is going on in other minds (Geertz 1983: 55–70; Holy and Stuchlik 1983). Nor are notions of choice and decision-making unproblematic, as discussed with respect to Goffman; exactly the same cautions apply in Barth's case.

Perhaps the most significant problem, however, is with the notion of 'boundary'. It is clear that Barth understands identity boundaries as ongoing products of social interaction, particularly between people holding different identities. It is in these ongoing transactions that what is or is not relevant as markers of the identities in question – and what 'being A' or 'being B' *means* in terms of consequences – is produced and reproduced. However, with its topological or territorial overtones, 'boundary' is a metaphor the use of which demands vigilance; witness the ease with which one talks about *the* boundary. It may be precisely Barth's emphasis on boundaries which allows many other anthropologists to draw on his work while persisting in the reifying view of the ethnic group as corporate and perduring which he intended to demolish (R. Cohen 1978: 386–7).

It is in fact far from clear where or what the boundary of any particular identity 'is'. This is not surprising, since it is not, really, anywhere or anything. Boundaries are to be found in interaction between members of different identities, which can in principle occur anywhere or in any context. Identification is not a simple matter of the 'cultural stuff' which is associated with any specific identity, and which may appear to constitute the solid criteria of membership. Identity is about boundary *processes* (Wallman 1986) rather than boundaries. As interactional episodes, those processes are temporary check-points rather than concrete walls (and even the latter are permanent only in their makers' conceit: witness Maginot and Berlin). Boundary processes may be routinised or institutionalised in particular settings and occasions – something which I will discuss subsequently with respect to the institutional-isation of identity – but that is a different matter.

Lastly, Barth's notion that revision of an identity occurs if it is 'objectively' incorrect requires more attention. As a moderate caution it is sensible, reminding us that the capacity of humans to define social reality in the face of 'the material world of causes and effects' is finite. But there may be a little more to it than environ-ment, and in this it harks back to discussions in earlier chapters. The embodiment of identities, for example, is a case in point. Gender is the obvious case: as transsexuals and transvestites attest, it is to some extent manipulable. But the definitive embodiment of female and male means that the scope for and ease of revision and change are limited. The same is true for other identities which are defined in embodied terms, such as 'race' or age. Embodiment aside, there is also a general point which is not to be denied. A group of people with no discoverable historical connections to Norway, and speaking no Norwegian, cannot, for example, simply arrive at the Norwegian border and have any expectation of mounting a plausible claim to Norwegian identity or nationality. Even social categorisation, as I argued in the previous chapter, can never be wholly arbitrary.

Thus actors' definitions of the situation cannot be unilaterally paramount. To begin with, not everything is thinkable in any given context; not everything that is thinkable is situationally practical; and not everything that occurs in practice is thinkable (or, at least, thought). Another of the issues is always *whose* definition of the situation counts; this returns us to the importance of power, authority, and resources. In recognising this, Barth – like Goffman – is espousing a middle-of-the-road materialist realism which resonates with the core themes of pragmatism.

This is one of the senses in which Barth stands in a line of thought which, via Goffman and the Chicago sociologists of the 1940s, reaches back to Mead and beyond. However, whereas Mead begins with the whole (society) and goes to the part (the individual), Barth works from individuals to society. Each makes his biggest error in conceptualising the matter in terms of a vector of one *to* the other. And in each case, the error is largely one of expression: they actually both imply models of the relationship between the collective and the individual as a perpetual and more or less simultaneous dialectic or feedback.

Barth's is among the most developed and empirically well substantiated[4] explorations of the interaction between internal and external collective identification, between group identification and social categorisation, and between the individual and the collective. His work is particularly important for two related reasons. First, he is concerned to understand how difference is organised in and arises out of social interaction. Rather than taking identity differences for granted and then looking at how they affect interaction, Barth's approach is the reverse. He wants to know – and he *really* wants to know, rather than paying the idea conventional lip-service – how identity and difference are socially constructed. Second, in exploring what he has called (1994) the 'median' level of social life, he offers a bridge between individuals, their practices and their identities, and the macro level of social forms and collective identities.

It is now time to justify my remark that Barth's arguments are applicable to social identities other than ethnic identity. Oblique support for this proposition comes from a paper by Yehudi Cohen which is contemporaneous with Barth's ethnicity symposium (1969). In a discussion which appears to owe nothing to reading Barth and draws on the literature about social networks, Cohen applies a model of 'boundary systems', which is similar to Barth's in that intra- and inter-group relationships are seen as mutually dependent across a boundary, to collective identities such as kinship and town membership. And, to anticipate the next chapter, many of the analyses which have been undertaken under the umbrella of Anthony Cohen's model (which explicitly owes much to Barth) are of social identities other than the ethnic.

In *Ethnic Groups and Boundaries*, however, Barth himself said little about this issue. He suggested, for example, that, like 'sex and rank',

> ethnic identity implies a series of constraints on the kinds of roles an individual is allowed to play, and the partners he may choose for different transactions. . . . ethnic identity is superordinate to most other statuses, and defines the permissible constellation of statuses, or social personalities, which an individual with that identity may assume.
>
> (1969: 17)

Fifteen years later (1983; 1984), discussing the intricacies of social life in Sohar, Oman, Barth painted a picture of the social organisation of difference using a wider palette, albeit with a fine brush:

> the diversity of identities that entails membership in distinctive culture-carrying groups in Sohar was not one that I had expected. I arrived in the field with the expectation that ethnicity would provide the primary ordering identities. . . . The dismantling of this picture . . . [was] my response to empirical findings in Sohar. . . .
>
> (1983: 81n.)

To understand the cultural pluralism of the town, it proved necessary to develop a model of diversity (Barth 1983: 81–93; 1984) which could encompass the following universes of discourse or streams of tradition:

- ethnicity (Arab, Baluchi, Persian, Zidgali, Indian Banyan), each with its own language, with Arabic as the *lingua franca*;
- religion (Sunni Islam, Shiah Islam, Ibhazi Islam, Hindu);
- history/descent (10 per cent of the population are the stigmatised descendants of former slaves);
- occupation and class;
- settlement and life-style (the distinction between townspeople and recently settled bedouin);
- gender, including institutionalised transsexualism (Wikan 1977); in Barth's view this is the deepest and most ubiquitous distinction of all.

To this list, although Barth might not conceptualise them as aspects of cultural pluralism, one could append further universes of discourse such as kinship or age.

The domains of identity which Barth explored in Sohar are bounded, but only weakly: there is coming and going across them, and little in the way of mutual reinforcement between them. The overlaps are complex. There is a varied range of processes of group identification and social categorisation. Some people, some collectivities, are in a stronger position to construct their identities and resist the imposition of identification by others; some are in a weaker position.

Soharis in their daily lives, and in the pursuit of their varied interests, spin the different strands into distinctive threads of biography and individual identity; in their transactions and interactions they weave a carpet of complex cultural plurality. In doing so, the mundane preoccupations of their daily lives emerge out of and are channelled by the histories to which they further contribute, and the local is brought to bear upon and is framed by wider networks and 'external' events and processes. The town is a 'kaleidoscope of persons' (Barth 1983: 165).

This summary of the ethnographic riches of Barth's (and his collaborator Wikan's) study makes a *prima facie* case for arguing that his model applies to a universe of social identity wider than ethnicity. It also supports Barth's recent, perhaps slightly ironic, observation that the original ethnicity symposium,

> contains, perhaps, one of the first anthropological applications of a more postmodern view of culture. Though we lacked the opaque terminology of present day postmodernism, we certainly argued for what would now be recognised as a constructionist view. Likewise in our view of history: we broke loose from the idea of history as simply the objective source and cause of ethnicity, and saw it as a synchronic rhetoric – a struggle to appropriate the past, as one might say today.
>
> (1994: 12–13)

Barth offers a *general* model of collective social identity, within which all of the domains of identity (my term) or universes of discourse (his) encompassed by the Sohar study are understandable. The same general model was implicit in 1969 in *Ethnic Groups and Boundaries*.

First, social identities are processual, aspects of the ongoing organisation of interaction and everyday life. They are not to be understood as part of a superstructure of 'culture'. Second, the analytical emphasis falls on the social construction of identities in interaction at and across the boundaries which they share with other identities, and upon process of recruitment. Third, collective identities are thus generated in transaction and interaction and are, at least potentially, flexible, situational and negotiable. Barth begins with embodied individuals in interaction and works up to collective social forms. Fourth, identity is a matter of ascription: *by* individuals of themselves, and *of* individuals by others. Collectively, the same holds good: groups identify themselves and are categorised by others. Finally, collective identification is inherently political; this is an important implication of Barth's emphasis upon transaction.

This is a model of the collective dialectic of identification, of the entanglement and interplay of group identification and social categorisation, of how that occurs in interaction between individuals. In emphasising the social organisation of difference, however, Barth arguably underplays the question of similarity. It is to this that I now turn.

11
The symbolic construction of similarity

Although the previous chapter focused on the role of difference in collective identification, it still makes sense to say that the emphasis in collective identification is upon similarity. Group identification, by definition, presupposes that members will see themselves as minimally similar. Social categorisation is predicated upon the proposition that those who are categorised have a criterion of identification in common. Collectivity means having something in common, whether it be 'real' or imagined, trivial or important, strong or weak. Without some commonality there can be no collectivity.

These issues have a long history in social theory. In particular, there is the theme that the less people have in common with each other, the more problematic social cohesion becomes. Marx's writings on alienation, and his subsequent discussions of class conflict and mobilisation, are about this. When Ferdinand Tönnies, writing in 1887, posited a historical shift from *gemeinschaft* ('community') to *gesellschaft* ('association'), he too was concerned with what people had in common and how it was changing. Durkheim's distinction between the mechanical solidarity of traditional rural society, in which their similarity bound people together – an image reminiscent of Marx's description, in *The Eighteenth Brumaire of Louis Bonaparte*, of the French peasantry as 'potatoes in a sack' – and the differentiated complementarity, or organic solidarity, of industrial society, evokes the same theme. So does his notion of the *conscience collective*.

One sociological topic around which these issues cluster is 'community'. Discourses of community belong to the romantic intellectual tradition in European thought, responses to the uncertainties and conflicts of modernisation and industrialisation which imagine a past when the meaning of life was relatively secure and consensual, in which cooperation rather than conflict prevailed, in which people 'knew their place'. 'Community' is also, however, a powerful everyday notion in terms of which people organise their lives and understand the settlements and localities in which they live and the quality of their social relationships. 'Community' is among the most important sources of collective identity. It has generated a huge sociological literature (Bell and Newby 1971; Crow and Allan 1994; Stein 1960), and an approach to doing social research, in the 'community study'.

Anthony Cohen's model of the 'symbolic construction' of communal and other collective identities is useful and suggestive (1982; 1985; 1986). He is trying to understand how people construct a sense of themselves and their fellows as 'belonging' *in* a particular locality or setting, and *with* – if not *to* – each other. This is what he means by 'community'. Although his interest has consistently been in peripheral communities within large-scale polities, he offers his arguments as general propositions about communal life. Community membership, for Cohen, depends upon the symbolic construction and signification of a mask of similarity which all can wear, an umbrella of solidarity under which all can shelter. The similarity of communal membership is thus imagined; inasmuch as it is a potent symbolic presence in people's lives, however, it is not imaginary.

Like most social theory, Cohen's is a creative synthesis. Drawing on the Durkheimian tradition of British social anthropology – emphasising the role of symbolism in creating social solidarity – Cohen's understanding of the significance of communal boundaries also owes much to Barth. With respect to the politics of symbolism, he acknowledges the influence of the Manchester

School of social anthropologists, particularly Max Gluckman (1956), Victor Turner (1967) and Abner Cohen (1974), while his emphasis upon meaning draws on Geertz (1973; 1983) and, ultimately, Weber. Cohen's starting point is that 'community' encompasses notions of similarity and difference, 'us' and 'them' again. This focuses attention on the boundary, which is where the sense of belonging becomes most apparent:

> The sense of difference . . . lies at the heart of people's awareness of their culture and, indeed, makes it appropriate for ethnographers to designate as 'cultures' such arenas of distinctiveness. . . . people become aware of their culture when they stand at its boundaries.
>
> (Cohen 1982: 2, 3)

Recognition of culture and community stems from the awareness that things are done differently *there*, and the sense of threat which that poses for how things are done *here*. The debt to Barth is obvious: in particular note that collective social forms – such as 'cultures' – are produced by the local sense of difference at the boundary.

However, 'community' is not material or practical for Cohen in the way that identity is generated in interaction for Barth. But neither, for Cohen, is 'community' a 'structural' phenomenon. It is definitively cultural, and as such, mental or cognitive:

> culture – the community as experienced by its members – does not consist in social structure or in 'the doing' of social behaviour. It inheres, rather, in 'the thinking' about it. It is in this sense that we can speak of the community as a symbolic, rather than a structural, construct.
>
> (Cohen 1985: 98)

Emphasising the symbolic construction of 'community', Cohen advances three arguments. First, he says that symbols generate a sense of shared belonging. A sports team, for example, can excite allegiance from, and thus unite, all or most of a community's members, coming, in time, to symbolise the community to its members and to outsiders. Shared rituals – be they weddings and funerals, or rituals explicitly focused on the community itself such as the annual fête or the works outing – can also act *for* the community as symbols *of* community.

Second, Cohen argues that 'community' – and its analogues in other languages – is itself a symbolic construct upon which people draw, rhetorically and strategically. To claim to do something in the best interests of the 'community', or to represent the 'community', are powerful claims indeed. We are all supposed to be in favour of 'community'. It is a feel-good word carrying a powerful symbolic load; hence its political uses, as in 'community care', for example (Bulmer 1987). Cohen is alerting us to the ideological nature of 'community': it not only says how things are, it says how they *should* be. 'Community' is also, according to Cohen (1985: 14), 'essentially enshrined in the concept of boundary'; so it symbolises exclusion as well as inclusion. Hence its rhetorical potency in ethnically divided situations such as Northern Ireland.

Third, Cohen argues that community membership means sharing with other community members a similar 'sense of things', participation in a common symbolic domain. But this does not entail either a local consensus of values or conformity in behaviour. 'Community', for example, covers a range of meanings and means different things to different community members. A similarly wide range of meanings can be expressed through it. So too with symbols of community. The rugby club in a south Wales valley, for example, will be experienced and understood differently by an ex-player, by a teacher who has only recently come to live in the town, and by the wife of an unemployed ex-miner who spends too much money in the club bar. But all may see themselves as supporting the team, particularly if it is doing well in the Cup. And to each of them the club will in some way represent the community. What is significant is not that people see or understand things in the same ways, or that they see and understand things in ways which differ from other communities, but that their shared symbols allow them to *believe* that they do.

Whether we are talking about symbols *of* community or community *as* a symbol, the power of the notions and the images thus mobilised depends on the capacity of symbols to encompass and condense a range of, not necessarily harmonious or congruent, meanings. By definition, symbols are abstract to a degree, imprecise to a degree, always multifaceted, and frequently implicit or taken-for-granted in their definition. As a consequence, people can to some degree bestow their own meanings on and in symbols; they can say and do the 'same' things without saying or doing the same things at all. This returns us to the distinction between the nominal and the virtual. The nominal – the name or description of an identification, and thus linguistic – is always symbolic. It may be further symbolised in heraldry, dress, ritual, or other material and practical forms. Which is precisely why the nominal can be associated with a wide range of virtualities without change or abandonment.

So the apparent sense of homogeneity or uniformity within local communities is just that: apparent, and every inch a social – and symbolic - construct:

> the members of a community may all assent to the collective wisdom that they are different from other communities in a variety of stereotypical respects. But this is not to say that they see each other, or themselves, manifesting these differences similarly.
>
> (Cohen 1986: 11)

Using an expression which recalls Barth (1981: 12, 79–81) Cohen argues that the ties or bindings of 'community' are *aggregating* rather than *integrating*: 'what is actually held in common is not very substantial, being *form* rather than content. Content differs widely among members' (1985: 20). Differences of opinion – and more: of world-view, cosmology, and other fundamentals – among and between members of the same community are normal, even inevitable. They are masked by the appearance of agreement and convergence generated by shared communal symbols, and participation in a common symbolic discourse of community membership which constructs and emphasises the boundary between members and non-members. Thus members can present a consistent face to the outside world. One might also say – although Cohen doesn't put it like this – that the symbolic construction of community allows people who have to get on with each other, to do so without having to explore their differences in damaging detail. Here Cohen introduces a distinction between the public and the private:

> The boundary thus symbolises the community to its members in two quite different ways: it is the sense they have of its perception by people on the other side – the public face, or 'typical' mode; and it is their own sense of the community as refracted through all the complexities of their lives and experience – the private face, and 'idio-syncratic' mode. It is in the latter mode that we find people thinking about and symbolising their community.
>
> (1986: 13)

This is almost a communal 'I' and 'me'. The symbolisation of community is, once again, to be found in 'thinking' rather than in 'doing'.

Finally, Cohen argues that symbolic boundaries – of hearts and minds – become more important as geo-social boundaries become less important, with centralisation and political integration. This is a response to the cultural and social homogenisation of nation-building and the incorporation by metropolitan centres of their peripheries. Further, the more pressure there is on communities to change as part of this process, the more vigorously boundaries will be symbolised. Difference will be constructed and emphasised and we-ness asserted in opposition to *them*. A symbolically contrived sense of local similarity may be the only available defence. In some cases the hardening of an apparently 'traditional' identity may actually serve as a smokescreen, behind which substantial change can take place with less conflict and dislocation.

A number of criticisms can be made of Anthony Cohen's work. The contrast between 'thinking' and 'doing' which runs through his analysis is problematic (R. Jenkins 1981). So is his distinction between social structure and culture. It is particularly difficult to defend his emphasis upon what people *think*. Apart from any cat-calls of 'idealism' which such a model might provoke, the epistemological difficulties should not be underestimated. His discussion of the private 'thinking of community' anticipates (1986: 9) his recent discussion of the essential privacy of self-consciousness and identity (1994), discussed in Chapter 5. As suggested there, an analysis developed on these terms is somewhat opaque, falling back on assertions which are inaccessible to argument.

Fortunately, Cohen's emphasis upon people's private thoughts is actually difficult to maintain in the face of his own writing. In his work on collective identity it is almost an irrelevant tangent. In advancing his argument by means of apt ethnographic case-study and illustration, the supporting data which he presents are, over and over again, accounts of people *doing* things: saying this or that, participating in rituals, mounting political protests, fishing together, or whatever. It is in and out of what people *do* that a shared sense of things and a shared symbolic universe emerge. It is in talking together about 'community' – which is, after all, a public *doing* – that its symbolic value is produced and reproduced.

Focused on the anthropologised margins, Cohen over-emphasises the homogenising, flattening effect on communities of integration into nation-states and wider polities. More important, he exaggerates the uniformity, and the monolithic tendencies, of large-scale political units. Doing what most anthropologists do – treating 'beyond the community' as the modern equivalent of 'here be dragons' on a medieval map – he doesn't attend to the complexity, divisions, and tensions of state and nation and their constituent institutions. Which is ironic. Almost every thread in his analysis of the 'symbolic construction of community' could be woven into a model of the 'symbolic construction of the nation' (and indeed, in many respects, it already has: see, for example, B. Anderson 1983). What Cohen is telling us is that the 'community' of locality and settlement is no less imagined than the 'community' of the nation, and no less symbolically constructed.

Another, related difficulty is that he doesn't explore situations in which communal solidarity is *not* symbolically re-asserted in the face of external pressure. He has replaced structural-functionalism's image of social consensus with a model of imagined consensus or homogeneity which is unlikely to fit all situations. What, one wonders, might he make of the fractured 'communities' of Sicily (Blok 1974; Gambetta 1993; Sabetti 1984; Schneider and Schneider 1976) or the inner cities of the United States (E. Anderson 1978; Hannerz 1969; Liebow 1967; MacLeod 1987; Rainwater 1973)? The evidence of the ethnographies is that these cases cannot be explained away as anomic disorder. Nor is Cohen's model incapable of expansion to include them: the symbolic elaboration of non-communal collective identification – within families, networks or associations, for example – should be grist to his mill. But in contexts such as these the mask of community – of 'belonging' – has slipped, that particular umbrella is in tatters. The fragmentation of communal identity within localities – its symbolic deconstruction, if you like – is one possible consequence of flux and change, and of categorisation, which Cohen neglects.

None the less, Cohen has much to offer a sociology of identity. In the first place, as suggested above, his model is not confined to localities of co-residence (1985: 97–118). Although his emphasis on community as a mental construct has its problems, it facilitates the application of his model to a wide variety of collectivities: communities of interest, ethnic communities, occupational communities, religious communities, etc. These are all collectivities to which one can 'belong'. Cohen's arguments have a relevance wider than the village or the neighbourhood: in his edited volume sub-titled *Identity and Diversity in British Cultures* (Cohen 1986), households, kinship, adolescence, and a farm are among the communities of identity discussed by the contributors.

Second, his work complements Barth's, offering a more developed model of the relationship between identity boundaries and their 'contents' – the culture of the people inside the boundary – which still emphasises flexibility and variability. Although Cohen's notion of boundary, bearing in mind his emphasis upon cognition and his concomitant de-emphasis of process, may actually be more reified than Barth's, he takes more seriously the 'cultural stuff' within the boundary and in emphasising symbolisation rather than values offers an advance on Barth. Collective identities are not 'internally' homogeneous or consensual. They can and do change; they can and do vary from context to context; they can and do vary from person to person; and yet they can and do persist. Without emphasising the symbolic dimensions of identification – in addition to the transactional and interactional – this cannot be fully understood.

Symbolisations of community are umbrellas under which diversity can flourish, masks behind which a considerable degree of heterogeneity is possible. In my terms, the mask or umbrella can be conceptualised as a *nominal* identification. This is always symbolised: in language, but also potentially in other forms, whether visual, musical, or whatever. The practice and experience of community membership, *vis-à-vis* other members and outsiders, is the *virtual* dimension of community identification; it may, in large degree, be individually idiosyncratic. Both nominal and virtual have internal and external moments of identification; each is a dialectic of group identification and social categorisation. Each feeds back upon the other (to return to Barth). The distinction between the nominal and the virtual allows my emphasis upon process and the practices of embodied individuals to be integrated into Cohen's scheme.

Cohen is saying, most convincingly, that the similarity emphasised by collective identities is a social construction, an ongoing historical contrivance, reminiscent perhaps of Bourdieu's 'cultural arbitrary'. It stems from the minimal sharing of a symbolic repertoire. But, of course, and Cohen would not disagree, in that the people concerned believe in it – in the sense of organising their lives with reference to it – it is not only socially 'real', it is consequential. And sometimes very powerfully consequential. A flag may only be a symbol of national unity, but there are too many historical examples of individuals perishing in its defence to take it anything but seriously. There is no such thing as *just* a symbol. Nor can a community ever be imaginary (or anything other than imagined).

And Cohen is saying more. If communal uniformity or similarity is a social contrivance, it is contrived in a comparative framework of similarity and difference. It is about our difference from them as well as our similarity to each other. But that's not all. Throughout Cohen's argument, and in his choice of examples, he emphasises that the 'belonging' of 'community' is symbolically constructed by people in response to, even as a defence against, their social categorisation by outsiders, whether they be the folk from the next village, tourists upon whose cash community members might depend, the representatives of an oil company, environmental protesters, or the officers and impersonal agencies of the state. Against these foils difference is asserted and similarity symbolically constructed; it is in their face that communal identity is necessary. Here, in Cohen's work, one can see the internal–external dialectic of collective identification at work.

To recall a point made elsewhere, words such as 'response' or 'defence' should not be misconstrued to imply necessary sequence. They do not mean that communal identity, the shared sense of living in and as a community, is absent until, one moment, along comes the outside world to conjure it up. There will always have been an 'outside world', even if only the next village. However, the outside world's salience, its power and size, and its perceived distance and difference from 'us', may all change. In the process, as part of an ongoing dialectic of collective identification, community may be more explicitly stressed and practices of communal symbolisation and differentiation increasingly called into play in the solidary affirmation of similarity and the defence of perceived collective interests. And, to reiterate another earlier point, collective identificatory strategies stressing symbolisations other than the strictly communal – family, friendship, gang, or whatever – may be alternatives to a communal response.

The internal–external dialectic allows us to think about identity boundaries – A/not A – without reifying them. One metaphor for boundaries might be the hyphen between the internal and the external (a hyphen means nothing without whatever it connects). In another image the boundary can be seen as the dialectical synthesis of internal thesis and external antithesis: the identity *is* in important senses the boundary. These ways of thinking about the matter converge, in that each involves at least two simultaneous points of view. The internal definition of A is external from the point of view of B, and vice versa; similarly A and B can be thesis, antithesis or synthesis, depending on starting point (of view). Boundaries are definitively relational, simultaneously connecting and separating one side and another.

The relational nature of boundaries of identification is closely connected to the symbolisation of social identity. In the first place, symbols only 'make sense' in relation to other symbols. Meaning is a product of system and relation; nothing means anything on its own. Similarity, for example, cannot be established without also delineating difference. The second place, however, is more interesting. This is 'the line of argument of the French sociologists of *L'Année sociologique* ... that the social relations of men provide the prototype for the logical relations between things ...' (Douglas 1973: 11). That line of argument stretches from Durkheim and Mauss, via Lévi-Strauss, to Michel Foucault, Mary Douglas herself, and Pierre Bourdieu. In the present context it points to a reciprocal mutuality of signification between symbolisation and social identification. This means that social identification is not just a sub-set of the general symbolic domain of culture. As the symbolic constitution of relationships of similarity and difference between collectivities and individuals, social identification provides the basic template – via analogy, metaphor, homology, etc. – for the wider constitution of the world as meaningful. Social identity emerges as fundamental to culture, a view which resonates with the arguments of Marx and Mead that interaction between humans is the a priori of consciousness, rather than vice versa.

If social relations provide the model for symbolic relations – for meaning – then it is important to remember that those are relations between individuals, and that those individuals are embodied. This is recognised by, among others, Douglas (1973) and Bourdieu (1977: 87–95; 1990: 66–79). The collective – cultural – point of view imagines a world with humanity at its centre; the individual point of view centres on the body. With respect to social identity, this is perhaps most significant in that the (individual) human body provides a basic metaphor for symbolising and imagining collective identities. It is not only social scientists who 'see' society using organic analogies. In English, for example, we talk about 'the head of the family', 'the head of state', 'the heart of the community', or 'the backbone of the organisation'. We say that a particular group 'has guts'. Communities can be 'alive' or 'dead'. And one could doubtless find many other examples. Even collective identity, it seems, draws symbolically on embodiment as a model of consistency and integrity.

Looking at the symbolisation of identification offers a further perspective on the social processes in which the embodied individual and the abstract collective converge. Individual and collective identifications are inherently symbolised, particularly in the symbolic interaction of language (remember the discussion of Mead, in Chapter 5). This allows the individual to participate in the collective domain; according to Mead, it permits reflexive selfhood, in the capacity to take on the role of the Other. In condensing vast amounts of information about people into manageable forms, the symbolisation of identification also allows us, sociologically and in everyday life, to think about and to model – in other words to imagine – collectivities and the relations between them. Symbolisation permits the necessary abstraction of individuals and collectivities, and of the relationships between them, which is the constitutional basis of the notion of 'society'.

Among the most important aspects of the symbolisation of identity in this respect is that it allows individual diversity and collective similarity to co-exist within the same social space. There is no need to wonder about why people who 'are' the same don't all 'do' the same. For certain purposes and in certain contexts, they simply imagine that they are more or less the same. And that imagining is socially 'real'. The symbolisation of identification works, what is more, in a similar fashion whether individually or collectively. One way of talking about selfhood, for example, is as a symbolisation of the complexities of individuals, glossing them with enough consistency to allow others who are acquainted with them to decide how to act towards them. The identification of individuals with respect to their membership of collectivities contributes in the same way to the expectations which others have of them. The point is not that this consistency is actual, but that it provides a plausible basis for a minimum of predictability in relations between people.

The unity of selfhood is in one sense an umbrella or mask, under or behind which the diversity and contradictions of the individually embodied point of view over time and across situations can co-exist without having to be perpetually in the public limelight (to the likely confusion of self and others). The parallel with the 'symbolic construction of community' is clear; selfhood is no less imagined than any other social identity. Identity, whether individual or collective, is always symbolically constructed.

Cohen's focus on symbolisation draws our attention to the unavoidable abstraction of social identification. Sociologically speaking, images of identity – selfhood, community, or whatever – look like what Max Weber called 'ideal types' (1949: 90–106). An ideal type is an abstract model, of any particular social pattern or social form, with two basic characteristics. First, it is a synthesis of/from a myriad of 'more or less present and occasionally absent' social phenomena. Not everything which is a specified feature of an ideal type is necessarily present in any actual case. Second, phenomena are included as elements of an ideal type on the basis of the 'accentuating' point or points of view – in the sociological case, theoretical positions and interests – from which it is constructed.[1] Among the examples of social science ideal types which Weber offers are the 'city-economy', 'capitalistic culture', 'feudalism', 'the state' and 'Christianity'. The construction of ideal types by social scientists is a heuristic procedure which permits comparison and hypothesis formulation in the face of the extreme diversity and density of social life.

Weber recognised that many ideal types are not only *analytical models*, but are also socially meaningful *folk* models (which harks back to the discussion of groups and categories in Chapter 9). Sociologists are not the only people who need to compare things, or frame working hypotheses. Nor do they have any monopoly on the complexity of social life. Alfred Schutz (1967: 176–250) expanded upon Weber's conception of the ideal type to make this point more thoroughly. Schutz argued that all of our knowledge of the world – whether common-sensical or sociological – is in the form of ideal typifications. Given the inherently symbolic nature of language this is perhaps no more than we might expect.

Schutz distinguished our direct face-to-face knowledge of our *fellows* in the everyday social world, from our indirect social experience of *contemporaries*, who we have never met and may never meet.[2] Our ideal typical models of our contemporaries are likely to be more abstract than the typifications – based in direct social experience – upon which we draw to understand and render more predictable people whom we 'know'. There is a continuum, from more concrete to more abstract, which Schutz expressed from an ego's point of view, as a move from *We* to *Thou* to *They*. From the direct vividness of my face-to-face interaction with known others, the social world becomes ever more 'remote and anonymous' as I look out into the world of my contemporaries. Eventually the boundary of that world is reached in artifacts which 'bear witness' to their meaning for some unknown Others, but don't identify those Others to me. Beyond that boundary my contemporaries are inaccessible. What Schutz is saying has relevance with respect to similarity and difference:

> All our knowledge of our fellow men is in the last analysis
> based on personal experience. Ideal-typical knowledge of
> our contemporaries, on the other hand, is not concerned
> with the other person in his given concrete immediacy but
> in what he is, in the characteristics he has in common with
> others.
>
> (1967: 193)

This is similar to my proposition that individual identification
emphasises difference, while collective identification emphasises
similarity. The 'concrete immediacy' of our fellows differentiates
one from another as complex individuals; our contemporaries have
'in common' their collective similarity as members of a particular
category.

Schutz's distinction between fellows and contemporaries
illuminates the nuanced relationship between similarity and difference with respect to individuals and collectivities. For example,
despite Schutz's stress on what they have in common, it is clear that
contemporaries are definitely individuals, even though they may
be shadowy and anonymous. I know that the Mexican Navy, for
example, is made up of real sailors; I don't recognise any of their
faces, however. Even in the case of contemporaries with faces, in
the absence of knowledge based in direct personal experience one
relies on more superficial, less individualised knowledge about
them, among which their participation in collective identifications –
gender, ethnicity, residence, class, occupation, etc. – will be to the
fore. With one of my fellows, however, that she is Mrs Oswald's
daughter, baby Helena's mother, owner of a red Mazda coupé, and
that she dropped a bag full of groceries outside my door yesterday
(which I helped her to pick up at the same time as having a chat
about the new couple who have just bought the house two doors
away), are all likely to be more relevant to me than her collective
identifications as female, Afro-Caribbean, middle-class and a
lawyer.

But this example itself prompts further elaboration. I cannot,
for example, *forget* that Mrs Oswald's daughter is female. Otherwise she would be Mrs Oswald's son, and could not possibly
be Helena's mother. And the relevance of gender depends upon
point of view: whether 'I' am male or female, regardless of closeness
of relationship and directness of knowledge (and not actually
regardless: the opportunity for, and nature of, intimacy between

individuals is likely to be influenced by gender). Gender, the embodied intersection of one relationship of similarity and one of difference, is simultaneously and definitively individual and collective.

Nor is ethnicity – 'race' in this case – disregardable: 'my' ethnic point of view matters, depending on context. When I first encountered the woman who I now know to be Helena's mother, that she was Afro-Caribbean may have been the most significant thing that I noticed about her. And *is* Mrs Oswald Afro-Caribbean? And what might it tell me if she were not? Similarly the fact that her daughter owns the red Mazda tells me something about her class, which in itself may call up knowledge about her profession. And that she is a lawyer is a significant aspect of her individual identity as one of my fellows: you never know when you might need a bit of informal legal advice. Etcetera. And, no less important, there is the place of collective identifications in her self-image, which none of the above begins to touch on.

Our knowledge of our fellows – their individual identity in our eyes – can never, whether in the last analysis or not, be completely 'based on personal experience' as Schutz claims. I do not, for example, have to experience Mrs Oswald's daughter practising law to know, for all practical purposes and until otherwise proven wrong, not only that she is a lawyer, but also (approximately) what being a lawyer entails. That is a matter of the things she has in common with other members of the collective professional identity – lawyers – which she claims as her own. What we know about individuals as fellows in our everyday lives, and the plausible expectations we have of them, are as much a matter of their collective identifications as our direct experience of them.

Nor are our contemporaries only known to us in terms of their collective similarities to specified others. The President of the United States – as I write it is Bill Clinton – is not one of my fellows. I would, however, recognise him if I bumped into him in the High Street. And his wife. I know a great deal about both of them, although the accuracy of my knowledge is another matter: from their marriage, to their politics, to their business dealings, and so on. But do I know any less about Bill Clinton than I know about the neighbour with whom I pass the time of day every day, discussing only the garden and the weather, and is what I know any less accurate, less verifiable, or less concrete?

One resolution of these questions might suggest that all of our fellows are, in some aspects of their lives and in some circumstances, also our contemporaries. That this is so may, when it becomes apparent, be a potent source of distress in close relationships: 'To think I thought I knew her' . . . etc. We simply can't have full direct experience of even our closest intimates. Each of our fellows is identified individually by us as an idiosyncratic combination of their collective identifications and the synthetic, rolling account provided by our direct experience of them. And we know about our contemporaries in vastly different degrees of detail and individuality.

The arguments put forward by Cohen and Schutz suggest that the more people have to do with each other in everyday life, the more likely they will be to identify each other as fellow individuals, rather than primarily by reference to collective identifications. From the outside or a distance, looking into the scene of everyday life, others, however, will be more likely to identify them first as members of a collectivity, as contemporaries. Whether someone is my fellow or my contemporary is always a function of my point of view. At the boundary, in encounters between insiders and outsiders, when insiders come to see themselves as collectively belonging – in the internal–external dialectic of collective identification – there is a constant interplay of similarity and difference. As symbolic constructions, each is imagined. In their consequences, however, neither is imaginary.

12
Predictability

Consistency, as distinct from consensus, is important in social life. The symbolisation of communal identity generates an imagined similarity, and, as Anthony Cohen argues, this allows difference and heterogeneity to prosper. But if diversity was all, social life would be complex and unpredictable to the point of being *un*imaginable. Because people orient their behaviour in terms of it, communal identity – for example – is 'socially real' in W.I. Thomas's sense. People may or may not think the same, but there must be *some* reciprocal and consistent similarity, if not uniformity, in what co-members *do*. Identity is a practical matter of what people do, and it involves similarity as well as difference.

This brings me back to Barth, for whom consistent patterns of behaviour generate identity boundaries and collective social forms more generally. Goffman is concerned with this when he talks about 'routines' and 'presentation'. Schutz also seems to allude to it in his definition of a 'personal ideal type' – a model or typification of a particular kind of person and of what it is plausible to expect of them – as '*by definition* one who acts in such and such a way' (1967: 190). Should the behaviour not conform to the ideal type, then eventually the individual will be re-identified with reference to another ideal type.

One way to look at *collective* consistency is in terms of conformity. Social psychology's conventional wisdom (Aronson 1991: 12–55), which resonates with Mead and Goffman, suggests that two motivational goals inspire conformism: the desire to be correct, and the desire to remain in the good graces of others. The first has its greatest impact on backstage private decision-making, the second on frontstage public behaviour. Each is rooted in primary socialisation and each is an emotional allotrope of the desire to *belong*. External factors which impinge upon conformist orientations vary culturally, situationally and individually. Non-conformity may come most easily to those whose group membership is secure in the mainstream. Insecure membership may thus encourage conformity, although one would expect to find a point of marginality beyond which this is no longer true. This puts a different spin upon Cohen's argument about the symbolic power of boundaries to license or accommodate within them a degree of dissensus and heterogeneity.

Aronson recognises that conformity may have sources other than these conscious goal-orientations. *Compliance*, for example, is produced by compulsion. It may only be weak conformity, which won't survive relaxation of the coercion, but it is significant. *Identification* depends upon affective powers of attraction, in intimate dyadic relationships and in more collective or public contexts. Identification, of course, is related to the desire to stay in the good graces of others. *Internalisation*, finally, results from learning and rationalisation. Here, conformity results from doing whatever is thought – within local canons of rationality – to be the most sensible response to the demands of the situation; it is also routinely reflected in the thoughtlessness of habitual routines.

Aronson's scheme is not wholly straightforward, however. Attempting to distinguish internalisation from the desire to be correct, for example, looks like hair-splitting. Culturally or locally specific accounts of 'correctness' are central to both, and in both there is a presumed motivation to be 'right' or to avoid being 'wrong'. Similarly, the perceived rational thing to do may be to stay in the good graces of others. Compulsion apart, the distinction between goal-oriented and non-goal-oriented conformism is, therefore, only analytical, at best.

Max Weber's discussion of the nature of domination (1978: 53–4, 212–301) is pertinent here. From Weber's point of view, conformity is the product and expression of domination. In his model the exercise of *power* – the capacity to dominate others through coercion of one kind or another – is the pursuit of compliance. The alternative to power, however, is more interesting and more routine: *authority* is legitimate domination, the conformity of those who accept its demand or expectation as justified (Smith 1960: 15–33). Identification and internalisation fall within Weber's categorisation of legitimate domination: the first is the basis of charismatic authority, the second of either legal or traditional authority. There are many modes of domination, and many sources of conformity. They are all intimately bound up with the symbolisation of collective identities (cf. Bourdieu 1991; Bourdieu and Passeron 1977; Gledhill 1994). To identify oneself or one's people in a particular way, is to assume as legitimate, if not as axiomatic, the arbitrariness of one's way of life and social relations.

As discussed in the previous chapter, the social construction of conformity is also in part an attempt to render interaction predictable. It affords individuals some expectations of the behaviour of others (and Others), on the basis of which to go about their everyday life without having to consider consciously everything in advance, and without excessive uncertainty. Conformity of a kind may also, however, result from uncertainty. When one is unsure of local rules or customs, the behaviour of others may be the single most important source of information about the right thing(s) to do. Hence conformity. This is of major significance for childhood learning, but it remains important throughout adult life (think, for example, about driving in a foreign country), and offers another understanding of why behavioural conformity may be at a premium at the boundary.

Looking at these matters anthropologically, Mary Douglas (1966) argues that notions of ritual pollution and supernatural danger reinforce other pressures towards conformity. Both tend to be associated with the boundaries of identity: examples might be marriage rules forbidding certain alliances, or ghost stories associated with the territorial spaces between groups. Her particular emphasis is upon symbolic classifications and their boundaries: between different membership roles within groups, between appropriate and inappropriate behaviour, between dirt and cleanliness, etc. Without classificatory systems, social life is unthinkable. Every social group has such a system or systems, some competence or participation in which is a criterion of practical group membership. *Inter alia*, classification systems focus our attention on boundaries: of the group, of acceptable behaviour, of purity, of humanity, of whatever. Issues of classification are always issues of identification.

Ritual pollution and supernatural danger combine in the 'incest taboo'. Conventional anthropological wisdom suggests that a ban on incest, in one local form or another, is *the* universal social rule, the ultimate boundary. From Frazer to Lévi-Strauss, and since, debates about incest have a long history within anthropology. Their relevance for this discussion is brought out by Fortes.[1] He argues that the notion of incest, the identification of particularly close categories of kin between whom sex is prohibited, provides a basic 'us–them' model, creates a need to form relationships between us and them, and offers the basic model for the rules of social life in general. It is thus the foundation of human society: 'without rules there can be neither society nor culture. . . . it was the emergence of the capacity to make, enforce, and, by corollary, to break rules that made human society possible' (Fortes 1983: 6). The argument is plausible, although one qualification would be that social organisation involves more than rules. Fortes suggests that there is an intimate relationship between identity and our capacity to live social, cultured, *human* lives. One can overstress the order-liness of society, but human social relations are certainly ordered. The original sin of incest is to generate disorder, a confusion of identities. Incest places individuals in two incompatible social places at once: how can one's mother also be one's sister, for example? Fortes also suggests that rules do not create identities. The message of incest prohibitions is that, if anything, rules emerge from the categorical differentiation of individuals. Social identity – knowing who we are, who others are, and what that involves – is an irreducible aspect of being human and living together.

Stereotyping and attribution are important dimensions of classification (Aronson 1991; Tajfel 1981). Stereotyping, the label-ling and classification of social collectivities, albeit in a partial fashion, simplifies information flows about complex situations. It is an extreme example of the general classificatory process of ideal typification. In its concern with predictability, stereotyping underlies habituation and facilitates institutionalisation (Berger and Luckmann 1967: 74–5). I will return to this in the next chapter. At this point the important thing to grasp is the mundane nature of stereotyping. Although the word has come to attract wholly negative connotations, stereotyping is a routine, everyday cognitive process upon which we all to some extent depend.

However, stereotyping is about more than the social and cognitive demands of information management. Boundary mainte-nance and symbolisation, *pace* Barth and Cohen, are also important

(McDonald 1993). Stereotypes, almost before they are anything else, are powerful symbols: 'symbolic discourse . . . only retains from experience a minimum of fragments to establish a maximum of hypotheses, without caring to put them to the test' (Sperber 1975: 4). Stereotypes of the inhabitants of either side of an identity boundary demarcate its contours with a particular, albeit illusory, clarity. Stereotypes are at best partial and always – like all ideal typifications – constructed from a point of view. They are not, however, necessarily hostile: a stereotype can flatter (a similar point was made in Chapter 8 about labelling). Apropos Schutz and my general argument about collective identities, it is in the nature of stereotypes to emphasise a small number of putative similarities between the stereotyped rather than their infinite array of differences. Stereotypes are extremely condensed symbols of collective identification.

Attribution, the attempt to understand others – particularly the motivations of others – by inference from the limited information provided by their verbal and non-verbal behaviour, is also at work within stereotyping. Attribution is another attempt to understand the social world and render it more predictable. All people, all of the time, need to explain and anticipate the behaviour of others. To do so, we frequently need to go beyond the available information. Ambiguity and uncertainty in such situations leads, Aronson suggests, to the use of stereotypical attributions. It may, therefore, be no coincidence that, according to Douglas, anomaly and ambiguity are likely to attract a symbolic load (1966: 41–53). Ambiguity or anomaly, uncertainty about which way to jump or what to do, are characteristic of boundaries and borders, hence the need to map them with imaginary precision or to dramatise them ritually (and it is, of course, precisely the ambiguity of boundaries which underlies Barth's understanding of them – and of identities – as fluid and permeable).

To recapitulate a core theme of this discussion, although individual and collective identity are matters of symbolic classification and boundary maintenance, they are matters of classification *in interaction and practice*. Group membership, for example, demands, as a practical accomplishment, some behavioural conformity: some consistent similarity in what individual members do. Every member has to be able, to some extent, to 'bring it off'. As we have seen, however, this doesn't entail consensus. The symbolisation of group boundaries and identity (the 'umbrella'), the distinction between private judgements and public behaviour, and the variety of types of domination, all suggest that normative consensus is not necessary for the existence of a shared social identity.

Nor do marginality, deviance or non-conformity necessarily imply normative dissent. At the margins of the group, where the frameworks of predictability are less firm, there is likely to be ambiguity about membership criteria and appropriate behaviour. Group boundaries may thus be generated by uncertainty, emerging as an ordering response to the relative unpredictability of encounters. Strong pressures encouraging conformity – with penalties attaching to deviance – may oppress most those whose membership or social identity is insecure. Powerful signals about conformity and deviance, dramatising group membership and boundaries, are easily expressed in stereotypes of in-siders and out-siders. For individuals on the collective margins, the price of admission may be some subordination of their own ambiguity, submission to the minor tyranny of the predictability demanded by others. The less securely one belongs, or the more one wants or needs to, the higher that price is likely to be. And in this, once again, it is possible to see an internal–external dialectic of identification at work.

Symbolisation is, however, central to more than individual and collective dialectics of identification. For Abner Cohen symbolisation underlies 'the whole process of institutionalisation. . . . Social relations are developed and maintained through symbolic forms and action' (1974: 5). Institutionalisation is one of the most consequential ways in which individuals participate in, or take on, collective identities. It also contributes to the establishment of environments of relatively predictable collective behaviour.

To follow the thread of the argument back as far as Mead, I have been considering predictability as an emergent and symbolically constructed property of social life. People identify themselves in particular ways at least in part in order that others may know what to expect of them. This involves a minimum of appropriate behaviour: a performance. In identifying myself within any minimally shared cultural setting I render the behaviour of others easier to predict (or imagine). I can imagine their position or orientation *vis-à-vis* myself. In presenting myself, I may make an active contribution to their behaviour towards me. Similarly, identifying others in particular ways permits me to imagine that I know what to expect of them. I will, more often than not, orient my behaviour towards them in terms of their presentations of identity. And so on. Throughout, one can see the interactions of internal and external moments of identification.

Nor must predictability be 'objectively' well-founded or accurate, or identification actually predictive of behaviour. It may be, but that isn't the point. Our ideal typifications of ourselves and others allow us to proceed in our everyday lives without fretting perpetually about what other people are going to do. On the basis of who we think they are, who we imagine them to be, we accept them at behavioural face value until there is reason not to do so. Most people most of the time 'know' who they are, 'know' who others are, and 'know' what to expect. This is fundamental to understanding social identity.

Talk about institutions and institutionalisation means something more than this, however. Institutions are organised and organising with respect to social identity and behaviour. No less imagined than any other social phenomena, they are enormously consequential in everyday life. In the next chapter I discuss institutions and institutional identity, and explore further arguments about the importance of social identity as a conceptual bridge linking the individual and collective within a unified understanding of social life.

13

Institutionalising identity

Having understood that social collectivities are more than the sum of their embodied parts, Durkheim, following Comte and Spencer, made an error in adopting an organic analogy – society as a corporeal entity (a 'living thing') – in order to understand and communicate this. In this, he was adopting an essentially common-sensical symbolisation of collective identity. Margaret Thatcher, approaching the same issue, made what is arguably a worse mistake, however, in declaring that there is *no* such thing as society, other than 'you and me and our next-door-neighbour and everyone we know in our town' (Raban 1989: 29–30).

A worse mistake, but an easy one to make. Although their existential status is not straightforward, individuals are at least embodied and obvious. Collectivities are altogether more nebulous; they are often difficult to 'see', whether in common sense or socio-logically. An army on the march or a stadium full of partisan sports fans has an embodied physicality that presents itself with material immediacy. But even their tangible presence – and many collectivities don't have that kind of presence – is a small part of what constitutes each as a collectivity. There must be something else if an aggregation of individuals is to be anything other than arithmetical. The fact of a lot of breathing human bodies occupying a territory is not enough to constitute a collectivity.

Collectivities and collective identities are to be found, in the first instance, in the practices of embodied individuals which generate or constitute them. Two different kinds of identificatory process have been outlined: group identification and social categorisation. These correspond, respectively, to the internal and external moments of the process of collective identification. These processes take place most definitively at the boundaries of identity. At the risk of repeating myself once too often, this doesn't mean a territorial boundary, nor is it like the physical boundary of an organism. It is a cumulative social construction which occurs when people who are identified as, say, Laputans interact with others who are identified differently, in any context or setting in which being Laputan matters. In the process the relevant criteria of membership of Laputa are developed, as are the consequences of being Laputan. These are political processes: negotiation, transaction, mobilisation, imposition, resistance.

In these processes, an image of similarity which is the defining characteristic of collective identities is symbolically constructed. But in the shade of that image a range of diversity and heterogeneity exists with respect to what people do. Collective identity emphasises similarity, but not at the expense of difference. Similarity and difference are irretrievably entangled in each other and where the emphasis falls depends on the point of view. Difference is no less socially constructed than similarity: both are culturally arbitrary, but neither, to remember W.I. Thomas, is any less 'real'.

Individual and collective identities coincide in complex ways. A useful perspective on this can be gained by looking at institutions. Institutions are patterns of behaviour in any particular context which have become established over time as 'the way things are done'. An institution has relevance and meaning in the social situation concerned; people will recognise it – will know it – if only in the normative specification of 'how things are done'. Institutions are an integral part of the social construction of reality, with reference to which, and in terms of which, individuals make decisions and orient their behaviour. The study of institutions is a staple of the sociological diet, and their constitution as appropriate objects for our attention is a matter of fundamental methodological importance. Institutions can be understood as ideal types, in both common-sensical and sociological discourse. Abstractions from the complex ebb and flow of interaction, they allow us to think about, to imagine, the patterns and regularities of social life. Once again, however, they are anything but imaginary: they are consequential and constraining.

First and foremost, institutions – very like identities, in fact – are emergent products of what people do as much as they are constitutive of what people do. They don't 'exist' in any sense 'above the action'. Institutions are our collective ideal typifications of continuing processes of institutionalisation. One of the most lucid accounts of those processes, rooted in the ideas of Schutz (see Schutz and Luckmann 1973), comes from Peter Berger and Thomas Luckmann in their classic, *The Social Construction of Reality* (1967: 70ff.).

They identify habit as the precursor of institutionalisation. Whatever else we are, human beings are creatures of habit. The habitualisation or routinisation of behaviour brings with it important cognitive and other psychological gains. Choices are narrowed to the point where many courses of action or ways of doing things do not have to be chosen at all. Since we don't have to think and decide about every little aspect of our daily lives, space for 'deliberation and innovation' is opened up; there is no need for every situation to be perpetually encountered and defined anew. More than simply rendering the social world predictable, habitualisation almost obviates the need for predictability in many situations: it creates a substantial, and secure, social environment of 'the way things are', which may not be easy to reflect upon consciously, much less change (cf. Bourdieu 1977; 1990).

When a number of people begin to share the same habitualised pattern of activity, to possess some sense that they are doing it, and to communicate to each other in the same terms about what they are doing, that is the beginnings of institutionalisation. If it persists for any length of time, a pattern of activity acquires a history. People encounter it as 'the way things are done'. It has become institutionalised as a taken-for-granted feature of the social landscape.

As part of this process, sanctions are likely to become associated with deviation from institutionalised routine: 'the ways things are done' may quickly become 'the way things should be done' (if, indeed, there is much difference in the first place). Institutions, perhaps before anything else, involve social control. Lest this be misunderstood, however, Berger and Luckmann are clear that the very existence of the institution, as an axiomatic part of the social world – 'the way things are' – is the primary form of social control. Doing things otherwise is simply difficult to imagine.

Additional processes of control are necessary only if institutionalisation is less than complete or effective.

The social world that we encounter as axiomatic in the course of socialisation is a world of institutionalised practices. As the products of history, we encounter them as 'objective', not to be questioned, and we seem to move in and out of their shadows. It is, of course, actually we who cast those shadows:

> Knowledge about society is thus a *realization* in the double sense of the word, in the sense of apprehending the objectivated social reality, and in the sense of ongoingly producing this reality.
>
> (Berger and Luckmann 1967: 84)

This is how institutions 'hang together'. They are 'real' – W.I. Thomas again – because we think they are and behave as if they are. The logic which institutions appear to possess derives not (only) from their own organisation, but is imposed by the reflective consciousness of actors. We 'know' that they are logical and integrated and therefore *de facto* they are. Language – discourse – is the pre-eminent source of this superimposed order, in the form of ritualised speech, rules and laws, written records, narratives, etc.

Institutions order social life, provide predictability, and permit actors to exercise lower levels of attention than might otherwise be demanded by a complex social world. They provide templates for how things should be done. But they do require legitimation in order to be presented successfully to each new generation: 'The same story, so to speak, must be told to all the children' (p. 79). The more meanings and canons of relevance are shared in any collectivity, the greater scope there is for the thoroughgoing and interpenetrating institutionalisation of social life. This we may call 'axiomatic legitimation' (R. Jenkins 1983: 7). Where a range of constituencies each constructs the world from differing points of view – which is likely, no matter how 'simple' or 'complex' the society in question – then the institutional order will be more fragmented or limited in scope; legitimation is more problematic in the presence of alternatives. Berger and Luckmann (1967: 110–46), while drawing in the first instance on Weber, broaden the notion of legitimation to encompass more than the overtly political; they insist that the legitimation of the institutional order is a matter of *knowledge* rather than *values*. Legitimation is bound up with the production and reproduction of 'symbolic universes': cosmologies, implicit and explicit specifications of the nature of the world and the place of people and their creations within it. In my terms, symbolic universes may be thought of as collective points of view:[1]

> bodies of theoretical tradition that integrate different provinces of meaning and encompass the institutional order in a symbolic totality . . . symbolic processes are processes of signification that refer to realities other than those of everyday experience.

> (ibid.: 113)

One of the key words in the above is 'processes'. At the heart of these processes is language, the primary constituent and framework of symbolic universes.

While wishing to avoid the reification which bedevils discussions of this nature, a symbolic universe is, if you like, the story which a collectivity tells about itself, the world and its place in the world. A symbolic universe – and Anthony Cohen later said something very similar – is, for Berger and Luckmann, the unifying umbrella under which the discrepant diversity of social life can come together. Nor is this just a collective matter:

> By the very nature of socialization, subjective identity is a precarious entity. It is dependent upon the individual's relations with significant others, who may change or disappear . . . symbolic universes . . . are sheltering canopies over the institutional order as well as over individual biography.

> (ibid.: 118, 120)

For Berger and Luckmann, then, symbolic universes are the sources of collective *and* individual consistency and continuity: 'psychology always presupposes cosmology' (p. 196). Returning to the concerns of this discussion, one paraphrase of this might suggest that psychology is to cosmology, as individual is to collective identity.

Unfortunately, Berger's and Luckmann's conception of the symbolic universe is perhaps a little grandiose. It is certainly too integrative. A kind of back-door functionalism, consensus in the final instance, lurks in the 'totality' of it all. As earlier chapters have argued, consensus – whether normative or cognitive – is neither necessary nor likely. We might do better to imagine the social world as a complex of greater and lesser symbolic universes – 'provinces of meaning' in the quotation above? – which interlock and conflict with each other in a variety of ways and with uncertain outcomes. Modest examples of symbolic universes in this sense might be godparenthood, the profession of medicine, a local community, a bureaucracy, or a voluntary organisation (each of which integrates within it a certain amount of institutional diversity).

The centrality to Berger's and Luckmann's model of cognition – symbolisation and knowledge – is also problematic. When it first appeared, *The Social Construction of Reality* offered a welcome corrective to structural-functionalism's emphasis upon normative integration and values. However, as discussed above, the model of ultimate cognitive integration with which Berger and Luckmann replaced it had many of the same problems. Even more serious – and there is a similar problem in the work of Anthony Cohen – is their neglect of the materiality of the social world as a source of its 'hanging together'. This is most significant, in the present context, with respect to the location and sedimentation of institutions in embodied individuals, artefacts, and territorial space.[2]

This of course varies, depending upon which institutions we are talking about. Marriage is an institution, for example. It exists, it hangs together, it persists, as a fairly abstract institution, because people believe in it as a symbolic universe within wider symbolic universes. But it also hangs together in a very material sense: in the sexual, domestic and economic practices of cohabitation, in common property, in the physical presence in the social world of married couples, in specific places which one has to attend and specific rituals – whether secular or religious – which one has to perform there in order to be married, in the ring and the ring finger, etc. Without the full symbolic consecration of marriage it is possible to be married after a fashion by *doing* it: cohabiting, behaving as a married couple, and even wearing rings. And symbolic consecration alone may not be sufficient: without cohabitation, without 'being' a married couple in the social world, is it a 'proper' marriage? Each scenario is recognised, for example, in British law and everyday discourse: one is a common-law marriage, the other grounds for divorce (or refusal of admission by an immigration officer). How often have we heard people say things such as, 'The marriage was *really* over years ago'? Nor do the commonplace practices of marriage and its symbolic specification have to accord. They appear not to for many people at the moment; but that doesn't mean that marriage as an institution, rooted in a symbolic universe, is necessarily weakening.

A more straightforward example is a university. A university is an institution in two senses: as an example of 'the university' – a type of institution of higher learning – and as *this* particular university (of Poppleton or wherever). Symbolically it is conjured up within a rich universe of statutes, traditions, ideals of scholarship, rituals of consecration, funding mechanisms, recruitment processes, business plans and so on. This constitution has developed historically within the broader institutional field of education, although these days it also has something of the air of a commercial enterprise (and does this undermine it as a university?). More mundanely, however, it also exists as a body of people and as a collection of buildings, a campus, playing fields. Getting off the train at Poppleton, for example, it is possible sensibly to ask for, and expect to receive, directions to 'the University'.

Thus one can see and 'bump up' against both marriage and a university. Metaphorically, where marriage is a shifting archipelago of particular and historically ephemeral marriages, a university is a substantial land mass (which is not to ignore its eventual historical impermanence). The point is not that Berger and Luckmann are wrong to emphasise the symbolisation of institutions. Quite the reverse: everything about the materiality of marriage and a university which I have described above is, in fact, definitively symbolised and cannot be otherwise. The point is, rather, that symbolisation is always embodied in the materiality of practices, their products, and three-dimensional space (which also involves time, since space does not make sense outside a temporal framework, and vice versa: Giddens 1984: 110–44). In their desire to move beyond the materialist–idealist impasse this, perhaps, was something that Berger and Luckmann neglected. Collective life hangs together as much in the visibly embodied doing as in the thinking (and the two are, indeed, not easily disentangled). Berger's and Luckmann's notion of 'society as objective reality', meaning symbolically objectified reality, does not take the embodiment of society – in people and in things – seriously enough. Social forms may be imagined, but they are not imaginary: the practices of people, and their products, constitute them as tangible in space and time.

There are other criticisms of Berger and Luckmann. The cognitive and the normative, for example, are not as distinct as they sometimes seem to imply: the way things *are* done and the way things *should* be done often amount to much the same thing. And the distinction between habituation and institutionalisation is not hard and fast. In this respect, there is a continuum from the individual to the collective: collective habit is a form of institutionalisation, and habit is often the individual expression of institutionalised patterns (hence Bourdieu's notion of the habitus).

Berger's and Luckmann's underplaying of power and compulsion is more telling. Their emphasis upon legitimation is an important recognition of particular aspects of domination, and of the stratification which is an inherent characteristic of knowledge and symbolic universes. Nor do they wholly ignore power: 'He who has the bigger stick has the better chance of imposing his definitions of reality' (1967: 127), is only one example. But power could be more central to their model than it is. This is particularly important for our understanding of internal–external dialectics of identification. An external moment of identification does not have to be legitimated or accepted by those who are its subject and object – they don't necessarily even have to *know* it – in order to be consequentially real for them.

Criticism notwithstanding, Berger's and Luckmann's account of institutionalisation offers a plausible and straightforward model of how it happens, which allows us to think about institutions that are flexible, fluid and loosely specified, as well as about those that are more formally constituted. It also helps us to understand the nature of collectivities and collective identification. Collective identities are institutionalised: as 'ways of being' they are 'the way things are done'.[3] With the emphasis upon identification, upon identity as process, collective identifications are institutionalised processes. Ethnic identifications are institutionalised. So are locally specific gender identifications. Even the most loosely knit friendship group or temporary interest-based coalition is institutionalised.

And, to reverse the thrust of the argument, institutions – events (e.g. an annual village fête), estates (e.g. marriage), corporate groups (e.g. universities), or whatever – are sources and sites of identification. They may not in themselves be collective identities, but they are productive – in Barth's terms, generative – of identifications. The annual village fête, for example, has an organising committee and a structure of tasks and offices. These are occupied by individuals, whose incumbency differentiates them from each other, from those who merely attend the fête, and may have wider resonance within the village. Being married differs from being single, being divorced, or being widowed; all of these, however, are identities which are rooted in the institution of marriage. Being a university lecturer is an identity constituted in and by the institution of the university, which contributes to the frameworks of similarity and difference which situate it – and any particular university lecturer – with respect to, say, a university porter, on the one hand, or a lecturer in a college of further education, on the other.

Collectivities and collective identifications are institutionalised: they are 'the way things are done'. And institutions are sources and sites of identification for individuals. But what, for example, about the relationship between institutional identities and the individuals who occupy them? Ralph Linton addressed this issue with his well-known distinction between *status* and *role* (1936: 113–31). A status is an institutionalised identification viewed in the abstract; it is 'simply a collection of rights and duties' (p. 113). For example, 'husband' and Professor of Culture and Media Studies at the University of Poppleton are both statuses. Neither says anything about particular individuals who may be identified with the status at any particular moment. Every status has a processual element, which is the role attached to and specified by it: this is what the occupant of the status does when acting in that status. Status and role are inseparable; one cannot exist without the other. In Linton's notion of role, with its implied theatrical analogy, one can see the roots of Goffman's dramaturgical model.

The dyad of status–role proved to be a basic conceptualisation in the development of social theory. However, it is problematic in at least three key respects. As Merton pointed out (1957: 369), 'a particular status involves, not a single associated role, but an array of associated roles'. Merton preferred to refer to the 'role-set' attached to a status: 'that complement of role-relationships which persons have by virtue of occupying a particular social status'. Taking Merton's point further, any institutionalised identity – any status – can be operationalised or put into effect in a variety of ways, depending upon the individual occupant, the contextual constraints and possibilities, and the demands of significant others.

The second problem is that the practical concomitants of any particular institutionalised identification are unlikely to be as clear and unambiguous as Linton and Merton appear to think. No doubt some of the practical role-expectations of any status are obvious and definite: fidelity is part of the role of 'husband' in western Christian societies, for example. But much will be situationally responsive and improvisatory within the mutual ebb and flow of the interaction order, as recognised by Goffman and Bourdieu. Moreover, the role-expectations of a status may be contradictory or incongruent: fidelity figures prominently in Christian marriage vows, but locally it may also be regarded as perfectly appropriate for a 'good' husband discreetly to take a mistress. But in that same local context, failure to take a mistress does not amount to failure as a husband.

Finally, a source of difficulty at the heart of Linton's definition may in part account for the 'difficulties and weaknesses of general role theory' (Jackson 1972: 5). Put simply, if a status is a collection of rights and duties, why do we need a further concept of role to define its performative aspects, unless those performances are somehow different from the rights and duties concerned? Both rights and duties are specifications of practice: rights are what you can expect of others, duties what they can expect of you. Since Linton and many sociologists subsequently have understood role as the operationalisation of the rights and duties of status, the former entailed in the latter, the concept of role seems redundant (Coulson 1972). Status–role looks suspiciously like a version of the problematic distinction between thinking and doing, and its associated allotropes of structure:action, and culture:society.

These criticisms might suggest that the notions of status and role are not particularly helpful. And, indeed, from the point of view of the 1990s, they look somewhat antediluvian; they are certainly no longer widely used. But they should not simply be forgotten. For example, in suggesting that rights and duties are definitive of institutionalised identity, the notion of status encourages an emphasis upon the internal–external dialectic of identification. Rights are what I expect of others; duties what can be expected of me. And Linton's choice of words suggests more than this. *Rights* may be what I expect of others as an aspect of my institutional identity, but they have no effect – they don't in fact exist – if those others don't recognise them. I cannot simply assert this or that 'right'; it has to be specified in a legitimate collective discourse about rights and about the entailment of rights in particular identifications. This is the whole point about institutionalisation. And the point in reverse can be made about my *duties*: the call of duty may be collectively issued, but it has to be recognised – and that duty done – by me as an individual.

Status, as a collection of rights and duties, alerts us to the complexity of a dialectic involving more than one mutually entailed moment of identification. Nor is it the only one of Linton's formulations which is useful:

> *A status*, in the abstract, is a position in a particular pattern. It is thus quite correct to speak of each individual as having many statuses. . . .However, unless the term is qualified in some way, *the status* of any individual means the sum total of all the statuses that he occupies.
>
> (Linton 1936: 113)

This is perhaps a little over-simple, but using the same word for the abstractly institutional and the concretely individual encourages an appreciation of the interpenetration of the individual and the collective. Individual identity is revealed as, to a considerable extent, a customised collage of collective identifications.

The problems with status–role seem to centre largely on the role side of the equation. The distinction between the *nominal* and the *virtual* may offer a more promising way forward. It allows us to think about the fact that abstractly collective institutionalised identifications (statuses) are occupied by embodied individuals yet independent of them. The nominal in this case is the ideal typification of the institutionalised identity – its name or title, the notional rights and duties which attach to it, etc. – while the virtual is how that identification is worked out, given local vagaries of context and allowing for individual variation, by any particular incumbent. This permits comparison of the range of differentiation in everyday life between *individual* incumbents of the same institutionalised identity, such as 'husband' or lecturer at the University of Poppleton. It also allows us to compare *local* differences in typification and practice with respect to institutionalised identities; we might look, for example, at lecturers at the Universities of Poppleton and Old Sarum to see what they have in common and how they differ. Thus, instead of persisting with the concepts of status and role, we might talk about institutionalised identities in their nominal and virtual aspects. This might also diminish the scope for confusion between the Weberian notion of status – that dimension of social stratification which relates to social honour or social standing, judged according to a range of ascribed or achieved criteria (B. S. Turner 1988) – and status as abstract institutionalised identification.

So far I have been talking about institutions in very general terms. But what about different kinds of institutions? Clearly there is, for example, a difference between 'marriage' and an event such as the village fête. Both are institutionalised, both are sources of identifications; but I don't have to be a sociologist to appreciate that they are not really the 'same kind of thing'. A first move towards clarifying the matter is to distinguish *institutions* from *organisations*.

Institutions have already been defined. Organisations are particular kinds of institutions in which:

- members combine in the pursuit of explicit objectives, which serve to identify the organisation;

- there are criteria for identifying, and processes for recruiting, members;
- there is a division of labour in the specification of the specialised tasks and functions performed by individual members; and
- there is a recognised pattern of decision-making and task allocation.

By this definition the category of organisations includes many possibilities: from a rhythm 'n' blues band, to a New Guinean men's house, to an Ashanti matrilineage, to a bowling club, to the KGB, to Microsoft, to the United Nations. Marriage is not an organisation (although any particular marriage may be), while the village fête is.

The sociological study of organisations is well-established. Building on Weber's understanding of bureaucracy, there is a huge literature, on formal organisations in particular,[4] that need not be reviewed here. But looking at organisations will help us understand the interplay between individual and collective identifications. Organisations are composed of members, actual individuals. My organisational memberships are an aspect of my individual identity, although each is not equally relevant. Being a member of the University of Sheffield has greater salience than being a member of the History Book Club. Once again, however, this depends on point of view and context: to the staff of the Book Club my membership of the Club is likely to be my only significant identification.

Organisations are also networks of specialised nominal identifications: positions, offices, functions, etc. This is where the organisation as a division of labour comes into its own. Although occupied at any point of time by individuals, these positions are identified with or part of the organisation: at least in principle, their existence is independent of their occupancy by specific individuals. Organisations create, in fact, the possibility of social identities which are not, at any particular point in time, embodied (whether individually or collectively). That an office or a post is vacant does not necessarily mean that it ceases to exist.

The organisation of social identification is an important part of what social scientists talk about, often with a glibness that does them little credit, as 'social structure'. If social structure is to be found anywhere other than in the aggregate abstraction of statistics, it is in institutions and organisations, and the pattern of relationships between organisations and their members. In the organisation of social identification, the interaction order and the institutional order – to hark back to Goffman – are routinely and mutually

implicated in each other. An appreciation of social identity is vital
if we are to steer the structuration debate – concerned with linking
analytically micro and macro, structure and agency, collectivity and
individual – out of its present doldrums. In any society, organised
processes of identification are central to the allocation of rewards
and penalties, resources and costs, honour and stigma; they are at
the heart of the social construction of hierarchy and social stratification. Furthermore, since the degree to which social identity is
organised is likely to be a function of social complexity – scale and
institutional heterogeneity – there is also something to be said in this
respect about modernity and social identity. These issues are taken
further in the closing chapters.

14

Organising identities

The English word 'organisation' can refer to the *act* of organis*ing*, to the state of *being* organis*ed*, or to an organis*ed* system. Each meaning emphasises social activity, process and practice. Organisations are bounded networks of people – distinguished as members from non-members – following coordinated procedures: *doing* things *together* in inter-related and institutionalised ways. These procedures are specified explicitly or tacitly, formal or informally, in bodies of organisational knowledge: organisationally specific symbolic universes, which may be subject to revision or confirmation and are transmitted to members through processes of organisational socialisation. Organisations are also networks of identifications – individually and collectively – which influence strongly who does what within those procedures, and how. These identifications – positions, offices, functions, jobs, etc. – are specified informally and formally by and in organisational knowledge, as are the procedures for allocating or recruiting individuals to them.

Understood in this way, everything from families to nation-states (and beyond) can be described as organisations. If so, doesn't this suggest that the term is too vague and general to have analytical value? I don't think so. First, as discussed in the previous chapter, not all institutions are organisations. Second, not all collectivities are organisations. Categories, for example – collectivities which cannot speak, do not in fact know, their own name – are not organisations. Nor are spontaneous collectivities (crowds, audiences, mobs, refugees in flight, etc.). Nor are loosely knit networks of individuals pursuing the same or congruent goals but lacking organised divisions of labour or authority structures (Boissevain 1968; Mayer 1966). The word 'organisation' covers most collectivities, but not all.

In terms of identity, organisations are constituted simultaneously in a distinction between members and non-members, on the one hand, and in an internal network of differentiation among members, on the other. An organisation without internal differentiation doesn't make much sense: organisation *is* the harnessing and orchestration, under a symbolic umbrella, of difference. Thus between the members of any organisation there is a relationship of similarity and a range of relationships of difference.

If organisations were only concerned with their own internal affairs they would be of limited sociological interest. However, organisational members rarely live their lives all day and every day wholly within the organisation: the 'total institution' (Goffman 1968b) is the exception rather than the rule. Nor are most people members of only one organisation. Furthermore, an organisation's *raison d'être* is the coordination of the activities of a plurality of individuals – not all of whom will necessarily be members – in collective pursuit of some specified purpose. This defining purpose is the organisational charter; it is what calls the organisation into existence, and is another element of the organisationally specific symbolic universe. Such purposes are, however, typically located in a wider, external social world. Organisations are open to and part of their social environments. Their boundaries may be permeable and osmotic; it isn't always easy to see where they are drawn.

One other defining feature of organisations requires emphasis. Without relations of authority (or, indeed, power), the successful coordination of activities would not be possible. Some subordination to others is the reciprocal precondition of individual autonomy, in the same way as similarity is the precondition of difference (and rules of deviance). Organisations – small or large – are institutionalised networks of hierarchical relationships, of sub- and superordination, of power and authority. Organisational collectivity is, in fact, the source of the legitimacy without which authority carries no weight.

For the purposes of this discussion, I will concentrate on two aspects of organisations:[1] first, the ways in which individuals become identified as organisational members (and as particular organisational members), and second, the ways in which organisations influence the identification of non-members. Surveying the historical, cross-cultural, and institutional variety of either, let alone both, would be a task more appropriate to an encyclopaedia. Instead, in order to illustrate the range of possibilities, I shall discuss a limited selection of procedural types or cases with respect to each, as examples of general organisational processes. I will also discuss the consequential nature of organisational identification with respect to the lives of individuals and the production and reproduction of patterns of social differentiation: hierarchy, stratification, inclusion and exclusion, etc. In this chapter I focus on organisations and their members; in the next, on their impact on non-members.

Without personnel renewal and replacement, the life-span of any organisation could be no longer than that of its most long-lived individual member. Since a characteristic of organisations is that they can persist despite routine attrition of personnel, procedures for recruiting replacement members are vital. There are two basic trajectories of organisational membership. In the first, the qualifying criteria of recruitment are 'givens' such as parentage, age and position in the life course, gender, etc. These identities are socially constructed – typically in terms of embodiment and folk notions of biology – as basic, natural, or primordial. They are typically also collective: they identify the individual as a member of a group or category. They are understood socially as aspects of the individual for which she has little or no responsibility, and over which she has little or no control. Although in any specific situation the possibilities may exist of a renunciation of membership by a candidate, a refusal to recognise a candidate, or her subsequent expulsion, organisational membership of this kind is generally taken-for-granted, even if not inevitable. If a boy wants to join the Scouts, for example, his age and gender render him unproblematically eligible.

In the second trajectory, criteria of membership may be many and varied, but membership is not entailed in pre-existent personal characteristics. It is also much more a matter concerning the individual *as* an individual. Membership is, therefore, always to some degree uncertain and must typically be sought and endorsed; it is a matter of negotiation at the organisational boundary, and more or less competitive. However, the presence or absence of self-determination and choice is not a defining feature. Both trajectories can involve involuntary or imposed organisational membership.

The two different routes into organisational membership may be characterised thus: in the first an individual is a member or a prospective member by virtue of *who* she is, in the second by virtue of *what* she is. Often seen, erroneously, as a contrast between 'traditional' and 'modern' modes of social identity, this has much in common with the distinction between *ascribed* and *achieved* statuses drawn by Linton (1936) in his original formulation of status and role.[2] Ascribed identities are socially constructed on the basis of the contingencies of birth. Achieved (or, to adopt Merton's subsequent and more accurate terminology, *acquired*) identities are assumed during the subsequent life course, and are generally – although not necessarily – the outcome of a degree of self-direction. This general distinction between the ascribed and the acquired is not specific to organisational identifications; it can in principle, be applied to all social identities.

The key distinction of this discussion, between the *internal* and *external* moments of the dialectic of identification, is heuristic, drawn as an opposition for explanatory purposes. Much the same can be said about ascription and achievement/acquisition. In everyday life the difference between them is likely to be at most a matter of emphasis. Organisational membership, no less than any other identity, is thus a particular combination of the acquired and the ascribed. The ins and outs of biography conspire to ensure that who I am and what I am are not easily disentangled.

This can be explored a bit further. Primary identities such as gender, rooted in very early social experience, are massively implicated in the embodied point of view of selfhood. Following Linton and Merton, they are ascribed identities and criteria of organisational membership. But they are also – *qua* selfhood – important influences upon the self-direction that can be so influential in the achievement of identity. However, the purposeful acquisition of achieved organisational identities depends upon more than unilateral self-determination. Most significantly, it involves negotiation and transaction with others – organisational gatekeepers of one kind or another – who are in a position to recruit individuals to the organisation or to exclude them, and to decide to which organisational positions individuals will be recruited. In making their choices, gatekeepers will frequently have recourse to (ascriptive) criteria such as gender or age. Where acquired organisational identities are *imposed* on *non*-members – such as selection for conscription or imprisonment – ascriptive criteria are likely to be particularly influential. Imposition can evoke many possible responses. It may not produce any apparent reaction at all; it may be internalised; it may be resentfully endured; it may spark resistance. But as long as categorisation is recognised by those upon whom it is visited, or produces consequences in their lives, it is never a question of imposition *only*. Whatever it might be, there is always a response; there is always the dialectic between internal and external identification.

Indeed, *all* the above scenarios can be understood with reference to an internal–external dialectic of identification, albeit with different emphases in each case. In each there is a relationship of mutual signification between the ascribed and the achieved/ acquired. Even so, a loose analytical distinction between ascribed and acquired identities continues to make sense, and particularly, perhaps, with respect to organisational identity. They differ – as Nadel, for example, seems to have appreciated (1957: 36–41) – in the manner in which individuals assume them. With respect to organisations, this difference is largely (which doesn't mean only) procedural. Recruitment to organisational identities where the emphasis falls upon ascription is a matter of *affirmation*. Membership is immanent; it must be publicly confirmed, registered, solemnised, consecrated, or whatever. Recruitment to organisational identities which are achieved or acquired is, however, a matter of *rationalisation* (cf. Collinson *et al.* 1990: 110ff.). Membership must be justified, reasons have to be offered. Affirmation and rationalisation reflect different sources or kinds of legitimate authority. In Max Weber's terms (1978: 212–41), affirmation is rooted in *traditional* understandings of legitimacy, and rationalisation – unsurprisingly – in *rational-legal* legitimacy.

Affirmation can take many forms. The Christian ritual of confirmation or First Communion, in which the young person is received into full membership of the Church, is one example. The Jewish *Bar Mitzvah* and *Bat Mitzvah* rituals also come to mind (Mars 1990). And there are options other than the strictly religious: many societies around the world could be drawn upon to provide examples of life-course rituals in which young people are initiated into organised age-sets of one kind or another (Bernardi 1985; La Fontaine 1985). Coming-of-age ceremonies often touch upon more than the membership of specific organisations: 'These rites of initiation transform individuals by investing them with socialness'

(A. P. Cohen 1994: 57). It may be nothing less than full membership of the society in question which is at issue (see Richards [1956] for one of the classic anthropological accounts). Although the ritual dimensions of coming of age have atrophied in the industrialised societies of modernity, they can still be found, for example, in the notion of the 'key of the door', or in the informal humiliations which often attend the 'last night of freedom' of brides- and grooms-to-be.

More obviously organisational memberships can also depend primarily on the ascription of 'who you are'. In rural Northern Ireland, for example, membership of the Orange Lodge depends upon as many as three ascriptive criteria: being protestant, being male, and apropos *which* Lodge one joins, family (R. Harris 1972: 163, 192–4). And if we recognise the family as an informal organisation – or even, in the bureaucratised modern state, as a formal organisation – then the rite of baptism, for example, is *inter alia* a public affirmation of the full organisational membership of a new infant.

Common to all of the above is a transition from immanent membership to actual membership – literally, confirmation – and an element of ritualised initiation. These are important dimensions of rites of passage, a general category of ritual first identified by Arnold van Gennep nearly a century ago (van Gennep 1965). Building on his ideas, there is now a relatively settled anthropological consensus that humans experience life as a series of social transitions from one identity to another, that these transitions are ritualised to a greater or lesser extent, and that the transitions have a tripartite form (Leach 1976: 77–9; Morris 1987: 246–63). That form is not a structural universal, it simply makes sense logically and situationally: first *separation* from the present state or identity; then *transition* or *liminality* (a state of limbo which may draw upon a symbolised vocabulary or repertoire relating to death); then finally *incorporation* into, or *aggregation* with, the new state or identity (which may use birth as a metaphor). In ritual, these phases may be represented spatially; they always have a temporal sequence, one after the other. A processual structure of this kind appears in all explicit and organisationally marked identity transitions.

Rites of passage and the internal-external dialectic of identification have a bearing on each other. The enhancement of experience which ritual offers, cognitively and particularly emotionally, plays an important role in the internalisation of identification. To say this, is, in most significant respects, to agree with Durkheim about the power of ritualised communion. Ritual can invest the symbols of organisational membership – flags, uniforms, logos, songs, etc. – with an affective weight that transcends occasion or ceremony. It is likely to be of particular moment in generating individual internal identification with the external collectivity: making the recruit *feel* that she belongs and is part of the greater organisational whole. It may also distance her from previous identities. Even the formal pattern of separation, transition and incorporation is amenable to interpretation in this light: separation weakens existing internal self-identification(s); during transition the new identity is intro- duced 'from outside' and dramatised; incorporation affirms and strengthens the new identification.

Victor Turner (1974: 119ff.), inspired by the theologian Martin Buber, understood that although the 'we' of collective identifica- tion is enormously powerful, it is always fragile and contingent, always vulnerable to subversion. In my terms, it is imagined but not imaginary. Among other things, this reflects a contradiction between the egalitarian inclusiveness of 'us' and the internal hierarchical differentiation of an organisational division of labour. Similarity and difference play against rather than with each other within organisations. Hence the organisational importance of rituals of identity transformation and initiation. While these are generally significant as occasions for acting out and practically participating in the symbolisation of identity, they are particularly momentous in combining an affirmation and re-affirmation of what Turner calls 'communitas' – undifferentiated 'we-ness', if you like – with a recognition and legitimation of internal organisational structure.

Ritualised affirmation of ascriptive identity is not only a matter of individual membership, however, nor is it confined to initiation or recruitment. In addition to rites of passage, there are many other ritual occasions which organise, orchestrate and *re*affirm collective identities. Public pageantry provides many obvious examples of rituals of communal affirmation. From the great totalitarian set-pieces of state occasions in the USSR (Lane 1981), to the more modest ceremonial of 'traditional' African states (Gluckman 1963: 110–36), to the parades of the protestant 'marching season' in Northern Ireland (Bell 1990), the theme is similar: the public reaffirmation and consecration of ascriptive collective identities. Similar themes can be discerned in more secular rituals (Moore and Myerhoff 1977) such as carnivals (A. Cohen 1980) or beauty contests (Wilk 1993). Organised collective identities which claim to be more than merely socially constructed are also likely – for both internal and external consumption – to use ritualised public ceremonial to affirm and symbolise their a-historical essence. Examples of this include the characteristic and inevitable carnivals of nationalism, and festivals such as the gay and lesbian Mardi Gras in Sydney, Australia.

As well as being an analytical category, social class is an ascriptive identity of sorts. Class is equated in common sense with 'background', referring to family of origin, and often with 'breeding' too. A sophisticated version of this is the argument – with which the Eugenics movement, for example, identified itself – that class differences reflect differential genetic endowments; a view which probably persists more widely than we know. A mirror-image of this, glorifying the essential nobility of working people, can be seen in Soviet socialist realist public art. Ceremonial or ritualised (re)affirmations of class identities are easy to exemplify: on the one hand, May Day marches of international solidarity, and the Durham Miners' Gala; on the other, Oxbridge May Balls and the set-pieces of the upper-class sporting and social circuits. It is no surprise that the middle class(es) – often in upwardly mobile flight from their 'background', generally thanks to achievement – appear less keen to affirm publicly the primordiality of their identity.

So, with respect to ascriptive identifications such as family, age, ethnicity, gender, and even class, ritual (re)affirmation is of considerable significance. It may actually be fundamental: identity – as a definitively social construct – can never be essential or primordial, so it has to be made to *seem* so. We have to be made to *feel* 'we'. Nor are collectivities embodied in quite the way that individuals are. In addition, the potential tension between ascriptive inclusion (similarity) and hierarchy (difference) should be borne in mind. These difficulties are all addressed when the power of symbol and ritual is brought to bear. Organised collective identity is endowed, via collective ritual and 'communitas', with personal authenticity and experiential profundity. Inasmuch as public ritual is performative, it is a powerful and visible embodiment of the abstraction of collective identity (cf. Connerton 1989: 41–71). Rituals gather together enough members for embodied collectivity to be socially 'real'. The individual – whether participating as an individual or as 'one of the crowd' – is included in the organised collectivity in the most potent fashion. Individual diversity finds a place within symbolised unity. The imagined ceases to be imaginary.

Ascription is, however, as much a principle of exclusion as inclusion; it encourages expulsion as well as recruitment. The refusal to admit women, Jews, and black people – and these are only the most obvious cases – to membership of exclusive clubs is one such situation. More consequential are the less thorough-going but none the less significant discriminations which operate in the labour and education markets of a country such as Britain. At its most comprehensive, ascriptive exclusion can plumb the depths reached by various regimes of slavery, by the Republic of South Africa during the period of *apartheid*, or by the racialised state created in Nazi Germany.

We are now approaching situations in which important elements of rationalisation figure. The point that ascription and achievement/acquisition are not easy to disentangle in everyday life can be made in many ways. Ascriptive exclusion may, for example, define the arena within which the principle of competition comes into play in recruitment. A club may not admit women, Jews or black people, but that doesn't mean that *any* white male can join. The choice of *which* white males is a matter for rationalisation, even if only at the level of procedural correctness. Ascriptive inclusion – the organisational boundary – may delineate the space within which internal position and office are competitively achieved. And there are subtler possibilities. An employer who would rather not hire black employees is not committed to hiring whites regardless of their capacity to do the job in question. But nor, in the absence of a white person fitting the bill, is she totally constrained from hiring a black worker. Rationalisation permits both options.

These examples illustrate the interaction of criteria of 'accept-ability' and 'suitability' (R. Jenkins 1983: 100–28; 1986: 46–79). In competitive organisational recruitment, ascriptive criteria – 'who you are' – are most likely to influence the identification of acceptability, which can be broadly defined as whether or not an individual will 'fit in' to the social networks and relationships of the organisation, or be the right 'kind of person' in general. Suitability, however, emphasises achieved or acquired characteristics relating to 'what you are'. This is typically a matter of competence; how-ever, it can also be, in voluntary organisations for example, a question of interests or attitudes. Suitability is more an issue when a particular organisational position, rather than just membership (or a broad category of membership), is at stake. Notions of suitability are definitively involved in employment recruitment, for example, but are less likely to influence recruitment to club membership. Where both criteria are influential, permutations are possible: individuals may be suitable but unacceptable, or vice versa.

The distinction between suitability and acceptability is rarely clear-cut. Being apparently the most suitable person for an organisational position doesn't guarantee your recruitment to it. 'Whether your face fits' may contribute to colleaguely relations and, hence, to fulfilling the organisational charter. So is it a kind of competence? Suitability can't always be easily specified; there may be a number of equally suitable candidates; the threshold of suitability may be low. In situations such as these, questions of acceptability – now concerning the individual and the idiosyncratic, rather than the categorical – may once again become influential. And both suitability and acceptability offer a basis for competitive recruitment. There is no straightforward equivalence between the ascribed and the acceptable, or the acquired and the suitable. It is possible to argue that gender, for example, is sometimes a criterion of suitability. And acceptability can depend on factors such as marital or domestic situation, or attitudes to abortion or nuclear disarmament (or whatever), which are unlikely to be a matter of ascription. And so on.

There may be no straightforward equivalences, but there is a modern discourse which emphasises opportunity, achievement and access, particularly with respect to economic activity and benefits. Or there are, rather, two related modern discourses: of meritocracy and of equality. The two do not always make happy partners – the idea of meritocracy, for example, owes a frequently unacknowledged debt to notions of 'liberty' which are not readily compatible with equality – but they come together in the western democracies in the political project of equality of opportunity (Paul *et al.* 1987). This is relevant here because of its emphasis upon access for all to fair competitive organisational recruitment. From the point of view of the promotion of equality of opportunity, ascriptive criteria or criteria of acceptability require special justification.

And here we can begin to appreciate the importance of the organisation of identity for the production and reproduction of large-scale patterns of social differentiation and stratification. Ascriptive social identities are not only collective, they are typically widely recognised. Significant numbers of people agree on the nominal boundaries of male and female, black and white, etc. The understandings of 'us' and 'them' across those boundaries – the virtual identifications – are less consensual; it depends on point of view. But the basic outlines, the scaffolding around which virtual identification – played out in the history of consequences – is constructed, will be relatively clear.

Ascription may be socially constructed as the inevitability of natural causes, but it isn't innocent of self-interest or competition for collective advantage. It informs widespread processes of social categorisation: the defining of others in the external moment of the dialectic of identification. Among those processes is recruitment into organisations. Organisational membership in any social context is therefore likely to reflect local ascriptive categories of identification. We know that this is often the case. At least two, analytically distinct, organisational processes produce this situation.

In the first, people organise themselves in terms of ascription: this is organisation for 'us', with 'us' understood in a particular way. The organisational charter defines membership: Poppleton *Working Men's* Club, the Eastend *Punjabi Youth* Association, Old Sarum University *Women's* Society, Boyne Square *Protestant* Defenders Flute Band, and so on. Organisation along these ascriptive lines is a potent political and economic resource. Among its advantages are an ideology of natural or primordial community and loyalty, the symbolisation and valorisation of identity, comradeship and mutual support, pooled resources, the organisation of collective action, and the creation of opportunities – jobs or whatever – or members.

In the second, the organisational charter does not define membership in ascriptive terms. It may in fact evince a commitment to competitive, achievement-based membership. However, those who are in a position to recruit or reject prospective members may draw upon ascriptive criteria in their decision-making. For example, a manager may refuse to employ men as production workers in a factory assembling electrical components, because he 'knows' that women are more dexterous, and don't want to work full-time, and that men can't tolerate the boredom. As a result of this managerial categorisation, the factory employs only women in the majority of jobs. If there is consistency in the working knowledge of managers in general – some participation in a shared symbolic universe – then their recruitment decisions will draw upon similar typifications and stereotypes, and will contribute to the production of a wider social pattern in which women are disproportionately represented in part-time, semi-skilled assembly work. Reflecting consistencies in *their* recruitment and careers, managers *are* likely to have things in common: class background, 'race', gender, politics, orientation towards business, organisational and professional socialisation, etc. That they should behave similarly in similar circumstances is not remarkable. The process may be even more avowedly exclusionary than the example given: racism and sexism, for example, remain potent forces in recruitment (Collinson *et al.* 1990; R. Jenkins 1986). Organisations – and although I have focused on employing organisations, discrimination operates in many other areas – may be nominally open to all but virtually closed to many categories of the population, excluded on the basis of ascription.

There are too many other possibilities to explore here. One thing must, however, be emphasised, apropos acquired identities. People join organisations for many reasons: to validate an existing self-identification, to change it, or for other reasons more idiosyncratic. This applies in employment and across the spectrum of political and social activities. Distinctions between identity and other aspects of the person (whatever *that* means) are difficult to maintain. Does someone become a hunt saboteur because she is opposed to cruelty to foxes, because she likes the image of herself as a 'sab', because 'that'll really make my mother mad', because she can't stand 'upper-class pratts on horses', or because she fancies that 'bloke with the dreads'? It is not easy to know. But it all contributes to identity.

People also *form* organisations as vehicles for identity projects. This has already been suggested in the case of ascription; it is no less true for acquired identities. The organisational charter may refer to facilitating and improving the wider public understanding of train-spotting, or sado-masochism, or whatever, but that cannot be divorced from the train-spotters or sado-masochists who are the members, and their cause(s). And many of the advantages that accrue in the case of organisations based on ascription – support, symbolisation, pooled resources, coordinated action – apply equally to organisations oriented around acquired identities.

Whether they emphasise ascription or acquisition, however, different organisations are of more or less moment in the implications of membership for individual identification. Scarcity is an obvious factor. Joining the Mickey Mouse Club, where the only qualification for membership is a small fee sent through the mail, is clearly less significant than finally, the day after your ninth birthday, having made yourself a pain in the neck for the last few months, being initiated as only the fifth member of your big brother's gang.

And exclusivity isn't just a matter of competitive scarcity: the membership criteria matter, too. Hence the power of ascription. In ascriptive theory, at least, you can only be in or out. The boundary between the two, dramatised as it often is by ritual, may also be the threshold between the sacred and the profane. On one side purity, on the other danger (Douglas 1966). Certainly other factors contribute to the strength of particular organisational identities – the affectiveness of initiation, external pressures on the group, the penalties attached to leaving, and so on – but the importance of exclusivity should not be underestimated.

Whatever the context, in competitive recruitment a degree of rationalisation is called for. This can be a matter of reasons, or a matter of procedure, or both. The question of reasons has already been discussed: is someone acceptable? and are they suitable? These are reasons. Procedures may not be easily separable from reasons, however. Sometimes procedural correctness provides sufficient legitimation for the outcome. That the proper procedure has been followed is reason enough.

A good example here is the *ordeal*, a category of ritual which figures in a variety of organisational initiations: from the theatrical pretension of the Masonic rite, to the violence of a motorcycle gang, to the psycho-sexual emotional trials of some New Guinean peoples, to the torment visited on new recruits to élite military units. In the ordeal, survival rationalises recruitment. As ritual, it dramatises and authenticates the achievement of membership, both for the recruit and for her or his new colleagues. In this sense it contributes to both internal and external identification. The other major context in which the ordeal figures historically – determination of guilt or innocence in the face of accusation[3] – also has serious implications for membership. An unfavourable outcome to a judgemental ordeal may result in expulsion from membership; recruitment may depend – and here we are back to initiation – upon satisfactory reputation or character.

More characteristic of modern organisational recruitment, however, is the *interview* and its associated screening procedures (although these may be experienced as an ordeal). Interviewing is rooted in the informally institutionalised or ritualised social world of Goffman's interaction order: one or more people talk to another person – this is a definitively oral social form – in order to find out sufficient about her to decide about her recruitment (or, indeed, whatever fate is in question). However, the organised interview has arguably become *the* generic form of bureaucratic social encounter. Its only rival is the committee (and the two are, of course, combined in the board or panel). The bureaucratic interview has a number of characteristic features (see R. Jenkins 1986: 128–9, for more extended discussion). There are always two sides, interviewer(s) and interviewee(s). There is a situational hierarchy. One side – the interviewer – is typically in charge of the procedure and of the determination of outcomes. This hierarchy derives from the interviewer's organisational position (particularly her control over resources), and, often, from her possession of the requisite cultural competences to carry off interviewing authoritatively. The business of the interview is the allocation of resources or penalties to the interviewee; the legitimacy of that allocation is grounded in adherence to more or less formally constituted procedures and in the reasons which inform the decision-making. However, the interview is not necessarily about decision-making; it may be at least as much about the *ex post facto* justification or rationalisation of decision-making (Silverman and Jones 1976). Finally, interviews are generally private. The protection of privacy is extended as much – indeed more – to interviewer(s) as to interviewee; decisions can be made without the scrutiny of an audience. The ordeal, by contrast, is typically a public or semi-public event which *requires* an audience for its legitimacy.

The ordeal and the interview are not the only forms of rationalisation: recruitment by *election*, by *nomination*, or by *lottery* can be important too, drawing on specific legitimatory rhetorics of democracy, authority and chance. And rationalisation does not preclude affirmation. Once an individual's recruitment to an organisation has been rationalised, nothing prevents that decision being subsequently ceremonially affirmed. There is every reason for doing so, if the argument about the affective power of ritual is correct. Rationalised membership is as much in need of authenticity as any other. Existing members can have their membership re-affirmed and re-authenticated too. A good example is the 'team-building' which figures in staff development programmes in many employing organisations in western industrial societies. One common model is the 'residential': staff are taken away from work and home to spend a few days 'out of time', engaging together in a range of activities – from outdoor pursuits, to intensive group work, to equally intense socialising – after which they return home, ideally somewhat transformed (otherwise what is the point?). Separation, limbo, and (re)incorporation: the rite of passage analogy is irresistible.

These are some, but only some, of the ways in which organisations affect the identities of their members. Organisations are, first and foremost, groups. As we proceed through life, our organisational memberships make a significant contribution to the diversity of the expanding portfolios that are our individual identities. The internal–external dialectic of identification can be seen at work between members, and between members and non-members. Organisations are constituted in the tension between solidary similarity, *vis-à-vis* outsiders, and the internal hierarchical differentiation of members from each other. Although the internal moment of group identification is a consistent and necessary thread of organisational identification, on balance categorisation – of outsiders by insiders, of members by other members – is the dominant theme of recruitment and initiation.

15

Allocation and classification

Every organisation is a group, with members who recognise it and their own membership of it. Organisations are also always networks of reciprocal identification: self-definition as a member depends upon recognition by other members. Specifically, membership must at least be registered by those who are authorised to do so (i.e. 'by the organisation'). This minimum requirement even makes it possible to have organisational 'members' who are authoritatively registered as such, but are not themselves aware of their 'membership', or may not even exist. Mutuality and reciprocity within organisations are framed by hierarchies of authority and control; even group membership is in part a matter of categorisation.

Organisational membership can be a penalty *or* a resource or benefit. When a would-be member is interviewed by the Committee of an exclusive Country Club, none of the participants doubts that something scarce and attractive is at stake. A job selection interview is also allocating an organisational membership which is usually seen positively, as a resource. However, an interview assessing someone for a place in a psychiatric institution or residential care home is deciding something more ambiguous.

These examples prompt the question, when are the two sides to the transaction actual or potential co-members of the same organisation? The successful applicant and the Country Club committee are co-members. On the face of things, so are recruiter and recruit in an employing organisation. But that may not be straightforward. If one is a manager and the other an hourly-paid worker, whose terms and conditions of membership – among which is security of membership – are dramatically different, in what sense are they co-members? Point of view is important here, as is the interplay of similarity and difference within organisations. Whether or not a psychiatric patient is a member of the institution will depend upon institutional policy. And also upon point of view. Membership may be demanded of the patient by a therapeutic regime emphasising inclusion and participation; she, however, may refuse to connive in it, which in its turn may have consequences. Nominally she may be a member, but virtually? Virtually she is an inmate. Therapeutic rhetoric aside, she cannot enjoy membership of the same kind as that of her psychiatrist.

And, of course, organisations deal with a range of people wider than their membership: customers, competitors, victims, clients, and so on. Organisations often have an impact on the identification of non-members. Take, for example, the inevitable, if perhaps unintended, consequences of organisational recruitment. An individual who applies unsuccessfully for organisational membership is affected by the experience. Recruitment is, after all, a labelling process: the rejected applicant's self-identification may change; she may find herself stigmatised and excluded from access to other organisations. Materially, the resources which she invested in the bid for membership may be lost. On the other hand, if successful, her recruitment may have consequences for the members of her social network, and for her position within it (if she joins the police, for example, or if her working hours are altered). Joining one organisation may mean having to resign from another. And so on. A change of identity is a stick poked into a pond: ripples spread in all directions. Organisational recruitment – or rejection – touches the lives and identities of more people than those immediately involved.

To make a point which resonates with the arguments of many other authors, not least Foucault, although modern organisations produce engine parts, meals, telecommunication services, government information, or whatever, they also contribute to the production of people, identified in particular ways. Some organisations, indeed, reflect this in their charter. Schools, colleges and other organisations of formal education are perhaps the most obvious examples, but they are not the only ones. The criminal courts, for example, administer membership and identification as penalty and stigmatisation. Instead of branding a felon on the forehead, modern criminal justice interrupts her official biography – her 'record' – with a prison sentence. This cancels or suspends most of her existing organisational memberships, locking her into a new one – convicted prisoner and inmate – which overrides practically all others. Branding iron and prison record are both effective stigmata; both change her identity.

To take another example, institutional psychiatry, in addition to its provision of therapeutic benefits and care, is in the business of containment and, arguably, punishment.[1] Both sides of the coin involve the authoritative – medical – identification of individuals as patients of a particular type, and their location in appropriate niches within organisational hierarchies. 'Psychiatric patient' ('person with a serious mental health problem' or whatever) is another identity, its origins organisational, which overshadows most other aspects of individual identity. In Becker's terminology (1963: 32–3) – borrowed from Everett Hughes – it is a 'master status', to which most other identities are subordinate.

Identity of any kind is consequential (otherwise it wouldn't *be* identity). Organisational identity is consequential in particular ways. Membership may offer access to resources and it may have costs; it may be a benefit or a penalty. For example, organisations are generally something more than a symbolised 'social umbrella': even if only in a modest way, they are often corporate groups, in which property and resources are vested and within which those resources are distributed. Furthermore, as hierarchical networks of authority and power, organisations entail the direction of the behaviour of members and at least minimal individual submission to collective routines (if not actual rule). Organisational membership closes some options as it opens others.

But organisations don't exist solely for their members. Organisations are typically in the *public* eye also: in buildings, artefacts and public symbols; in the organisation of time (timetables, the working day, the prison sentence, visiting time, opening hours, etc.); in the wearing of uniform or other visible identifications by members. In interaction, an individual's organisational identity may be framed at least as much by that organisation's public presence as by her presentation of self. This doesn't necessarily mean that, in the case of a railway employee, for example, passengers 'see' the organisational identity rather than the individual. But they certainly *do* see that, and to them it may be the most important thing about her in that situation.

The public presence of organisations is an important dimension of their impact on non-members. From the dawning of our experience of the social world – during the processes of primary identification – our environment is organised and signified by organisations of which we are not members. Space is defined in terms of its ownership or control by organisations. The skyline itself may be outlined by their buildings and monuments: think of the CNN Tower in Toronto, the medieval cathedral-building projects of Christian Europe, or the great earth- and stoneworks of prehistory. Most organisations are visibly symbolised more modestly: a flag flies over the general's tent; the Post Office has a sign outside it; the removal company van is covered in the firm's name and logo; the local football club's fans wear its colours on match day; and so on. Individuals in public may be identified with this or that organisation (which, as in the case of the football fans, doesn't necessarily mean they're members). The social world is a highly visible world of organisations.

It's not just a matter of visibility, either. For all sorts of reasons we deal with organisations and their representatives. Many organisations are definitively in the business of allocating resources or penalties to non-members; they organise the social world. It is either the theme of their organisational charter or a by-product of their main activities. The organised allocation of resources and penalties prompts questions. How do organisations classify collectivities in the abstract, and identify embodied individuals, in order to determine allocation? What are the consequences for the identification of those people of that organised allocation (or denial)? What is the relationship between social identity and the categorisation inherent in organisational allocation procedures?

In small-scale societies, without extensive markets or a state, the allocation of resources and penalties has, historically, been a matter for organisations of modest scale, with members typically recruited according to kinship or locality: family, lineage, village, 'tribe', etc. Here the criteria which inform allocation are implicit in the principles of organisation, and predominantly bound up with group membership (which does not obviate the need for decision-making, or the competitive allocation of scarce resources: Sahlins 1974).

It is different in the large-scale urbanised and industrialised societies of the modern world. I shall concentrate on them for the purposes of illustration. Modernity, perhaps before anything else, differs from other eras in the extent to which social life is framed within and by complex organisations, and by the number and heterogeneity of those organisations. The existence in most modern states of a welfare system – even in countries, such as the United States, which are not usually identified as welfare states – means that all social life is entangled in organisations.

Organised and organisational allocation is a pervasive aspect of administrative systems. *Administrative allocation* (Batley 1981) takes place in many contexts; some have been touched upon in the discussion of labelling in Chapter 8, and in the previous chapter with respect to organisational recruitment. A large literature discusses the topic in a range of organisational and cultural settings (Collmann and Handelman 1981; Hasenfeld *et al*. 1987). Administrative allocation procedures have some features in common. They are typically found in the organisations of the state and its licensees, although they also occur in market settings (particularly the most bureaucratised and regulated of markets, the labour market). They characterise agencies or enterprises (M. Weber 1978: 956), the main public spheres within and through which the large-scale allocation of resources and penalties occurs in modern, institutionally diverse societies.

Agencies and enterprises are bureaucracies, and the legitimacy of bureaucratic action is to a considerable extent grounded in procedural correctness. However, this doesn't necessarily mean that allocatory procedures are wholly, or even thoroughly, formalised. Formality and informality – much like control and deviance – are inescapably entailed in each other (Harding and Jenkins 1989: 133–8). The interview is at the heart of these procedures. As a ritualised encounter, between those-who-decide and those-about-whom-decisions-are-made, it requires the interviewee to engage in a presentation of self and the interviewer to categorise; each is involved in different identificatory work. The interview is an oral form, an organised encounter which blends the formal and the informal. Literate procedures, such as the written examination (Ong 1982: 55–6) or the diagnostic test (A. P. Cohen 1985: 183–96; Hanson 1993), are increasingly influential in some arenas of administrative allocation and do not depend upon the immediacy of interaction and situation. These are characteristically modern procedures; testing, in particular, exemplifies what Giddens describes as the increasing importance in the modern world of 'expert systems' (1990: 27–9). The test offers a vision of decision-making uncontaminated by its immediate social context, 'objectivity' guaranteed by scientific method. With the IQ test as a basic model, an array of standardised tests – promoted by an expansionist academic discipline, psychology, and exploited in their profession-alising strategies by personnel and training specialists – is now used to assess intelligence, motor skills, personality, aptitudes, etc. Formal testing adds apparent rigour and legitimate authority to bureaucratic classificatory processes. The relationship between testing and interviewing varies – either can rationalise decision-making – but testing, with its focus upon suitability rather than acceptability, is rarely determinate in itself.

Allocation is concerned, in large part, with rationing. Although scarcity is frequently exaggerated or constructed, if only to maxi-mise organisational control over resources and increase their value, resources are always in finite supply. Penalties too, if they are to have meaning, must not be devalued by over-use. One issue, therefore, is how to rationalise rationing. Legitimate procedure is important, but so are reasons; these reasons are categorising judge-ments about whether or not recipients *qualify*. The politics which frame administrative allocation mean that these judgements often derive from or reflect ideology and policy agendas.

Categorisation operates in two apparently contradictory, but actually complementary, modes: the use of discretion, and stereo-typing. Discretion is central to allocation. For a range of reasons it is inherent in the processes of policy formulation and implemen-tation in modern states (Ham and Hill 1984: 148–73). Far from being a departure from bureaucratic niceties, without discretion bureaucratic organisations don't function well. Discretion permits a flexibility of response and decision-making which is appropriate to conditions of scarcity – whether real or imagined – and to the complexity of individual differentiation and situational variety. The interview has become so central to bureaucratic work because it creates the formally constituted space within which discretion can operate. Organisations are structured by rules, but rules become meaningful in their interpretation, and in the elaboration of exceptions.

On the other hand, the necessary simplification that facilitates judgement encourages recourse to identificatory stereotypes. And, on closer inspection, discretionary exceptions are not easily made without stereotypes from which to depart. If classification without stereotyping is a contradiction – as argued in Chapter 12 – so stereotyping is inherent in institutionalisation. Stereotyping is a routine feature of human attempts to enhance predictability – or at least a *sense* of predictability – in everyday situations of complexity and/or uncertainty. The maximisation of predictability is one respect in which bureaucractic organisations can claim what Weber called 'technical superiority' (1978: 973), so we should not, therefore, be surprised to discover 'a close relationship between popular stereotypes and bureaucratic classification' (Herzfeld 1993: 71).

In everyday terms, what does all this mean? Some examples may help. Recruitment into employment, to take one such, was discussed in the previous chapter. Here, the resource being allocated or denied is also an identification; the two aspects of a job are not easily disentangled. As a competitive process, discrimination – in the non-accusatory sense of the evaluation of a number of options and selection between them – is inherent in employment recruitment. Apropos scarcity, however, the more vacancies there are, the more competition will favour the job-seeker and the less discriminatory recruiters can be. And, of course, vice versa. The recruitment process may be administrative, but market conditions are still important, not least in determining the intensity of competition.

Stereotypes which are systematically related to situationally-specific criteria of suitability and acceptability come into widespread play in employment selection (R. Jenkins 1983: 100–28; 1986: 46–79). The generality of this distinction is suggested by the range of analagous concepts in the literature – 'functional' and 'extra-functional' criteria (Offe 1976: 47–99), or 'quantitative efficiency' and 'qualitative efficiency' (Gordon 1976: 22–6), for example – and its subsequent use by other researchers (Collinson *et al.* 1990; Curran 1985). It is significant because acceptability is concerned with perceived identity as an indicator of employability.

Examinations and diagnostic tests are most likely to feature in employment recruitment in the context of decisions about suitability. Even when 'personality' is tested, this is typically with respect to effectiveness in a particular post, rather than organisational 'fitting in' or general reliability. Acceptability is arguably less predictable than suitability, if only because it is difficult to define and situational. So we might expect recourse to stereotypes to be more common when acceptability is in question. Not only does this seem to be true, but many of stereotypes are general enough to produce patterned outcomes across a range of unconnected recruitment occasions. There is ample evidence of the cumulative influence in employment recruitment of common stereotypes relating to 'race', ethnicity, gender, disability, class, and so on.

Take family responsibilities as an example. With respect to men, and particularly, but not exclusively, in secure manual jobs, a stereotypical model of the ideal employee as 'a-married-man-with-two-kids-a-house-and-a-car' has been documented (Blackburn and Mann 1979: 105; R. Jenkins 1986: 67–8; Nichols and Beynon 1977: 97, 199). It is strongly related to age-based notions of maturity. These are 'steadier' workers, recruiters believe, because the burden of their domestic responsibilities disciplines and habituates them to be so. If, as a consequence, men in this category stand a disproportionate chance of recruitment to secure manual jobs, then their perceived 'stability' will, at least in part, be a product of the stability of those jobs. In the process, a particular kind of worker is (re)produced: one who can afford a mortgage, a car, etc., who values a degree of predictable minor prosperity, who recognises the rewards attached to behaving in particular ways, who is tied in to consumerism. Organisational recruitment decisions, and the criteria which inform them, are among the processes whereby particular class identities – in this case, relatively affluent, 'respectable', politically conservative, and working-class – are constituted as distinct social 'types'. In this case, the process is also predicated upon, and reproductive of, a set of gendered identifications. For a woman, the same domestic responsibilities may be perceived by employers as a disincentive to recruitment, because it is believed that they will weaken her commitment to a stable work pattern (Collinson *et al.* 1990: 192–213; Curran 1985: 26–9). The example further illustrates the power of routine and axiomatic ethnocentrism in the specification of the 'normal' family.

Administrative allocation is significant in other contexts and with respect to other resources. Housing, for example. In the owner-occupier market, decisions are conditioned by a variety of factors, particularly the contingencies of supply and demand at any particular moment. Similarly in the private-rented sector. In the context of local relationships between identity and wealth, a great deal of the spatial materiality of identification – residential segregation – is generated in bilateral market transactions between

private individuals, mediated by financial and brokerage organisations. In public housing,[2] however, demand – particularly for
'desirable' housing – typically exceeds supply, and scarcity is the
norm. In the public housing sector – certainly in Britain, given
its recent contraction – the scope for tenant choice is limited.

The organisation of public housing is more bureaucratised
than other housing sectors. This scarce public resource is allocated
through assessment, involving the interviewing by officials of
individuals and families. Assessment is conditioned by implicit
or explicit stereotypes of eligibility and need, on the one hand,
and of particular categories of people – 'blacks', 'single-parents',
'problem families', 'roughs', the 'homeless', or whatever – on the
other. This may be reflected in policy formulation (Gill 1977).
More typically it operates in the immediacy and privacy of specific
allocatory decisions (Flett 1979; Karn 1983), involving classificatory
work such as the assessment and grading of housekeeping
standards. Desirable housing is a resource, undesirable housing a
penalty, and they may be allocated as such. Access to any public
housing may be denied. These tendencies may be encouraged by
the politics of clientage to which local government is vulnerable.
The end product is a spatial arrangement of public housing which
identifies individuals as of greater or lesser social worth according
to where they live, and places them where they live on the basis
of the identification of their worth. This is another way in which
identification becomes mapped on to public space. It also illustrates
the virtualities of identification. People are allocated a house in a
'good' area because they are judged to be worthy of it; because of
where they live they are judged to be 'respectable'. And so on (and
vice versa).

Administrative allocation is wide-ranging and pervasive.
Discretion and stereotyping in allocatory decision-making can be
seen at work in benefit allocation in social security offices in the
United Kingdom (Dalley and Berthoud 1992; Howe 1990: 106–35).
They have been documented in social work encounters of one kind
or another in the United States (Lipsky 1980; Prottas 1979). In
Prottas's expression this is a business of 'people processing'. The
'gatekeeping encounters' of the interview room are concerned with
'social selection' as well as with allocation (Erickson 1976). In fact,
social selection and allocation are the same process; a process of
authoritative classification (and in contexts such as the administra-
tion of immigration rules, for example, this is particularly clear).
Much policing work exhibits the same combinations of discretion

and stereotyping. Using Lipsky's and Prottas's model of the 'street-level bureaucrat', even this can be understood as administrative allocation, in this case largely of penalties (Cicourel 1968; Turk 1969).

Reference to policing is a useful reminder that I am talking about labelling processes here. Although the labelling model originated in the study of deviance, as argued in Chapter 8 it can be applied to social identity in general. Administrative allocation is a process of labelling, imbued with organisational and administrative authority, in which positive and negative stereotypes of particular social categories are applied to individuals, systematically influencing the distribution to them of scarce resources and penalties. It establishes stereotypical identificatory labels as consequential in the constitution of life-chances across a range of situations.

So, which stereotypes, and is there consistency in their mobilisation? Some are obvious: gender, sexual orientation, ethnicity, 'race', all of the usual suspects. Among the more interesting are stereotypes of the 'deserving' and the 'undeserving'. These are typically concerned with attributes of life-style – cleanliness, thrift, sobriety, honesty, etc. – many of which are understood to be visibly embodied, encoded in appearance and demeanour. Allied to categorical distinctions such as 'rough:respectable' and 'reputable:disreputable' (Ball 1970; Matza 1967), these are particularly applied to working-class people. With their origins in nineteenth-century ideals of self-help and social improvement, these ideas and social categories are implicated in the ideologies of free-market capitalism, and still constitute an influential thread in the formulation and implementation of social policy in industrialised societies (Handler and Hasenfeld 1991; Katz 1989).

Stereotypes of the 'deserving' and the 'undeserving' are significant in a number of respects. The research cited in previous paragraphs (see also Hutson and Liddiard 1994; R. Jenkins 1983) suggests that in a variety of allotropes they are very general, informing policy and administrative allocation in Europe, North America, and elsewhere. They are also conspicuous in everyday common sense. This is a cumulative and consistent classificatory process which is anything but trivial. Categorical boundaries are drawn that gloss morality and identity on to each other in a forthright manner. This moral register, summing up underlying notions about fairness and justice, makes these stereotypes so appropriate to allocatory decision-making. From its own point of view, the process appears, not as denial, but as a means of ensuring that the deserving are not deprived of scarce resources by the undeserving. What is more, stereotypical classifications such as these are sufficiently blunt to permit widespread application, yet sufficiently discriminating to allow their discretionary interpretation (and the two things are not unconnected). They are general collective categories which can be applied to individuals. They are flexible, and adapt well to changing circumstances. They can be mapped onto other stereotypes – such as gender or 'race' – to produce cumulative and potent classifications of ineligibility and exclusion (Karn 1983: 170–3). They also resonate with homologous themes such as the discourse of moral responsibility informing the modern medical model of the patient (the 'sick role', as in Parsons 1951: 428–54).

However, stereotypical classification doesn't only affect the disadvantaged, and it isn't always disadvantageous. Nor do written examinations or other formally 'objective' assessment procedures guarantee immunity from the influence of stereotyping or discretion. Allocatory decision-making is enormously consequential in education (Cicourel and Kitsuse 1963), and here too there is stereotyping and discretion. Bourdieu (1988: 194–208) analyses the relationship of generally mutual reinforcement between the formal marks given to students' written work and the stereotypical professorial judgements of that work (as 'clumsy', 'vigorous', 'brash', 'cultivated', etc.), and how this relates to the high or low cultural capital of the student, as indicated by class background. Bourdieu argues that social inputs (class) are converted into educational outputs (marks, scholarships, university places) through the mediation of those stereotypical categories of judgement. Stereotypes also come into play in the careful descriptive qualification of formal results – the discretion – which the writing of references demands. Even if students have similar formal achievements, their work – and their worth – may be evaluated differently (another example of the nominal and the virtual). Stereotypes enable social classification to be euphemised as academic classification. This is analogous to the way in which the various distinctions between the 'deserving' and the 'undeserving' combine with procedurally correct allocations of resources to represent collective social classification as the just satisfaction of legitimate individual 'need'.

Stereotypical categories of allocatory judgement do not arise wholly, or even mainly, within organisations. If they did they wouldn't be such common currency. Organisations aren't self-contained. The classifications which are evident in organisational categorisation are also mobilised and developed outside organisations. Indeed they feed *into* allocatory processes *from* the wider social environment (which, of course, consists, in part, of other organisations). Officials, managers, teachers, whomsoever; they have histories, upbringings and backgrounds, they go home at the end of the day, they read newspapers, they talk to their friends. They live lives which are more than organisational. The mass communication media – television, cinema, the press, advertising – and the political institutions and arenas of the state, are significant frames of everyday life in modern societies. The media and politics are not innocent with respect to each other. Each feeds the other in the promotion and agitation of public discourses and campaigns focusing upon particular issues and particular categories of the population.

Some of these campaigns are familiar to us as 'moral panics', following Stanley Cohen's seminal account (1972) of the political demonisation of working-class youth culture – 'mods' and 'rockers' – in England in the 1960s. However, the word 'panic' underplays the routine nature of many of these processes and overestimates their drama. Becker's notion of the 'moral crusade' (1963) is more downbeat, and has the virtue of emphasising organisation and direction. However we describe them, in important respects these campaigns are not new phenomena; the recurrent social construction of working-class youth as a threat, for example, has a considerable history (Pearson 1983). Their volume, variety and pervasiveness have increased – and this is doubtless something other than a mere increase in magnitude – but there is a remarkable degree of historical continuity. These collective public discourses affect what individuals do – in administrative allocation, for example – and, in turn, they reflect individual behaviour. Hutson and Liddiard's account (1994) of the relationship between the social construction of 'youth homelessness' as an issue and the bureaucratic processing of the young homeless illustrates this interplay between 'public issues' and 'personal troubles'.

Other social categories which have been the recent subject and object of public discourse in this way include black youth (Hall *et al.* 1978; Solomos 1988: 121–45), welfare recipients (Golding and Middleton 1982), and homosexuals and HIV-positive people in general (Cook and Colby 1992; Watney 1988). Some public moral campaigns, dealing with child abuse and paedophilia (P. Jenkins 1992) or satanism (Richardson *et al.* 1991), in addition to identifying deviant social categories – whether real or imaginary – dramatise and normalise identities and institutions such as the family and Christianity. To re-emphasise that these campaigns are not distinctively modern, a parallel can be found here with medieval and early-modern anti-semitic public discourses, for example (Dundes 1991; Hsia 1988). Other, more routine collective public discourses – for example, the signification of conventional gender roles – dramatise and promote 'normal', positively valorised identities. These are less likely to be crusades or panics, more ubiquitous themes in advertising, cinema, literature, and so on (Goffman 1979; McRobbie 1991).

The identification and social construction of the 'normal' has many facets, however. Returning to administrative allocation, the role of testing is important in this respect. Inspired in part by Foucault, Ian Hacking (1990) argues convincingly that the notion of 'normality' is in large part a modern artefact of the exponential growth of mathematics as a cultural discourse and a way of understanding the world. The development of statistics transformed the imprecise everyday probability of chance and experience into a hard image of predictability, legitimated by science and suitable to the needs of bureaucracy. This facilitated the imperialism of increasingly sophisticated and unforgivingly firm models of statistical 'normality'. Hand-in-glove with this went the elaboration of social categories in general: 'many of the facts presented by the bureaucracies did not even exist ahead of time. Categories had to be invented into which people could conveniently fall in order to be counted' (Hacking 1990: 3). The census of population, while it has antecedents in the empires of antiquity, is a product of the modern state's statistical governmentality. But the distance achieved by statistical abstraction does not mean that the everyday world is unaffected. Far from it. Hacking argues that a powerful framework has been created for social life and the experience of individuals:

> The normal stands indifferently for what is typical, the unenthusiastic objective average, but it also stands for what has been, good health, and for what shall be, our chosen destiny. That is why the benign and sterile-sounding word 'normal' has become one of the most powerful ideological tools of the twentieth century.

> (ibid.: 169)

One invented modern category – which definitively invokes 'normality' – is 'mental retardation' (in the US) or 'learning difficulties' (in the UK). Where once some individuals were seen as 'half-witted', 'dunces', a 'bit slow', or whatever, a distinct population category has been created out of the diffuse individual diversity of intellectual (in)competences. This category's coherence derives primarily from the exclusionary treatment of its members, and the services delivered to them on the basis of their categorisation (Trent 1994). The legitimacy of the category rests on authoritative psycho-medical diagnosis – that is, identification – and testing. Research in the USA by Mehan *et al.* (1986) and Mercer (1973) suggests that testing may be pre-eminently influential in the construction of individual educational careers and identities as 'mentally retarded'. The symbolic power of the statistical model of normality is such that internal individual differentiation is submerged in a dominant classification of similarity, constituted in an external relationship of difference *vis-à-vis* the rest of the population (and also serving to define their 'normality'). In the process, the imagined has become anything but imaginary, and is powerfully consequential in the lives of individuals.

F. Allan Hanson (1993), also drawing on Foucault, offers a further perspective on testing. His concepts of *authenticity tests* and *qualifying tests* seem to be homologous to my notions of acceptability and suitability. Authenticity is concerned with commitment, attitude, faith, or whatever; qualification is largely a matter of competence or ability. Whereas the assessment of authenticity, through procedures such as the ordeal, is documented throughout history, Hanson argues that the quantitative assessment of qualification is distinctively modern. He documents the centrality of testing to much administrative allocation in the contemporary United States.

Hacking and Hanson agree on the degree to which the categorising effects of normality-assessment procedures frame the identification of individuals and population categories. In the general contours of their argument and in their debt to Foucault they are not alone. Rose (1989) argues, for example, that the twentieth century has seen the increasingly authoritative (and authoritarian) social construction, by practitioners of expert systems such as psychology, of a normalised model of responsible, autonomous and 'healthy' selfhood. More generally, Cohen talks about the 'classified society' (1985), Polsky about the 'therapeutic state' (1991), and de Swaan of the 'management of normality' (1990).

In the historical background, imperialistic normalisation – in this case of culture – has roots other than the statistical. The increasing centralisation of the nation-state, beginning in Europe in the late eighteenth century, was manifest in the codification of law, state education, language policies, public health reforms, and public welfare (de Swaan 1988). The standardisation and centralisation of national identity went hand in hand with the project of cultural homogenisation. Not for nothing was one of the chosen vehicles of French cultural integration and the modernisation of the state called the *Ecole Normale* (E. Weber 1976: 303–38).

Finally, also with respect to historical background, it would be inappropriate to move on without pausing to remember the apotheosis – and the nadir – of the state categorisation of individuals and populations, and of the twentieth century's elaboration of normality. The genocide of Nazi Germany against Jews and gypsies, and its assault upon those of its own citizens who were identified as 'unfit' in one sense or another, derived from scientific models of the 'normal' and diagnostic procedures; they were, certainly in the first instance, in the hands of authoritative experts (Burleigh and Wippermann 1991; Müller-Hill 1988). The process was also thoroughly bureaucratised. It is chilling to recognise the continuity between allocation procedures which determined whether or not individuals should live, and our own mundane procedures of employment recruitment or educational assessment. As Bauman argues(1989), the Holocaust was a definitively modern phenomenon – with lessons for today – rather than an atavistic throw-back to barbarism.

This chapter has looked at some of the ways in which organisations have an appreciable impact on the identification of people other than their own members. This may, unusually, be purely nominal, a matter of name or category alone, as in the administrative formulation of census classifications. Most typically, however, processes of identification are bound up with the allocation of resources and penalties. A broad definition of resources, as something more than the common-sensically material or economic, is implied here. In this discussion I have focused on administrative allocation, the exercise of authority. The allocation of resources and penalties can, however, be achieved by other means – typically involving force – and they are no less relevant to identity. However achieved, the capacity of organisations to identify people – authoritatively or powerfully, as individuals or collectively – and to make those identifications 'stick' through the allocation of resources and penalties, should not be underestimated.

Identification and allocation are mutually and reciprocally entailed in each other. Identity is consequential in terms of allocation: how you are identified may influence what, and how much, you get. Allocation is part of the process which generates identification: being deprived of or given access to particular resources is likely to colour the sense of what it means to be an X or a Y. A shared experience of being treated in particular ways may even generate a sense of collectivity where none existed before. The significance of this lies in distinctions drawn in earlier chapters: between the virtual and the nominal, and between social groups and social categories. Identification is consequential in everyday life. It is in those consequences that what an identification *means* – whether individually or collectively – is generated. These consequences vary from place to place, and epoch to epoch, but in the consequences the virtualities of identity emerge. What it was to be Jewish in Germany in the late 1930s was utterly different, for example, from what it is to be Jewish in Israel during the 1990s. Nominally the same, virtually different: same name, different identity?

The reciprocal connection between identification and its consequences is in large part established in the allocation of resources and penalties. Organisationally, this may be allocation to members (internal), or to non-members (external). It is, however, generally – perhaps necessarily – organised. It is in the consistency over time and across organisations of (stereo)typifications of identification and patterns of allocation that a 'social structure' – an organised pattern of relationships between stable collective identities and allocation – can be discerned.

Theoretical points about structure aside, however, the consequential nature of identity must be central to our understanding of it. Alongside internalisation – which in itself isn't enough – consequentiality is the main thread of identification as experience. Coming back to groups and categories, this means that a collectivity – or indeed an individual – can be categorised, and that categorisation can produce major consequences for them, without their being aware of it. The example of people with learning difficulties – who often aren't aware of their categorisation as such – has been mentioned elsewhere in this book (see also Davies and Jenkins 1997). Although there are *particular* groups of people with learning difficulties – clubs, residential units, etc. – they are a category in the largest sense, not a group. That category is a social reality for the 'rest of society'; its consequences are real for people with learning difficulties and their families.

Another possibility is that the members of a group may know that they are (nominally) categorised by the Ys as Xs – indeed X may be what they call themselves – without understanding the consequences, the virtualities, of that categorisation. This is a common situation in times of change. Many German Jews, for example, took a long time to realise the implications for them of National Socialist racial policies; that something akin to a census classification had become massively and fatally consequential. This example further illustrates how consequences can eventually feed into internal definition, into internalisation. The post-1945 history of Israel – and of Jewish people the world over – has been a painful working-through of the internalisation of the Holocaust, a reworking and historicisation of individual and collective experience in the construction of new Jewish identities (Hartman 1994; Kaplan 1994).

Organisational processes of identification take many forms, from the mundane to the terrible. The extent to which they shape our lives – who we are and our experience of being who we are – seems to be characteristic of the modern world. In the closing chapter, I will return to some of the questions about modernity and identity which were raised early on in the present discussion.

16

Modernity, rationality and identity

Throughout this book, I have argued for an understanding of identity as an internal-external dialectic of identification. The previous chapter, however, emphasised the external moment of that dialectic. In taking that line, I was ploughing a furrow which owes much to Foucault, and even more perhaps to Max Weber's vision of the 'iron cage'[1] of modern life, in which the capitalist 'care for material goods', and the demands of rational conduct and bureaucratic organisation, diminish the human spirit to a point beyond despair (M. Weber 1976: 181). In Chapter 2, I suggested that reflexive self-identity is a ubiquitous, defining feature of being human, neither diagnostic of modernity nor peculiar to the modern world. The argument that I advanced in Chapter 15 suggested that, if anything, it is the power of social categorisation – the subjugation of the internal moment of identification in the external – which characterises the modern world.

This isn't the place to discuss comprehensively Weber's foundational contribution to our understanding of rationality and modernity (see Brubaker 1984; Schroeder 1992: 112–40; Whimster and Lash 1987). But, if we *do* find ourselves in an iron cage – and I don't for one moment believe that we do – it's clear that Weber intended us to understand that, in large part, *we* have manufactured the cage and imprisoned ourselves within it. The impositions of modern bureaucracy are both external and internal. To say this, however, begs fundamental questions: how constraining and imposing is bureaucracy (and, by extension, modern government), and how rational? There are a number of complementary grounds for scepticism about the existence, let alone the penal efficiency, of the bureaucratic cage.

The first of these reflects an impressive body of social research on formal organisations, from Alvin Gouldner (1954) onwards. Weber underestimated the capacity of individuals to subvert the formal rationalities – objectives and procedures – of bureaucracies. This applies as much to those who work in bureaucracies as to those who otherwise deal with them. The sources of this resistance include the 'rational' pursuit of other, non-organisational objectives, the boredom and distress engendered by over-routinisation, and the refusal to recognise organisational categorisations. Generations of managers have wrestled with these problems, and generations of management consultants and trainers have made a living offering solutions to them. None of them has been more than partially successful.

The second point is related. Formality and informality cannot be separated other than conceptually. Each is a presence and an absence in the other; each needs the other to make sense (Harding and Jenkins 1989: 133–8). Formal procedures *of necessity* bring the informal with them, for a number of reasons, of which the recurrent need to bypass bureaucratic formality simply in order to get things done with dispatch, and the fact that not everything can be legislated for, are only the most obvious. Weber defined the 'formal rationality of economic action', a version of *zweckrationaliteit* which is at the heart of his model of bureaucracy, as: 'the degree to which the provision for needs . . . is capable of being expressed in numerical, calculable terms, and is so expressed' (M. Weber 1978: 85). This is the realm of allocation and diagnostic testing. However, not everything is amenable to quantification. Not everything is susceptible to formal rationalisation. Nor are efficiency and formal rationality necessarily the same thing (Ritzer 1993).

A further related point concerns organisational size and complexity; these are significant in the construction (or not) of the iron cage. Size is a function of number of employees, number of transactions, volume of business, and geographical/spatial spread; complexity relates to spatial patterning, relations with the external environment, and specialisation of the division of labour. Size and complexity are inter-related. As size and/or complexity increase, the more irresistible one might imagine the impetus towards formal rationalisation. Paradoxically, however, the bigger and more complex the organisation, the greater the potential and opportunity for the disruption of that rationality and the more difficult it becomes to rationalise and communicate procedures. Large, complex social systems have their own inherent problems of coherence and consistency which are countervailing tendencies with respect to rationalisation.

Formal rationalisation is demanding of actors in terms of cognitive *and* social competences. Fortunately, however, *in*competence of both kinds is widespread and there are limits to the remedies which training and education can offer. Further, we must not forget one of the very few sociological laws of relatively universal application (an example of lay sociologising to warm an ethnomethodologist's heart). Sod's Law, under and in a variety of different names and formulations, predicts that whatever can go wrong, will go wrong. I would, personally, want to add a codocil to the effect that *everything* can (go wrong). The combination of everyday incompetence with Sod's Law is a powerful obstacle to successful rationalisation.

Comfort can also be taken from the fact that within the most efficiently rationalised bureaucracy, many things other than organisational procedures and objectives come into play to generate the practices of actors. The 'irrational' dimensions of social life – for example, symbolism, myth, notions of fate or luck, sexuality, religious or other ideologies, ethnic attachments, emotional ups-and-downs, etc. – are ubiquitous and significant, within organisations no less than in other walks of everyday life. Furthermore, as organisations with boundaries, memberships and recruitment processes, bureaucracies are themselves constitutive of all the devices and enchantments – rituals, symbols, *ésprit de corps*, history, etc. – which are implicated in the constitution of collective social identity. Upon close examination, rationalised bureaucracies are, in important respects, characterised by striking continuities with the 'pre-modern' social worlds which anthropologists claim as their special domains of expertise. The use of a term such as pre-modern is problematic; it is potentially, if not downright, misleading. But in this context it serves to emphasise that formal bureaucratic organisations are no less firmly under the sway of enchantments than other, less 'rationalised' areas of social life.

None of these arguments distracts from the organisational facts of life, or from the realities of inequality and stratification in the modern world. The inefficiencies of organisational procedure can be as much a burden as a liberation. Not everyone is equally well-placed to resist the compulsion and degradation which many organisational hierarchies routinely inflict on their members, particularly those at the bottom of the heap. The capacity to exercise self-determination – whether individually or collectively – is systematically related to wealth, in terms of both material and cultural resources. The power of rationality is no more to be underestimated than the power of enchantment.

But be that as it may, the complexities of modern social life run neither smoothly nor mechanically nor deterministically. Structure is metaphor as much as reality. The 'system' is creaky, partial, and contingent upon so much else that there is always room for some manoeuvre, space for some self-determination. Society is no more monolithic than history is the linear revelation of the inevitable.

Good, but what has all this to do with identity? In the first place, it emphasises the 'built-in' constraints on the capacity of organisations – and governments – to impose their categorisations. In the second, it suggests that humans persistently resist categorisation anyway. To do so is an important expression of their reflexive selfhood; if there is such a thing as 'human nature', this may be one area in which to look for it. This is something of fundamental importance, of which Weber, for example, wasn't sufficiently aware. Individuals and groups will insist on asserting their own sense of who and what they are. They may not always be very successful, but that is not the point. That resistance may often appear to be a response to categorisation doesn't undermine the point: if the internal–external dialectic *is* constitutive of identity, how could it be otherwise?

Nor is the issue only one of organisational categorisation: human beings are wont to resist categorisation in all sorts of ways, and whatever its source. Everyday life is the site of the most mundane and possibly the most important resistance. In terms of name and treatment, and in however modest a manner, human individuals assert themselves. Even the expression – asserting them*selves* – is telling. They may only do so 'in their heads', mindful of threat and constraint, waiting for a better day (even though that day may never come), but that is something. This is not to offer a naively idealised and utopian vision of the human spirit: it can be broken, and the body with it. But the point is not only that it *has* to be broken, *in extremis*, for complete domination, but that the cost of doing so is generally high enough to frustrate the object of the exercise.

Collectively, spontaneous resistance can take a range of forms: riot and protest, stoppages by workers, uprising on the plantation, passive non-cooperation – the possibilities are many and obvious. Organised resistance also takes many forms, in social movements and in parties, in neighbourhood groups and in guerilla bands, in persistent and delicate lobbying and in non-violent mass civil disobedience. And means and ends come together. Resistance, whether spontaneous or not, may be a potent affirmation of group identity; organising is necessarily so.

Struggles for a different allocation of resources and resistance to categorisation are one and the same thing. Weber ended *The Protestant Ethic* by enjoining us to avoid either one-sided material-ism or equally one-sided idealism in our attempts to understand social life and individual behaviour. That remains good advice today: human beings – blessed with sociable natures and dignified by a spirited embodiment – demand nothing less. Whether or not there is an explicit call to arms in these terms, something that can be called self-assertion – or 'human spirit' is at the core of resistance to domination. It may ebb to the point of invisibility, but it remains a consistent thread in human social life. It is as intrinsic, and as necessary, to that social life as the socialising tyranny of categorisa-tion. The internal and the external dance together in the unfolding of individual and collective identities. And although those identities are imagined; they are not imaginary.

Notes

3 COMMON SENSE

[1] This glosses over the differences between sociology and social anthropology; I use the generic term 'sociology' only for simplicity's sake in writing. However, despite their intellectual and institutional divergence, they share more than differentiates them.

5 SELFHOOD AND MIND

[1] The following are useful: Breakwell (1992), Burkitt (1991), Carrithers *et al.* (1985), Carruthers (1986), Erikson (1968), Finkelstein (1991), Freeman (1993), Heelas and Lock (1981), Morris (1991; 1994), Rorty (1976), Shoemaker and Swinburne (1984), and a thematic issue of *History of the Human Sciences* (vol. 7, no. 2, May 1994) dedicated to 'Identity, Self and Subject'.

[2] This just brackets the ontological questions, it doesn't deport them from my argument. However, I had to start somewhere, and this seemed to be the most modest position to adopt.

[3] Such a framework would be a more general version of the specific model of social identity which I develop here.

[4] For social anthropology from a mutualist viewpoint, see Carrithers (1992).

[5] Joas (1985) is an intellectual biography of Mead which discusses his relationship to Cooley and other pragmatist thinkers.

[6] On the affinities between Marx and Mead, see Goff (1980).

6 SOCIAL SELVES

[1] Ryle would probably have dimissed with scorn Mead's model, as an example of the absurd notion of the person as 'some sort of committee' (1963: 181).

[2] An idea which runs from Dewey all the way to Habermas (Thompson 1982).

[3] This point is obvious and not original (e.g. Parsons 1963: 34).

[4] I'm not ignoring the ubiquity of 'mental health problems' here. The acute/serious personality disorders to which I refer are, however, *relatively* uncommon, and it's important to emphasise their place on a continuum, towards the other end of which are 'most people, most of the time'.

[5] I am delighted to acknowledge and thank John Parker, my ex-colleague at Swansea, for the insights and some of the phrasing of this paragraph.

7 ENTERING SOCIETY

[1] The bibliography in Poole's article is indispensable for anyone interested in the matters which are being discussed here.

[2] One – regrettably unrealistic – assumption which I make here is the routine availability of adequate nutrition for the infant.

8 SELF-IMAGE AND PUBLIC IMAGE

[1] Also known as the 'social reaction' perspective.

[2] And Becker's concept of the 'secret deviant' (1963: 20) is, even within the labelling perspective's own terms, a contradiction.

9 GROUPS AND CATEGORIES

[1] The author of this encyclopaedia entry is Michael Banton.

[2] I could at this point have mentioned, for example, the classificatory schemes of medicine. These, however, are, by definition,
intervention-oriented.

[3] Both examples cited are historically associated with adminis-
tration and government. African 'tribal' identities were at least
in part the product of colonial government, while social class
has been a conceptual tool of government in industrial
societies since the nineteenth century. Both are important in
population monitoring and censuses.

[4] These words are generally used to refer to this idea of Marx.
Marxology is not, however, my specialism, and I haven't been
able to find, in the major texts by Marx (or Engels) which are
to hand, this exact form of words. The closest is a passage
in *The Poverty of Philosophy* (1847) discussing the English
working class: 'Economic conditions had first transformed the
mass of the people of the country into workers. The domination of capital has created for this mass a common situation,
common interests. This mass is thus already a class as against
capital, but not yet for itself. In the struggle, of which we have
pointed out only a few phases, this mass becomes united and
constitutes itself as a class for itself' (Marx 1975: 159–60).

10 THE SOCIAL ORGANISATION OF DIFFERENCE

[1] Barth studied at Chicago in the late 1940s. His theoretical
works, particularly *Models of Social Organisation* (1966) and
Ethnic Groups and Boundaries (1969), acknowledge Goffman's
influence. Hughes taught Goffman at Chicago; his essay
'The study of ethnic relations', originally published in 1948
(Hughes 1994: 91–6), strikingly anticipates many of Barth's
later arguments.

[2] Barth's reference to ecology (1969: 19) means *cultural* ecology;
it does not imply any material determinism from an external
'natural world'.

[3] Although it could as easily be a reference to Merton (1957:
421), who calls W.I. Thomas's dictum about the relationship
between social beliefs and social reality the 'self-fulfilling
prophecy'.

[4] Space constraints mean that I have underplayed this aspect of
Barth's work: he has undertaken field research in Norway,
Kurdistan, Pakistan, Iran, Sudan, New Guinea, Oman, Bali and
Bhutan. Although he is among the most acutely theoretical of

anthropologists, Barth's ideas have always been hammered out
on the anvil of empirical research, which is what he takes to be
the core task of social science: 'What we . . . need is not a deduc-
tive theory of what these [social] systems will be but exploratory
procedures to discover what they are: what degree of order and
form they show in each particular situation in question. This
needs to be discovered and described, not defined and assumed
. . . ' (Barth 1992: 25).

11 THE SYMBOLIC CONSTRUCTION OF SIMILARITY

[1] One thing which Weber was attempting in his discussion of
ideal types was to explicate the role in the analytical process
of the point of view (including the value orientations) of the
historian or the sociologist. He wasn't trying to banish values
and points of view, in the futile pursuit of 'objectivity'; he was,
rather, trying to make them more visible.
[2] Although there is no space to deal with it here, Schutz
also discusses our knowledge of our predecessors and our
successors.

12 PREDICTABILITY

[1] My use of Fortes here doesn't mean that I accept his
arguments, in the paper cited, about altruism or the centrality
to the emergence of humans as cultured beings of the development of the institution of fatherhood. Nor, however, should
one reject either proposition out of hand.

13 INSTITUTIONALISING IDENTITY

[1] I have avoided the word 'culture' wherever possible throughout this book. This is because of the multiplicity of contested
meanings to which the word is attached, and because I don't
want to encourage the culture:society dichotomy, which (if
I understand it at all) makes little sense and smuggles in
further dichotomies – thinking:doing, mind:body, etc. – which
are even more problematic.
[2] There is an analogous problem in Berger's and Luckmann's
work with respect to their neglect of embodiment as the site
of the point of view of selfhood.
[3] This is another way of putting things which I owe to to John

Parker of the Department of Sociology and Anthropology at the University of Wales, Swansea (see Chapter 6, note 5 above).

[4] Most of the literature addressing organisations from a broadly sociological point of view has only limited relevance here. Among the interesting exceptions are Blau and Scott (1963), Alvesson (1993), Herzfeld (1993), and Silverman (1970).

14 ORGANISING IDENTITIES

[1] A third important contribution that organisations make to the construction of social identities, which space constraints exclude from consideration here, is the process whereby positions and functions are produced (designed) as offices – abstract positions in the network – before they are occupied by actual incumbents.

[2] Much the same distinction is intended by Nadel in contrasting the 'contingent' and the 'achieved', and 'recruitment roles' and 'achievement roles' (1957: 36). One could widen the net to suggest that anthropologically familiar distinctions between 'incorporation' and 'alliance' (Leach 1961: 21), or 'incorporation' and 'transaction' (Barth 1966: 4, 23–4), may be addressing the same theme.

[3] The ordeal has a long history (Bartlett 1986) as an arbiter of guilt and innocence, producing an identity transformation from 'suspect', to either 'innocent' or 'guilty'. Systematic torture may, at least in part, be interpreted as a relatively modern grafting onto *procedural* judgement of the organisational need for *reasons* which is manifest in the quest for confession (Peters 1985).

15 ALLOCATION AND CLASSIFICATION

[1] None of what I say here is a denial of the authenticity of 'mental health problems' (see Chapter 6, note 4 above).

[2] For simplicity's sake I am ignoring here the publicly funded voluntary sector, and housing associations in particular.

16 MODERNITY, RATIONALITY AND IDENTITY

[1] In deference to Weber's original language, see Chalcraft's discussion (1994: 29–32) of the appropriateness of Parsons' translation.

Bibliography

Althusser, L. (1971) *Lenin and Philosophy and Other Essays*, London: New Left Books.

Alvesson, M. (1993) *Cultural Perspectives on Organizations*, Cambridge: Cambridge University Press.

Anderson, B. (1983) *Imagined Communities: Reflections on the Origins and Spread of Nationalism*, London: Verso.

Anderson, E. (1978) *A Place on the Corner*, Chicago: University of Chicago Press.

Aronson, E. (1991) *The Social Animal*, 6th edn, New York: W.H. Freeman.

Asad, T. (1972) 'Market model, class structure and consent: a reconsideration of Swat political organization', *Man* (n.s.) vol. 7, pp. 74–94.

Ball, D.W. (1970) 'The problematics of respectability', in J.D. Douglas (ed.) *Deviance and Respectability: The Social Construction of Moral Meanings*, New York: Basic Books.

Barth, F. (1959) *Political Leadership Among Swat Pathans*, London: Athlone Press.

—— (1966) *Models of Social Organisation*, Occasional Paper no. 23, London: Royal Anthropological Institute.

—— (1969) 'Introduction', in F. Barth (ed.) *Ethnic Groups and Boundaries: The Social Organisation of Culture Difference*, Oslo: Universitetsforlaget.

—— (1981) *Process and Form in Social Life: Selected Essays of Fredrik Barth, vol. 1*, London: Routledge and Kegan Paul.

—— (1983) *Sohar: Culture and Society in an Omani Town*, Baltimore: Johns Hopkins University Press.

—— (1984) 'Problems in conceptualizing cultural pluralism, with illustrations from Sohar, Oman', in D. Maybury-Lewis (ed.) *The Prospects for Plural Societies: 1982 Proceedings of the American Ethnological Society*, Washington, DC: American Ethnological Society.

—— (1987) *Cosmologies in the Making: A Generative Approach to Cultural Variation in Inner New Guinea*, Cambridge: Cambridge University Press.

—— (1989) 'The analysis of culture in complex societies', *Ethnos*, vol. 54, nos 3–4, pp. 120–42.

—— (1992) 'Towards greater naturalism in conceptualizing societies', in A. Kuper (ed.) *Conceptualizing Society*, London: Routledge.

—— (1994) 'Enduring and emerging issues in the analysis of ethnicity', in H. Vermeulen and C. Govers (eds) *The Anthropology of Ethnicity: Beyond 'Ethnic Groups and Boundaries'*, Amsterdam: Het Spinhuis.

Bartlett, R. (1986) *Trial by Fire and Water: The Medieval Judicial Ordeal*, Oxford: Clarendon Press.

Bateson, G. (1972) *Steps to an Ecology of Mind*, New York: Ballantine.

—— (1991) *A Sacred Unity: Further Steps to an Ecology of Mind*, New York: HarperCollins.

Batley, R. (1981) 'The politics of administrative allocation', in R. Forrest, J. Henderson and P. Williams (eds) *Urban Political Economy and Social Theory*, Aldershot: Gower.

Bauman, Z. (1989) *Modernity and the Holocaust*, Cambridge: Polity.

—— (1990) *Thinking Sociologically*, Oxford: Blackwell.

Becker, H.S. (1963) *Outsiders: Studies in the Sociology of Deviance*, New York: Free Press.

Bell, C. and Newby, H. (1971) *Community Studies*, London: George Allen and Unwin.

Bell, D. (1990) *Acts of Union: Youth Culture and Sectarianism in Northern Ireland*, London: Macmillan.

Bentley, G.C. (1987) 'Ethnicity and Practice', *Comparative Studies in Society and History*, vol. 29, pp. 24–55.

Berger, P.L. and Luckmann, T. (1967) *The Social Construction of Reality*, London: Allen Lane.

Bernadi, B. (1985) *Age Class Systems*, Cambridge: Cambridge University Press.

Berne, E. (1968) *Games People Play: The Psychology of Human Relationships*, Harmondsworth: Penguin.

Blackburn, R.M. and Mann, M. (1979) *The Working Class in the Labour Market*, London: Macmillan.

Blau, P.M. and Scott, W.R. (1963) *Formal Organizations: A Comparative Approach*, London: Routledge and Kegan Paul.

Blok, A. (1974) *The Mafia of a Sicilian Village: A Study of Violent Peasant Entrepreneurs*, Oxford: Blackwell.

Blumer, H. (1986) *Symbolic Interactionism: Perspective and Method*, Berkeley: University of California Press (first published 1969).

Boissevain, J. (1968) 'The place of non-groups in the social sciences', *Man* (n.s.) vol. 3, pp. 542–56

Boon, J.A. (1982) *Other Tribes, Other Scribes: Symbolic Anthropology in the Comparative Study of Cultures, Histories, Religions and Texts*, Cambridge: Cambridge University Press.

Bourdieu, P. (1977) *Outline of a Theory of Practice*, Cambridge: Cambridge University Press.

—— (1988) *Homo Academicus*, Cambridge: Polity Press.

—— (1990) *The Logic of Practice*, Cambridge: Polity Press.

—— (1991) *Language and Symbolic Power*, ed. J.B. Thompson, Cambridge: Polity Press.

—— and Passeron, J.-C. (1977) *Reproduction in Education, Society and Culture*, London: Sage.

Breakwell, G.M. (ed.) (1992) *The Social Psychology of Identity and the Self Concept*, London: Academic Press.

Brubaker, R. (1984) *The Limits to Rationality: An Essay on the Social and Moral Thought of Max Weber*, London: George Allen and Unwin.

Bulmer, M. (1987) *The Social Basis of Community Care*, London: George Allen and Unwin.

Burkitt, I. (1991) *Social Selves: Theories of the Social Formation of Personality*, London: Sage.

—— (1994) 'The shifting concept of the self', *History of the Human Sciences*, vol. 7, no. 2, pp. 7–28.

Burleigh, M. (1994) *Death and Deliverance: 'Euthanasia' in*

Germany, 1900–1945, Cambridge: Cambridge University Press.

—— and Wippermann, W. (1991) *The Racial State: Germany 1933–1945*, Cambridge: Cambridge University Press.

Burns, T. (1992) *Erving Goffman*, London: Routledge.

Burton, J. W. (1981) 'Ethnicity on the hoof: on the economics of Nuer identity', *Ethnology*, vol. 20, pp. 157–62.

Campbell, J. (1994) *Past, Space and Self*, Cambridge, Mass.: MIT Press.

Carrithers, M. (1985) 'An alternative social history of the self', in M. Carrithers, S. Collins and S. Lukes (eds) *The Category of the Person*, Cambridge: Cambridge University Press.

—— (1992) *Why Humans Have Cultures: Explaining Anthropology and Social Diversity*, Oxford: Oxford University Press.

—— Collins, S. and Lukes, S. (eds) (1985) *The Category of the Person: Anthropology, Philosophy, History*, Cambridge: Cambridge University Press.

Carruthers, P. (1986) *Introducing Persons: Theories and Arguments in the Philosophy of Mind*, London: Croom Helm.

Chalcraft, D. (1994) 'Bringing the text back in: on ways of reading the iron cage metaphor in the two editions of *The Protestant Ethic*', in L.J. Ray and M. Reed (eds) *Organizing Modernity: New Weberian Perspectives on Work, Organization and Society*, London: Routledge.

Cicourel, A. V. (1968) *The Social Organization of Juvenile Justice*, New York: Wiley.

—— and Kitsuse, J. (1963) *The Educational Decision Makers*, Indianapolis: Bobbs Merrill.

Clark, G. (1992) *Space, Time and Man: A Prehistorian's View*, Cambridge: Cambridge University Press.

Cockburn, D. (ed.) (1991) *Human Beings*, Cambridge: Cambridge University Press.

Cohen, A. (1974) *Two-Dimensional Man: An Essay on the Anthropology of Power and Symbolism in Complex Society*, London: Routledge and Kegan Paul.

—— (1980) 'Drama and politics in the development of a London carnival', *Man* (n.s.) vol. 15, pp. 65–87.

Cohen, A.P. (1982) 'Belonging: the experience of culture', in A.P. Cohen (ed.) *Belonging: Identity and Social Organisation in British Rural Cultures*, Manchester: Manchester University Press.

—— (1985) *The Symbolic Construction of Community*, London: Tavistock.

—— (1986) 'Of symbols and boundaries, or, does Ertie's greatcoat hold the key?', in A.P. Cohen (ed.) *Symbolising Boundaries: Identity and Diversity in British Cultures*, Manchester: Manchester University Press.

—— (1994) *Self Consciousness: An Alternative Anthropology of Identity*, London: Routledge.

Cohen, R. (1978) 'Ethnicity: problem and focus in anthropology', *Annual Review of Anthropology*, vol. 7, pp. 379–403.

Cohen, S. (1972) *Folk Devils and Moral Panics: The Creation of the Mods and Rockers*, London: MacGibbon and Kee.

—— (1985) *Visions of Social Control: Crime, Punishment and Classification*, Cambridge: Polity.

Cohen, Y.A. (1969) 'Social boundary systems', *Current Anthropology*, vol. 10, pp. 103–26.

Collins, R. (1988) 'Theoretical continuities in Goffman's work', in P. Drew and A. Wooton (eds) *Erving Goffman: Exploring the Interaction Order*, Cambridge: Polity.

—— (1989) 'Towards a neo-Meadian sociology of mind', *Symbolic Interaction*, vol. 12, pp. 1–32.

Collinson, D.L., Knights, D. and Collinson, M. (1990) *Managing to Discriminate*, London: Routledge.

Collmann, J. and Handelman, D. (eds) (1981) *Administrative Frameworks and Clients*, thematic issue of *Social Analysis*, no. 9 (December).

Connerton, P. (1989) *How Societies Remember*, Cambridge: Cambridge University Press.

Cook, T.E. and Colby, D.C. (1992) 'The mass-mediated epidemic: the politics of AIDS on the nightly network news', in E. Fee and D.M. Fox (eds) *AIDS: The Making of a Chronic Disease*, Berkeley: University of California Press.

Cooley, C.H. (1962) *Social Organization: A Study of the Larger Mind*, New York: Schocken (first published 1909).

—— (1964) *Human Nature and the Social Order*, New York: Schocken (first published 1902).

Coulson, M. (1972) 'Role: a redundant concept in sociology? Some educational considerations', in J.A. Jackson (ed.) *Role*, Cambridge: Cambridge University Press.

Crow, G. and Allan, G. (1994) *Community Life: An Introduction to Local Social Relations*, London: Harvester Wheatsheaf.

Curran, M.M. (1985) *Stereotypes and Selection: Gender and Family in the Recruitment Process*, London: HMSO.

Dalley, G. and Berthoud, R. (1992) *Challenging Discretion: The*

Social Fund Review Procedure, London: Policy Studies Institute.

Damon, W. and Hart, D. (1988) *Self-Understanding in Childhood and Adolescence*, Cambridge: Cambridge University Press.

Davies, C.A. and Jenkins, R. (1995) *Lives in Context: The Transition to Adulthood of Young People with Learning Difficulties*, Swansea: unpublished report to the Joseph Rowntree Foundation.

—— (1997) '"She has different fits to me": How people with learning disabilities see themselves', *Disability and Society*, forthcoming.

Delamont, S. (1995) *Appetites and Identities: An Introduction to the Social Anthropology of Western Europe*, London: Routledge.

de Swaan, A. (1988) *In Care of the State: Health Care, Education and Welfare in Europe and the USA in the Modern Era*, Cambridge: Polity.

—— (1990) *The Management of Normality: Critical Essays in Health and Welfare*, London: Routledge.

Douglas, M. (1966) *Purity and Danger: An Analysis of Concepts of Pollution and Taboo*, London: Routledge and Kegan Paul.

—— (1973) *Natural Symbols: Explorations in Cosmology*, Harmondsworth: Pelican.

Dundes, A. (ed.) (1991) *The Blood Libel Legend: A Casebook in Anti-Semitic Folklore*, Madison: University of Wisconsin Press.

Dunn, J. (1988) *The Beginnings of Social Understanding*, Oxford: Basil Blackwell.

Eller, J.D. and Coughlan, R.M. (1993) 'The poverty of primordialism: the demystification of ethnic attachments', *Ethnic and Racial Studies*, vol. 16, pp 185–202.

Epstein, A.L. (1978) *Ethos and Identity: Three Studies in Ethnicity*, London: Tavistock.

Eriksen, T.H. (1993) *Ethnicity and Nationalism: Anthropological Perspectives*, London: Pluto.

Erikson. E.H. (1968) *Identity: Youth and Crisis*, London: Faber.

Erickson, F. (1976) 'Gatekeeping encounters: a social selection process', in P.R. Sanday (ed.) *Anthropology and the Public Interest*, New York: Academic Press.

Evens, T.M.S. (1977) 'The predication of the individual in anthropological interactionism', *American Ethnologist*, vol. 79, pp. 579–97.

Fentress, J. and Wickham, C. (1992) *Social Memory*, Oxford: Blackwell.

Finkelstein, J. (1991) *The Fashioned Self*, Cambridge: Polity.

Flett, H. (1979) 'Bureaucracy and ethnicity: notions of eligibility in public housing', in S. Wallman (ed.) *Ethnicity at Work*, London: Macmillan.

Fortes, M. (1983) *Rules and the Emergence of Society*, Occasional Paper no. 39, London: Royal Anthropological Institute.

Foucault. M. (1970) *The Order of Things: An Archaeology of the Human Sciences*, London: Tavistock.

—— (1980) *Power/Knowledge: Selected Interviews and Other Writings 1972–1977*, ed. C. Gordon, Brighton: Harvester.

Freeman, M. (1993) *Rewriting the Self: History, Memory, Narrative*, London: Routledge.

Freud, S. (1984) *On Metapsychology: The Theory of Psycho-analysis* (Penguin Freud Library no. 11) ed. A. Richards, Harmondsworth: Pelican.

Friedman, J. (1994) *Cultural Identity and Global Process*, London: Sage.

Gambetta, D. (1993) *The Sicilian Mafia: The Business of Private Protection*, Cambridge, Mass.: Harvard University Press.

Geertz, C. (1973) *The Interpretation of Cultures*, New York: Basic Books.

—— (1983) *Local Knowledge: Further Essays in Interpretive Anthropology*, New York: Basic Books.

Gibson, J.J. (1979) *The Ecological Approach to Visual Perception*, Boston: Houghton Mifflin.

Giddens, A. (1984) *The Constitution of Society*, Cambridge: Polity.

—— (1990) *The Consequences of Modernity*, Cambridge: Polity.

—— (1991) *Modernity and Self-Identity: Self and Society in the Late Modern Age*, Cambridge: Polity.

Gill, O. (1977) *Luke Street: Housing Policy, Conflict and the Creation of the Delinquent Area*, London: Macmillan.

Gledhill, J. (1994) *Power and its Disguises: Anthropological Perspectives on Politics*, London: Pluto.

Gluckman, M. (1956) *Custom and Conflict in Africa*, Oxford: Basil Blackwell.

—— (1963) *Order and Rebellion in Tribal Africa*, London: Cohen and West.

Goff, T.W. (1980) *Marx and Mead: Contributions to a Sociology of Knowledge*, London: Routledge and Kegan Paul.

Goffman, E. (1961) *Encounters: Two Studies in the Sociology of Interaction*, Indianapolis: Bobbs Merrill.
—— (1968a) *Stigma: Notes on the Management of Spoiled Identity*, Harmondsworth: Pelican.
—— (1968b) *Asylums: Essays on the Social Situation of Mental Patients and Other Inmates*, Harmondsworth: Pelican.
—— (1969) *The Presentation of Self in Everyday Life*, London: Allen Lane (first published 1959).
—— (1970) *Strategic Interaction*, Oxford: Basil Blackwell.
—— (1971) *Relations in Public: Microstudies of the Public Order*, London: Allen Lane.
—— (1975) *Frame Analysis: An Essay on the Organization of Experience*, Harmondsworth: Peregrine.
—— (1979) *Gender Advertisements*, Cambridge, Mass.: Harvard University Press.
—— (1983) 'The interaction order', *American Sociological Review*, vol. 48, pp. 1–17.
Golding, P. and Middleton, S. (1982) *Images of Welfare: Press and Public Attitudes to Poverty*, Oxford: Basil Blackwell.
Goldthorpe, J.H. and Hope, K. (1974) *The Social Grading of Occupations*, Oxford: Clarendon Press.
Goodman, M.E. (1964) *Race Awareness in Young Children*, rev. edn, New York: Collier.
Gordon, D.M. (1976) 'Capitalist efficiency and socialist efficiency', *Monthly Review*, vol. 28, no. 3, pp. 19–39.
Gouldner, A.W. (1954) *Patterns of Industrial Bureaucracy*, New York: Free Press.
Gove, W.R. (ed.) (1980) *The Labelling of Deviance: Evaluating a Perspective*, 2nd edn, Beverley Hills: Sage.
Haaland, G. (1969) 'Economic determinants in ethnic processes', in F. Barth (ed.) *Ethnic Groups and Boundaries*, Oslo: Universitetsforlaget.
Hacking, I. (1990) *The Taming of Chance*, Cambridge: Cambridge University Press.
Hall, S., Critcher, C., Jefferson, T., Clarke, J. and Roberts, B. (1978) *Policing the Crisis: Mugging, the State and Law and Order*, London: Macmillan.
Ham, C. and Hill, M. (1984) *The Policy Process in the Modern Capitalist State*, Brighton: Wheatsheaf.
Handler, J.F. and Hasenfeld, Y. (1991) *The Moral Construction of Poverty: Welfare Reform in America*, Newbury Park: Sage.

190 Social identity

Hannerz, U. (1969) *Soulside: Inquiries into Ghetto Culture and Community*, New York: Columbia University Press.

Hanson, F.A. (1993) *Testing Testing: Social Consequences of the Examined Life*, Berkeley: University of California Press.

Harding, P. and Jenkins, R. (1989) *The Myth of the Hidden Economy: Towards a New Understanding of Informal Economic Activity*, Milton Keynes: Open University Press.

Harré, R. (1979) *Social Being: A Theory for Social Psychology*, Oxford: Basil Blackwell.

—— (1981) 'Psychological variety', in P. Heelas and A. Lock (eds) *Indigenous Psychologies: The Anthropology of the Self*, London: Academic Press.

—— (1983) *Personal Being: A Theory for Individual Psychology*, Oxford: Basil Blackwell.

—— (ed.) (1986) *The Social Construction of Emotions*, Oxford: Basil Blackwell.

—— and Gillett, G. (1994) *The Discursive Mind*, Thousand Oaks, Ca.: Sage.

Harris, C.C. (1990) *Kinship*, Milton Keynes: Open University Press.

Harris, R. (1972) *Prejudice and Tolerance in Ulster: Neighbours and 'Strangers' in a Border Community*, Manchester: Manchester University Press.

Hartman, G. (ed.) (1994) *Holocaust Remembrance: The Shapes of Memory*, Oxford: Basil Blackwell.

Hasenfeld, Y., Rafferty, J.A. and Zald, M.N. (1987) 'The Welfare State, citizenship, and bureaucratic encounters', *Annual Review of Sociology*, vol. 13, pp. 387–415.

Heelas, P. and Lock, A. (eds) (1981) *Indigenous Psychologies: The Anthropology of the Self*, London: Academic Press.

Herzfeld, M. (1993) *The Social Production of Indifference: Exploring the Symbolic Roots of Western Bureaucracy*, Chicago: University of Chicago Press.

Heskin, K. (1980) *Northern Ireland: A Psychological Analysis*, Dublin: Gill and Macmillan.

Hirst, P. and Wooley, P. (1982) *Social Relations and Human Attributes*, London: Tavistock.

Hobsbawm, E. and Ranger, T. (eds) (1983) *The Invention of Tradition*, Cambridge: Cambridge University Press.

Hollis, M. (1977) *Models of Man: Philosophical Thoughts on Social Action*, Cambridge: Cambridge University Press.

—— (1985) 'Of masks and men', in M. Carrithers, S. Collins and

S. Lukes (eds) *The Category of the Person*, Cambridge: Cambridge University Press.

Holy, L. and Stuchlik, M. (1983) *Actions, Norms and Representations: Foundations of Anthropological Inquiry*, Cambridge: Cambridge University Press.

Honneth, A. and Joas, H. (1988) *Social Action and Human Nature*, Cambridge: Cambridge University Press.

Howe, L.E.A. (1990) *Being Unemployed in Northern Ireland: An Ethnographic Study*, Cambridge: Cambridge University Press.

Hsia, R.P. (1988) *The Myth of Ritual Murder: Jews and Magic in Reformation Germany*, New Haven: Yale University Press.

Hughes, E.C. (1994) *On Work, Race, and the Sociological Imagination*, ed. L.A. Coser, Chicago: University of Chicago Press.

Hutson, S. and Liddiard, M. (1994) *Youth Homelessness: The Construction of a Social Issue*, London: Macmillan.

Jackson, J.A. (1972). 'Role – Editorial Introduction', in J.A. Jackson (ed.) *Role*, Cambridge: Cambridge University Press.

James, A. (1993) *Childhood Identities: Self and Social Relationships in the Experience of the Child*, Edinburgh: Edinburgh University Press.

Jameson, F. (1991) *Postmodernism, or The Cultural Logic of Late Capitalism*, London: Verso.

Jenkins, P. (1992) *Intimate Enemies: Moral Panics in Contemporary Great Britain*, New York: Aldine de Gruyter.

Jenkins, R. (1981) 'Thinking and doing: towards a model of cognitive practice', in L. Holy and M. Stuchlik (eds) *The Structure of Folk Models*, London: Academic Press.

—— (1983) *Lads, Citizens and Ordinary Kids: Working-class Youth Life-styles in Belfast*, London: Routledge and Kegan Paul.

—— (1986) *Racism and Recruitment: Managers, Organisations and Equal Opportunity in the Labour Market*, Cambridge: Cambridge University Press.

—— (1990) 'Dimensions of adulthood in Britain: long-term unemployment and mental handicap', in P. Spencer (ed.) *Anthropology and the Riddle of the Sphinx: Paradoxes of Change in the Life Course*, London: Routledge.

—— (1992) *Pierre Bordieu*, London: Routledge.

—— (1994) 'Rethinking ethnicity: identity, categorization and power', *Ethnic and Racial Studies*, vol. 17, pp. 197–223.

Joas, H. (1985) *G.H. Mead: A Contemporary Re-examination of his Thought*, Cambridge: Polity.

Kapferer, B. (ed.) (1976) *Transaction and Meaning*, Philadelphia: ISHI.

Kaplan, H. (1994) *Conscience and Memory: Meditations in a Museum of the Holocaust*, Chicago: University of Chicago Press.

Karn, V. (1983) 'Race and housing in Britain: the role of the major institutions', in N. Glazer and K. Young (eds) *Ethnic Pluralism and Public Policy: Achieving Equality in the United States and Britain*, London: Heinemann.

Katz, M.B. (1989) *The Undeserving Poor: From the War on Poverty to the War on Welfare*, New York: Pantheon.

Kaye, K. (1982) *The Mental and Social Life of Babies: How Parents Create Persons*, Brighton: Harvester.

Keesing, R.M. (1975) *Kin Groups and Social Structure*, New York: Holt, Rhinehart and Winston.

Kuhse, H. and Singer, P. (1985) *Should the Baby Live? The Problem of Handicapped Infants*, Oxford: Oxford University Press.

Lacan, J. (1977) *Écrits: A Selection*, London: Tavistock.

La Fontaine, J. (1985) *Initiation*, Harmondsworth: Penguin.

Laing, R.D. (1971) *Self and Others*, Harmondsworth: Pelican.

Lane, C. (1981) *The Rites of Rulers: Ritual in Industrial Society – The Soviet Case*, Cambridge: Cambridge University Press.

Leach, E.R. (1954) *Political Systems of Highland Burma: A Study of Kachin Social Structure*, London: Athlone Press.

—— (1961) *Rethinking Anthropology*, London: Athlone Press.

—— (1976) *Culture and Communication: The Logic by which Symbols are Connected*, Cambridge: Cambridge University Press.

Lee, R. and Morgan, D. (eds) (1989) *Birthrights: Law and the Beginning of Life*, London: Routledge.

Lemert, E.M. (1972) *Human Deviance, Social Problems and Social Control*, 2nd edn, Englewood Cliffs: Prentice-Hall.

Liebow, E. (1967) *Tally's Corner*, Boston: Little, Brown.

Linton, R. (1936) *The Study of Man: An Introduction*, student edn, New York: Appleton Century.

Lipsky, M. (1980) *Street-Level Bureaucracy: Dilemmas of the Individual in Public Services*, New York: Russell Sage Foundation.

McDonald, M. (1993) 'The construction of difference: an anthropological approach to stereotypes', in S. MacDonald (ed.) *Inside European Identities: Ethnography in Western Europe*, Oxford: Berg.

MacIntyre, A. (1985) *After Virtue: A Study in Moral Theory*, London: Duckworth.

MacLeod, J. (1987) *Ain't No Makin' It: Leveled Aspirations in a Low Income Neighbourhood*, London: Tavistock.

McRobbie, A. (1991) *Feminism and Youth Culture: From 'Jackie' to 'Just Seventeen'*, London: Macmillan.

Mann, M. (ed.) (1983) *The Macmillan Student Encyclopedia of Sociology*, London: Macmillan.

Mars, L. (1990) 'Coming of age among Jews: Bar Mitzvah and Bat Mitzvah ceremonies', in P. Spencer (ed.) *Anthropology and the Riddle of the Sphinx: Paradoxes of Change in the Life Course*, London: Routledge.

Marshall, G., Rose, D., Newby, H. and Vogler, C. (1988) *Social Class in Modern Britain*, London: Unwin Hyman.

Marx, K. (1975) *The Poverty of Philosophy*, Moscow: Progress Publishers.

—— and Engels, F. (1974) *The German Ideology, Part One*, ed. C.J. Arthur, London: Lawrence and Wishart.

Matza, D. (1967) 'The disreputable poor', in R. Bendix and S.M. Lipset (eds) *Class, Status and Power: Social Stratification in Comparative Perspective*, 2nd edn, London: Routledge and Kegan Paul.

—— (1969) *Becoming Deviant*, Englewood Cliffs: Prentice-Hall.

Mauss, M. (1985) 'A category of the human mind: the notion of person; the notion of self', in M. Carrithers, S. Collins and S. Lukes (eds) *The Category of the Person: Anthropology, Philosophy, History*, Cambridge: Cambridge University Press (first published 1938).

Mayer, A.C. (1966) 'The significance of quasi-groups in the study of complex societies', in M. Banton (ed.) *The Social Anthropology of Complex Societies*, London: Tavistock.

Mead, G.H. (1934) *Mind, Self and Society from the Standpoint of a Social Behaviorist*, ed. C.W. Morris, Chicago: University of Chicago Press.

Mehan, H., Hertweck, A. and Meihls, J.L. (1986) *Handicapping the Handicapped: Decision Making in Students' Educational Careers*, Stanford: Stanford University Press.

Memmi, A. (1990) *The Colonizer and the Colonized*, London: Earthscan (first published 1957).

Mercer, J.R. (1973) *Labeling the Mentally Retarded: Clinical and Social System Perspectives on Mental Retardation*, Berkeley: University of California Press.

Merton, R.K. (1957) *Social Theory and Social Structure*, 2nd edn, Glencoe: Free Press.

Mills, C.W. (1959) *The Sociological Imagination*, New York: Oxford University Press.

Milner, D. (1983) *Children and Race: Ten Years On*, London: Ward Lock.

Moerman, M. (1965) 'Ethnic identification in a complex civilization: who are the Lue?', *American Anthropologist*, vol. 67, pp. 1215–30.

Moore, R.I. (1987) *The Formation of a Persecuting Society: Power and Deviance in Western Europe, 950–1250*, Oxford: Basil Blackwell.

Moore, S.F. and Myerhoff, B.G. (eds) (1977) *Secular Ritual*, Assen: van Gorcum.

Morris, B. (1987) *Anthropological Studies of Religion: An Introductory Text*, Cambridge: Cambridge University Press.

—— (1991) *Western Conceptions of the Individual*, New York: Berg.

—— (1994) *Anthropology of the Self: The Individual in Cultural Perspective*, London: Pluto Press.

Müller-Hill, B. (1988) *Murderous Science: Elimination by Scientific Selection of Jews, Gypsies, and Others, Germany 1933–1945*, Oxford: Oxford University Press.

Murphy, R.F. (1990) *The Body Silent*, New York: Norton.

Nadel, S.F. (1951) *The Foundations of Social Anthropology*, London: Cohen and West.

—— (1957) *The Theory of Social Structure*, London: Cohen and West.

Newcomer, P.J. (1972) 'The Nuer are Dinka: an essay on origins and environmental determinism', *Man* (n.s.) vol. 7, pp. 5–11.

Nichols, T. and Beynon, H. (1977) *Living with Capitalism: Class Relations and the Modern Factory*, London: Routledge and Kegan Paul.

Offe, C. (1976) *Industry and Inequality*, London : Edward Arnold.

Ong, W.J. (1982) *Orality and Literacy: The Technologizing of the Word*, London: Methuen.

Paine, R. (1974) *Second Thoughts about Barth's Models*, Occasional Paper no. 32, London: Royal Anthropological Institute.

Parsons, T. (1951) *The Social System*, London: Routledge and Kegan Paul.

—— (1963) 'The interpenetration of two levels. Social structure and the development of personality: Freud's contribution to the integration of psychology and sociology', in N.J. Smelser and W.T. Smelser (eds) *Personality and Social Systems*, New York: Wiley.

—— (1968) 'Cooley and the problem of internalisation', in A.J. Reiss (ed.) *Cooley and Sociological Analysis*, Ann Arbor: University of Michigan Press.

Paul, E.F., Miller, F.D., Paul, J. and Ahrens, J. (eds) (1987) *Equal Opportunity*, Oxford: Blackwell.

Pearson, G. (1983) *Hooligan: A History of Respectable Fears*, London: Macmillan.

Peters. E. (1985) *Torture*, Oxford: Basil Blackwell.

Plummer, K. (1979) 'Misunderstanding labelling perspectives', in D. Downes and P. Rock (eds) *Deviant Interpretations: Problems in Criminological Theory*, London: Martin Robertson.

Polsky. A.J. (1991) *The Rise of the Therapeutic State*, Princeton: Princeton University Press.

Poole, F.J.P. (1994) 'Socialization, enculturation and the development of personal identity', in T. Ingold (ed.) *Companion Encyclopedia of Anthropology*, London: Routledge.

Prottas, J.M. (1979) *People Processing: The Street-Level Bureaucrat in Public Service Bureaucracies*, Lexington: Lexington Books.

Raban, J. (1989) *God, Man and Mrs Thatcher: A Critique of Mrs Thatcher's Address to the General Assembly of the Church of Scotland*, London: Chatto and Windus.

Rainwater. L. (1973) *Behind Ghetto Walls: Black Families in a Federal Slum*, Harmondsworth: Pelican.

Richards, A.I. (1956) *Chisungu: A Girl's Initiation Ceremony in Northern Rhodesia*, London: Faber.

Richards, M.P.M. (ed.) (1974) *The Integration of a Child into a Social World*, Cambridge: Cambridge University Press.

Richardson, J.T., Best, J. and Bromley, D.G. (eds) (1991) *The Satanism Scare*, New York: Aldine de Gruyter.

Ritzer, G. (1993) *The McDonaldization of Society: An Investigation into the Changing Character of Contemporary Social Life*, Thousand Oaks: Pine Forge.

Rorty, A. (ed.) (1976) *Identities of Persons*, Berkeley: University of California Press.

Rose, N. (1989) *Governing the Soul: The Shaping of the Private Self*, London: Routledge.

Rosenthal, R. and Jacobsen, L. (1968) *Pygmalion in the Classroom*, New York: Holt, Rhinehart and Winston.

Ryle, G. (1963) *The Concept of Mind*, Harmondsworth: Peregrine (first published 1949).

Sabetti, F. (1984) *Political Authority in a Sicilian Village*, New Brunswick: Rutgers University Press.

Sahlins, M. (1974) *Stone Age Economics*, London: Tavistock.

Samuel, R. and Thompson, P. (eds) (1990) *The Myths We Live By*, London: Routledge.

Schneider, J. and Schneider, P. (1976) *Culture and Political Economy in Western Sicily*, New York: Academic Press.

Schroeder, R. (1992) *Max Weber and the Sociology of Culture*, London: Sage.

Schutz, A. (1967) *The Phenomenology of the Social World*, Evanston: Northwestern University Press (first published 1932).

—— and Luckmann, T. (1973) *The Structures of the Life-World*, Evanston: Northwestern University Press.

Sharpe, S. (1976) '*Just Like a Girl': How Girls Learn to be Women*, Harmondsworth: Pelican.

Shoemaker, S. and Swinburne, R. (1984) *Personal Identity*, Oxford: Blackwell.

Shotter, J. (1974) 'The development of personal powers', in M.P.M. Richards (ed.) *The Integration of a Child into a Social World*, Cambridge: Cambridge University Press.

Silverman, D. (1970) *The Theory of Organisations*, London: Heinemann.

—— and Jones, J. (1976) *Organizational Work: The Language of Grading/The Grading of Language*, London: Collier-Macmillan.

Simmel, G. (1950) *The Sociology of Georg Simmel*, ed. K.H. Wolff, New York: Free Press.

Smith, M.G. (1960) *Government in Zazzau 1800–1950*, London: Oxford University Press for the International African Institute.

Solomos, J. (1988) *Black Youth, Racism and the State: The Politics of Ideology and Policy*, Cambridge: Cambridge University Press.

Southall, A. (1976) 'Nuer and Dinka are people: ecology, economy and logical possibility', *Man* (n.s.) vol. 11, pp. 463–91.

Sperber, D. (1975) *Rethinking Symbolism*, Cambridge: Cambridge University Press.

Stein, M.R. (1960) *The Eclipse of Community: An Interpretation of American Studies*, Princeton: Princeton University Press.

Stewart, A., Prandy, K. and Blackburn, R.M. (1980) *Social Stratification and Occupations*, London: Macmillan.

Still, A. and Good, J.M.M. (1991) 'Mutualism in the human sciences: towards the implementation of a theory', *Journal for the Theory of Social Behaviour*, vol. 22, pp. 105–28.

Tajfel, H. (1981) 'Social stereotypes and social groups', in J.C. Turner and H. Giles (eds) *Intergroup Behaviour*, Oxford: Blackwell.

Tannenbaum, F. (1938) *Crime and Community*, New York: Columbia University Press.

Taylor, I., Walton, P. and Young, J. (1973) *The New Criminology: For a Social Theory of Deviance*, London: Routledge and Kegan Paul.

Thompson, J.B. (1982) 'Universal pragmatics', in J.B. Thompson and D. Held (eds) *Habermas: Critical Debates*, London: Macmillan.

Trent, J.W. (1994) *Inventing the Feeble Mind: A History of Mental Retardation in the United States*, Berkeley: University of California Press.

Troyna, B. and Hatcher, R. (1992) *Racism in Children's Lives: A Study of Mainly-White Primary Schools*, London: Routledge.

Turk, A. (1969) *Criminality and the Legal Order*, Chicago: Rand-MacNally.

Turner, B.S. (1988) *Status*, Milton Keynes: Open University Press.

Turner, V. W. (1967) *The Forest of Symbols*, Ithaca: Cornell University Press.

—— (1974) *The Ritual Process: Structure and Anti-Structure*, Harmondsworth: Pelican.

van Gennep, A. (1965) *The Rites of Passage*, London: Routledge and Kegan Paul (first published 1908).

Wallace, A.F.C. (1970) *Culture and Personality*, 2nd edn, New York: Random House.

Wallman, S. (1986) 'Ethnicity and the boundary process in context', in J. Rex and D. Mason (eds) *Theories of Race and Ethnic Relations*, Cambridge: Cambridge University Press.

Watney, S. (1988) 'AIDS, "moral panic" theory and homophobia', in P. Aggleton and H. Homans (eds) *Social Aspects of AIDS*, Brighton: Falmer.

Weber, E. (1976) *Peasants into Frenchmen:The Modernisation of Rural France,1870–1914*, Stanford: Stanford University Press.

Weber, M. (1949) *The Methodology of the Social Sciences*, ed. E.A. Shils and H.A. Finch, New York: Free Press.

—— (1976) *The Protestant Ethic and the Spirit of Capitalism*, London: George Allen and Unwin.

—— (1978) *Economy and Society: An Outline of Interpretive Sociology*, ed. G. Roth and C. Wittich, Berkeley: University of California Press.

Whimster, S. and Lash, S. (eds) (1987) *Max Weber, Rationality and Modernity*, London: Allen and Unwin.

Wikan, U. (1977) 'Man becomes woman: transsexualism in Oman as a key to gender roles', *Man* (n.s.) vol. 12, pp. 304–19.

Wilk, R.R. (1993) 'Beauty and the feast: official and visceral nationalism in Belize', *Ethnos*, vol. 58, pp. 294–316.

Williamson, L. (1978) 'Infanticide: an anthropological analysis', in M. Kohl (ed.) *Infanticide and the Value of Life*, Buffalo, NY: Prometheus.

Wisdom, J. (1952) *Other Minds*, Oxford: Blackwell.

Wittgenstein, L. (1974) *On Certainty-Über Gewissheit*, ed. G.E.M. Anscombe, Oxford: Basil Blackwell.

Wollheim, R. (1984) *The Thread of Life*, Cambridge: Cambridge University Press.

Wright, E.O. (1985) *Classes*, London: Verso.

Wrong, D.H. (1961) 'The oversocialized conception of man', *American Sociological Review*, vol. 26, pp. 184–93.

Index

Dewey, J. 36, 177
diagnostic testing: in social
    construction of identity
    158–9, 166–7
difference 3–5, 19, 29, 52–3,
    80–1, 90–103, 104, 106, 111,
    114, 123, 127, 140, 145–6, 167
Dinka: Sudanese people 84, 86
disability 51, 54–6
Douglas, M. 74, 113, 121, 123,
    151
domination: modes of 120–1
Dundes, A. 166
Dunn, J. 49, 58
Durkheim, E. 31, 36, .38, 42,
    44, 81, 92, 105, 113, 126, 145
duties 135

Eller, J.D. 65
embodiment 18, 21, 22, 27, 38,
    40, 47, 49–53, 54, 60, 69, 71,
    94, 99, 102, 111, 113–4,
    126–7, 132, 141, 146–7
Epstein, A.L. 65
ethnicity 2, 21, 23–4, 49, 51,
    90–103, 107, 117; as primary
    identity 65–6
Engels, F. 38
English identity 94
epistemology 33 –8, 70, 109
equal opportunity 148
Eriksen, T.H. 96
Erickson, F. 162
Erickson, E.H. 40
European Union, 6
Evens, T.M.S. 96
experience: central to identity
    21, 168–70

feminism 7
Fentress, J. 28
Firth, R. 91

Flett, H. 162
formality 137, 158, 159, 172–3
Fortes, M. 122, 179
Foucault, M. 25, 85, 113, 155,
    167, 171
Freud, S. 41, 44, 45–6
Friedman, J. 14–16

Gambetta, D. 110
gay identities 2, 3, 5, 78
Geertz, C. 90, 98, 106
generalised other 42–3
gender 7, 51, 99, 101, 161, 163,
    164; as primary identity, 21,
    49, 58, 60–4
German identity 93–4
Gibson, J.J. 59
Giddens, A. 7, 10, 13–16, 20,
    26, 40, 43, 44, 45, 62, 68, 132,
    159
Gill, O. 162
Gillett, G. 36
Gledhill, J. 121
globalisation 7, 13–16
Gluckman, M. 106, 145
Goffman, E. 20, 21, 22, 57, 66,
    68–76, 92, 94, 95, 98, 99,
    119–20, 134, 137, 140, 151,
    166, 178
Golding, P. 165
Goldthorpe, J.H. 84
Good, J.M.M. 36
Goodman, M.E. 65
Gordon, D.M. 160
Gouldner, A.W. 172
Gove, W.R. 74
groups 92–3, 96, 100, 101, 111,
    123, 149–5 154; defined 23,
    82; fundamental to identity
    23–4, 60, 80–89

Haaland, G. 92